Praise for *Shall Not Be Infringed*

"If you're wondering whether this year's candidates support or oppose your Second Amendment rights, this book, *Shall Not Be Infringed*, is a book you'll want to read!"

—**Dick Cheney,** former Vice President of the United States

"This timely book highlights the critical importance of electing officeholders who will protect our Second Amendment freedoms. Keene and Mason tell a troubling story about how the Obama State Department, led by Hillary Clinton, helped advance an UN effort to restrict the rights of law-abiding gun owners. As the book reveals, Hillary Clinton herself was personally involved in the effort. It is essential that we elect a president this fall who respects the Second Amendment and who will work to reverse the harm Barack Obama and Hillary Clinton have done to our constitutional rights."

—**Senator Orrin Hatch**

"The current assault on gun rights threatens our most basic rights as citizens— and our most sacred foundational principles. This book lays bare the dangers of the movement to disarm us and what's required to defeat it. It's a must-read for every American."

—**Monica Crowley,** PhD, editor and columnist for the *Washington Times* and political and foreign affairs analyst for Fox News

"In *Shall Not Be Infringed*, David Keene and Tom Mason have broken the code on the gun-grabbers' plot to make our Constitution's Second Amendment "irrelevant." For all who want to protect our precious civil liberties, this book is a mandatory must read!"

—**Lt. Col Oliver North,** USMC (Ret.), NRA Board Member, and bestselling author of *Heroes Proved*

"*Shall Not be Infringed* is warning to all of us that all of us must be freedom fighters in the defense of our storied and essential Second Amendment. I am proud to call David my friend and fellow warrior."

—**Thomas Millner,** CEO of Cabela's

"Chilling! David Keene and Tom Mason have fought on the front lines in the gun rights battles—in the US and around the world. Their clear description of how we arrived at the point where a major presidential nominee openly calls for banning guns in this country should be a clarion call for anyone who values the Constitution and the American way of life."

—**Tom Gresham**, Host of Gun Talk Radio

"*Shall Not Infringed* by Dave Keene and Tom Mason, a remarkable work by two of the most knowledgeable Second Amendment warriors I know, is must reading."

—**Stephen Hornady**, President of Hornady Ammunition

"Most recently in Germany, which has stringent anti-gun laws, a misguided young man illegally obtained an automatic weapon and killed many innocent people at a local McDonalds. We might as well outlaw automobiles if we want to curb violent death by restricting the instrument rather than the irresponsible actions of irresponsible people. Good moral people without guns are at the mercy of immoral people who will obtain them illegally. The Second Amendment protects good citizens—crippling it will leave them defenseless. We need to personally read this book to our kids who are being "brainwashed" by propaganda."

—**Pat Boone**, singer/songwriter

"Do we really need another book on the threat to the Second Amendment and the rights of America's gun-owners? Read *Shall Not Be Infringed* and your answer will be a resounding "yes!" Co-authors Tom Mason and David Keene have given us a timely, lucid, well-argued, and highly readable discussion of the threats "foreign and domestic" to our liberty. Fortunately, the Second Amendment is the only self-enforcing right in the Bill of Rights. Perennial gun-grabbers would be wise to keep that in mind."

—**Thomas Moore**, author and
consultant to the firearms industry

"David Keene's book, *Shall Not be Infringed*, is an essential read when advocates of our Second Amendment are under daily assault and America is one Supreme Court Justice away from reversing its affirmation that the Second Amendment is an individual right. In 2006, then-President George W. Bush asked me to serve on the Special United Nations Conference on "Illicit Trade in Small Arms and Light Weapons" led by John Bolton. We stopped a radical Draft Program of Action that would have sublimated the will and sovereignty of the America people to an un-elected band of NGO's and allied government—until our own American government let it happen. Our adversaries so miserably fail to recognize our God-given right of self-defense. One of our most important civil rights hangs in the balance. Backers of global gun control claim that civilian firearms are a genocidal threat. Yet in 1994 Rwanda, 800,000 innocents were killed or maimed by pangas (machetes), spears, and axes. An armed citizenry would have prevented this international atrocity, and all-too-many others."

—**Roy Innis**, National Chairman,
Congress of Racial Equality (CORE)

"History is often a collection of turning points where key individuals stood against the tyranny of the masses—be they media or others—and those champions made all the difference. With most in the mainstream press in a full-on assault of gun rights following the 2012 shooting at Sandy Hook Elementary, David Keene was one man who prevailed against the media's intellectual house of cards. For those who not only cherish the Second Amendment—but the rest of our constitution as well—David Keene was the right man at the right time and we owe him a great debt."

—**Chris Dorsey**, Founding Partner, Dorsey Pictures

SHALL NOT BE INFRINGED:

THE NEW ASSAULTS ON YOUR SECOND AMENDMENT

David A. Keene and Thomas L. Mason

Skyhorse Publishing

Skyhorse Publishing books may be purchased in bulk at special discounts
for sales promotion, corporate gifts, fund-raising, or educational purposes.
Special editions can also be created to specifications. For details, contact the
Special Sales Department, Skyhorse Publishing, 307 West 36th Street, 11th Floor,
New York, NY 10018 or info@skyhorsepublishing.com.

Skyhorse® and Skyhorse Publishing® are registered trademarks of
Skyhorse Publishing, Inc.®, a Delaware corporation.

Visit our website at www.skyhorsepublishing.com.

10 9 8 7 6 5 4 3 2 1

Library of Congress Cataloging-in-Publication Data is available on file.

Cover design by Tom Lau
Cover photo credit: iStockphoto

Print ISBN: 978-1-5107-1995-8
Ebook ISBN: 978-1-5107-1996-5

Printed in the United States of America

To Donna, to whom I owe everything and whom I adore. She organizes my life, encourages me when I need encouragement, prods me to always do better, puts up with my bullheadedness, and makes my life more meaningful. Without her, this book would never have been written or published.

—David Keene

To William "Gunner Bill" Montgomery—a scholar, a gentleman, and the nicest "pirate" one could ever know.

—Tom Mason

TABLE OF CONTENTS

ACKNOWLEDGMENTS

First, we thank gun owners worldwide and, particularly, the members of the National Rifle Association (NRA) who have supported our work on behalf of the Second Amendment. NRA members, including those who make up our families, have provided lifelong inspiration and are a lot of fun around the fire pit, at a gun range, or in a duck blind. Our experiences of the last decades would not have been possible had our NRA family, for whatever reason, not provided us the opportunity to play a small role in the fight to preserve the freedoms passed down to us by those who came before. For this we shall be forever grateful.

Second, the Second Amendment would have been lost without the tireless efforts of the elected Board, Officers, and professional staff of the NRA. Specifically, modern greats like Jim Baker, Alan Cors, Chris Cox, John Frazer, Sandy Froman, Marion Hammer, Jim Land, Wayne LaPierre, Woody Phillips, Jim Porter, Kayne Robinson, and, especially, Millie Hallow, on whom we depend for almost everything. On behalf of all Americans, thank you all for what you do, including the major players we may have missed.

We must also thank our wives for editing and coordinating between two busy men. Your back-and-forth and honesty made this book better. Any mistakes are entirely our own, as you will tell us if anyone finds any. Thank you, too, to Pam Leigh, a dedicated book agent who provides assistance and advice above and beyond, every step of the way. Jay Cassell and the Skyhorse team are terrific, especially in light of having needed to work their magic on short deadlines as they put up with newbies to the book world.

David would like to thank the editors and staff at the *Washington Times,* who should be rewarded with all the bonuses and praise possible (well, praise is probably all they will get or expect), for putting up with absences and my tendency to run the Opinion section of the paper from a laptop on the road, rather than my desk at the office. And to those I've worked with over the years who have given me an opportunity to volunteer so much time and effort to the causes about which I care so much—my friends and associates at the American Conservative Union, the Carmen Group, the Center for the National Interest, the Constitution Project, and other policy groups on whose Boards I have served or serve today.

Tom extends his thanks to Kaitlin Deasy and Annie Leonard, who were essential in preparing Part II, along with Lucas Taylor, who read the many thousands of Hillary Clinton emails that have been released to the public. Lucas would have cheerfully sorted through many more had the Justice Department let him get his hands on them. From what we know of the United Nations, Lucas could have had a lot more fun continuing to link Hillary Clinton to this betrayal of the American people and the Constitution.

Finally, to four generations of great family. Thank you all for being so flexible.

—David Keene, Tom Mason

FOREWORD

The liberal assault on the Second Amendment has taken many forms in recent years. When I arrived in Washington, Senators like the late Edward M. Kennedy of Massachusetts were railing on about "Saturday-night specials" and "cop-killer bullets" and insisting that guns, rather than those who misused them, were responsible for the crime and violence that spiked in the 1960s and '70s.

They derided gun owners and hunters as ignorant rednecks. They seemingly believed, sincerely, that, if we simply disarmed American citizens, registered and eventually outlawed the private ownership of firearms, and created a "gun-free zone" from sea to sea, all would be well. They weren't much interested in prosecuting the criminals they viewed as "misunderstood," nor were they interested in the victims themselves, and were instead offended by a "gun culture" they found intolerable.

Many of these same activists supported analogous international policies. They were supporters of what was known back then as the "nuclear freeze." They campaigned against U.S. defense policies in the belief that our international adversaries, much like Chicago street thugs, were simply misunderstood. World peace, they argued, would be achieved if we would simply disarm. It wasn't until Ronald Reagan moved into the White House, in 1981, that the nation effectively began to stand by its beliefs and values, to treat international gangster nations as a threat not to be accommodated, but defeated. It was those policies, rather than the willingness of those who continued to believe we, not our adversaries, were the problem, that led to the defeat of the Soviet Union and the freeing of millions of people who had suffered for decades under Communist tyranny.

Here at home, during those same years, we began to accept the reality that it was the criminals who misuse firearms and not the guns themselves that were the problem. We got tough on crime and, as a result, took back our streets and cities. Murder rates dropped precipitously, and the United States became a safer country, even as more and more of our citizens decided to take responsibility for their own defense and the safety of their families by buying and learning to use firearms.

Unfortunately, those, both here and abroad, who would disarm us in a dangerous world and leave us defenseless at home in the face of criminals, dope dealers, and gangbangers do not have much of a learning curve. They continue to argue for disarmament and refuse to accept the notion that we have actual enemies both domestic and foreign.

It amazes me that, in today's increasingly dangerous world, so many are willing to fall for this reasoning. In the aftermath of the June 2016 murder of 49 innocents in Orlando by a terrorist, the political elites and the media insisted it was not the killer's motives that were a problem, but the fact he was able to lay his hands on a gun. The problem, insisted the *New York Times*, was not radical Islamist terrorism, but the National Rifle Association and the Republican majority in our Congress. The President even argued that if any of the shooter's victims or potential victims had been armed, the carnage would have been worse.

Dave Keene and Tom Mason have fought for the Second Amendment for decades. Dave served as NRA President during the battle over the gun control measures proposed by President Obama in 2013, after having served as a "public delegate" to a United Nations (U.N.) conference on small arms at the request of the Bush White House. Dave and I have known each other for many years, and no one has worked harder to preserve American freedom.

Over the years, Dave has worked closely with Tom, who has been a central actor in the decades-long fight against international treaties deployed to undermine American rights. They were both of immense help to me as I served as our U.N. Ambassador. During that time, I had to contend with those who sought to use the United Nations to circumvent the Second Amendment rights of the American people, and I was there as anti-gun advocates from around the world argued for an international treaty that rejected the idea that anyone has a right to self-defense and would label a nation that permits its citizens the right to keep and bear arms a "human rights" abuser.

As President, George W. Bush opposed any such treaty and early in his Administration asked me to go to the U.N. and lay it on the line by establishing a "red line" that would make any agreement that might impinge on the freedoms and Second Amendment rights of Americans unacceptable. With Dave and Tom as allies, we stopped the U.N. effort to do that in its tracks.

Unfortunately, our efforts were reversed once President Obama and Secretary of State Hillary Clinton took over. They quickly let it be known that the "red line" was gone, that the new President wanted a U.N. treaty, and that they would work with those hostile to the United States to come up with one. Mrs. Clinton, as her own emails prove, was an active participant in the effort to develop a treaty that Senators of both parties have vowed never to ratify, but which will be used in future years to undermine the very Constitutional guarantees she and the President she served swore an oath to defend.

Dave and Tom, in this important book, provide facts and a warning about the fate of firearms in America. They know, because they've been involved in the struggle to defend our freedoms for decades, that we must all do our part or we will lose the freedoms, the culture, and the nation we have inherited from those who came before us. I hope this book helps everyone reading it to help in this defense.

—John Bolton
Former United States Ambassador
to the United Nations

PREFACE

Why Guns Matter

As we finish the writing of this book in the early summer of 2016, the coming presidential contest pitting Hillary Clinton against Donald Trump should be viewed as the most important election of our lifetime. Of course, someone says this at the beginning of every campaign, but this time it happens to be true.

When you hear this claim of importance from a candidate or party leader, its true meaning is easily inferred. A self-centered lot, politicians believe that every election in which they are candidates is, by definition, the most important. When John Kerry rose to accept his Democratic Party's nomination for President, in 2004, everyone within earshot knew what he meant when he referred to that fall's election as "the most important election of our lifetime." He meant, "This is my shot at the White House, and, believe me, this the most important contest of *my* lifetime." George W. Bush answered the question with his customary candor that same year when Larry King asked him during a televised interview, "Is this election the most important ever?" Without missing a beat, Bush said, "For me it is."

This time it is the most important election for the rest of us, all of us *not* running for office. The next President of the United States will have the opportunity to appoint as many as three Justices to the nine-member Supreme Court. As you read this, the Court is deadlocked with four liberal and four generally conservative Justices, because of the death of Associate Justice Antonin Scalia. The ideological deadlock that exists today will be broken when Scalia's replacement is confirmed. As other Justices leave over the next few years, the new President will be able to "lock in" the liberal or conservative majority that will determine just what the Constitution and Bill of Rights mean for decades to come—and the makeup of the Court has not been so obvious an issue since President Franklin Delano Roosevelt tried to pack the Court with liberals in the 1940s while America was at war.

During the 2008 presidential campaign, the National Rifle Association (NRA) and other gun groups realized that Barack Obama's record of hostility to the Second Amendment meant that his election could be a serious threat that should give gun owners pause. Yet Mr. Obama never openly attacked the Second Amendment and, in fact, assured all who would listen that he was a supporter of the individual right to bear arms. Even in June 2016, after his attempts to enact a strict gun-control agenda at every opportunity, he claimed, during what he called a "town hall" tour, not only that he supports the Second Amendment, but that he also ought to be regarded as pro-Second Amendment because so many guns were sold during his Presidency.

In this, Obama was acting as other Democratic progressives have since the 2000 elections, when Vice President Al Gore's open opposition to firearms rights cost him, according to then-President Bill Clinton, as many as five states and the White House. (You can read more about this at http://www.outsidethebeltway.com/bill-clinton-warns-democrats-against-overreaching-on-gun-debate/; and http://www.nytimes.com/2000/11/09/us/the-2000-elec tions-tennessee-loss-in-home-state-leaves-gore-depending-on-florida.html.) From 2000 to 2014, Democratic candidates made a point of appearing at gun ranges, alleging they were hunters and doing all they could to keep a discussion of guns and gun legislation "off the table." Many still chuckle at the image of John Kerry with the tags still on his hunting gear. But gun owners and Second Amendment supporters, like most other voters, were, in 2008, focusing on the war in Iraq and the economic collapse, which allowed Mr. Obama an opportunity to avoid the scrutiny he would have faced on other issues under different circumstances.

Gun rights advocates saw the threat and tried to sound the alarm, but were drowned out by the other pressing concerns. They knew Mr. Obama was a long-time gun-control advocate and that his most ardent supporters were urging him to impose new restrictions on the private ownership of firearms during his first term.

During his first term, President Obama resisted making gun control a major issue, knowing that it would hurt his re-election campaign in 2012. He did, however, authorize the State Department, under Hillary Clinton, to proceed in the United Nations to help craft an international treaty that many believe will impact Second Amendment rights in this country. All the while, his re-election campaign in 2012 ran ads in rural areas touting his commitment to the Second Amendment.

As subsequent events have demonstrated, the President was simply biding his time. Wayne LaPierre, Executive Vice President of the NRA, months before the election predicted that, if reelected, President Obama would do all he could to undermine the Second Amendment. This prediction was ridiculed by many in the media; pundit and television host Chris Mathews famously said LaPierre was "clinically insane" to suggest that Mr. Obama would do any such thing. (You can read more about this on the following links: http://freebeacon.com/politics/ leaked-audio-clinton-says-supreme-court-is-wrong-on-second-amendment/; http://www.bloomberg.com/politics/articles/2016-05-20/hillary-clinton- believes-pivotal-gun-rights-ruling-was-wrong-adviser-says; http://www.cnsnews. com/news/article/susan-jones/clinton-individual-right-bear-arms-if-it-constitu tional-right; http://nymag.com/daily/intelligencer/2016/05/hillary-clinton-candi dacy.html#; and http://www.breitbart.com/big-government/2016/01/06/dc-media- cover-up-actually-obama-and-hillary-have-said-they-want-to-confiscate-guns/.) Within less than 24 hours of his re-election, the President asked the United Na- tions to complete action on a controversial Arms Trade Treaty that Secretary of State Hillary Clinton had helped write. (He had asked the body to hold off on this as the election approached.) The U.N. moved quickly, abandoning the tra- ditional requirement that such treaties could move forward only if "consensus" had been reached and sending this treaty on for ratification. A month later, the mass shooting at the Sandy Hook Elementary School in Newtown, Connecticut, gave the newly reelected President the rationale he was looking for to launch a domestic political gun-control campaign that he characterized as a "common sense" series of reforms designed to prevent such tragedies. President Obama and his advisors, along with then-New York Mayor Michael Bloomberg and other like-minded groups and individuals, were certain they could exploit the Sandy Hook tragedy. Overnight, well-funded anti-gun nonprofits sprung up across the country, insisting that Congress and the states pass new firearms restrictions. Most of these had been rejected in other sessions of Congress, so the Adminis- tration and its supporters knew, even as the plan was being formulated, that to win the legislative and public support needed to succeed, they would have to go around or defeat the pro-Second Amendment efforts of the NRA and other gun groups. They hoped and believed that public outrage over what happened at Sandy Hook would allow them to do just that.

The President led the effort to demonize the NRA and marginalize the influence of its then-four million members by blaming the association for gun violence in his speeches and initiating a broad-based effort to isolate gun owners. Yet gun and ammunition sales soared, and gun owners in state after state attended rallies, called and wrote their representatives, and made it clear, in every way possible, that they would not be intimidated and were not about to roll over as a result of such pressure—and *this* is actually why so many guns were sold during Obama's Presidency.

That failure to regulate gun ownership has not deterred Mr. Obama or his supporters in their push for what he terms "common sense" gun-control measures. By early 2013, well into the Presidential campaign for his successor and in the beginning of his lame duck year, Mr. Obama began to define what he means by "common sense" more clearly. After denying for years that he or anyone else in his Administration wanted to outlaw the private ownership of firearms or confiscate privately held guns, he began to underscore that the two countries with what he considered the most sensible restrictions on firearms ownership are Great Britain and Australia—both of which have confiscated and outlawed citizens' guns—and that is why media coverage of the assassination of a pro-European Union British legislator during the Brexit election states that the shooter "must have been using an antique gun." Surely, if confiscation was so effective, such a thing is the only explanation.

The cumulative impact of Obama's rhetoric and the continuing assault on the very idea that responsible Americans should be able to own or use firearms, even for self-defense, is part of a larger effort to change, in the most fundamental ways, the traditional, historical, American acceptance of gun ownership. But firearms advocates and anti-gun advocates know the real fight is not about this restriction or that law, but about the nature of American culture and the acceptability of firearms by the average citizen.

That fight goes on daily in the media, various legislatures, and Congress, as well as in the courts and in the international arena. Yet these efforts have thus far failed to change America's public acceptance of the right to keep and bear arms. Indeed, firearms ownership increases by the day—one-third of American households own one or more guns. Poll after poll shows that more, rather than fewer, Americans support the Second Amendment, and the public backlash to the gun-control campaign has so increased the number of firearms in private hands that gun retailers only half-jokingly refer to President Obama as the "Gun Salesman of the Year."

But gun-control advocates do not give up. Again in 2016, Democrats and liberals launched a serious political effort to win public support for their desired restrictions. In the lead-up to her party's primaries, Mrs. Clinton focused on her long record of support for more restrictive gun laws partly to excite and motivate her party's base, who tend to favor such restrictions. She seemed to believe, like many of her fellow gun controllers, that the tide has changed and that firearms restrictions might attract rather than drive away voters. On this one issue candidate Clinton could get to the left of primary opponent Senator Bernie Sanders. Mrs. Clinton has talked about how the Supreme Court has been wrong on the Second Amendment and praised gun confiscation policies of Great Britain and Australia, then in the acceptance speech for her party's nomination assured voters that she supports the Second Amendment.

When Barack Obama first ran for President, in 2008, he promised change without really defining what he meant. As the 2016 elections approach, voters now know what change Obama had in mind, and they need to be reminded, in the midst of all the clutter and verbiage, just what Mrs. Clinton plans when it comes to the Second Amendment and to the private right to own firearms for any purpose, from self-defense to hunting and competitive shooting.

Voters, with the luxury that hindsight affords, have been able to judge the gap between what Obama has tried to do compared to what they expected—but these millions upon millions of gun owners and Second Amendment rights believers do not have to guess what Mrs. Clinton will do as President.

This will be the first election in which gun owners and Second Amendment supporters will all know from day one that their rights and freedoms are on the line. Second Amendment supporters have proven time and again that, when they know the nature of the threat, they will rally as volunteers, contributors, and voters, crossing party lines if necessary to protect their freedoms. In televised debates, Mrs. Clinton specifically named the NRA as one of her enemies. (You can read more about this here: http://www.cbsnews.com/news/democratic-debate-which-enemy-are-you-most-proud-of/.) The very survival of the Second Amendment is in the balance, and it will be up to voters to defend it—and voters know, without a doubt, they are facing the most important election of their lives.

Wisconsin Congressman Paul Ryan, as Chairman of the House Budget Committee and before becoming Speaker of the House, warned continually that the United States may well be at a "tipping point." He has said that unless we pull back from the precipice very soon, we will find ourselves living in a Europeanized nation, one with little hope of experiencing a restoration of its vibrant economy and free society bequeathed to us by our forebears. Ryan does not shave during hunting season until he gets his deer; he gets it.

Earlier generations of Americans have overcome domestic and international challenges to our freedoms. Other countries have not been so fortunate. Now, it is America's challenge. The chief threat to our way of life is not to be found on the battlefields of Syria, Iraq, or Afghanistan, but in the dedication of an American elite convinced that America must change in ways that would have appalled the Founders; if such changes continue, it could cost us our prosperity and, ultimately, our freedoms—unless we stop them.

Former President Ronald Reagan, in 1961, told the Phoenix Chamber of Commerce:

Freedom is never more than one generation away from extinction. We didn't pass it on to our children in the bloodstream. It must be fought for, protected, and handed on for them to do the same, or one day we will spend our sunset years telling our children and our children's children what it was once like in the United States where men were free.

There are voters who dismissed concerns about the direction America has taken, because they find President Obama "likeable" or because they have been persuaded that he is trying to do the "right" thing. History tells us that the greatest threats to liberty come not from those proclaiming a desire to obliterate the freedom of those they lead, but from leaders who persuade their citizens that trading just a little liberty for security is a trade worth making. Putting Obama on the Supreme Court poses just such a threat.

Sir Karl Raimund Popper, 20th-century philosopher and a professor at the London School of Economics, warned decades ago that:

> *[T]he attempt to make heaven on earth invariably produces hell. It leads to intolerance. It leads to religious wars, and to the saving of souls through the inquisition.*

Supreme Court Justice Louis Brandeis warned of these very threats to our liberty as long ago as 1928, when he wrote:

> *Experience should teach us to be most on our guard to protect liberty when the government's purposes are beneficent. Men born to freedom are naturally alert to repel invasion of their liberty by evil-minded rulers. The greatest dangers to liberty lurk in insidious encroachment by men of zeal, well-meaning but without understanding.*

Brandeis was observing a truth that Thomas Paine recognized at the time of our country's founding, when he warned, "The greatest tyrannies are always perpetrated in the name of the noblest causes." What was accurate then could have been seen as a prediction of the terrors of the 20th century. The prophets and leaders of the Communist world proclaimed themselves dedicated to creating an egalitarian utopia in which men and women would live and prosper, but which instead ended with the bloody deaths of hundreds of millions and enforced misery for those who survived.

From the beginning of history, the world has been divided into two basic camps. The first consists of those who, far from being obsessed with politics or the desire to rule others, simply want to be free to live their lives, raise and educate their kids, and enjoy what our Founders referred to as "the pursuit of happiness." The second camp is sure that they know better how those in the first camp should live their lives, raise and educate their kids, and channel their energies. The second camp thinks they are smarter and, knowing they are "right," are determined to rule the first camp. Sometimes these folks are simply harmless busybodies with advice for us all; we all know dozens of them, and while some can be incredibly annoying, most of them are pretty good people we might listen to because we are free to take their advice or ignore it. But while President Obama, Michael Bloomberg, and many who share their views may be sincere and may actually believe that a gun-free world would be a better world, they are badly mistaken. What is even worse is that they demonstrate a willingness to ig-nore evidence, experience, history, and the beliefs of the American people in their efforts to get the rest of us to accept their views. The current Administration in Washington is made up almost exclusively of busybodies who believe they know how we should live. They busily promulgate thousands of regulations to encour-age or, if necessary, force us to make the "right" decisions about how we live our lives, choose our doctors, educate our kids, heat our homes, and earn a living.

History teaches us that an unarmed populace is easier to rule, which is why the Founding Fathers gave constitutional protection to the right of individual American citizens to keep and bear arms. It is also why those same Founders emphasized "shall not be infringed," a definitive phrase that sets the Second Amendment in its own tier of rights. Today's liberals reject such thinking, in part because they place their faith not in the individual, but in the collective. They reject the very concept of self-defense, a rejection underpinning the Arms Trade Treaty negotiated on Secretary of State Hillary Clinton's watch, passed by the United Nations, and signed by her successor, Secretary of State John Kerry, at President Obama's direction.

The idea that people in modern society have an individual right to pro-tect themselves and their families seems anachronistic to the President and his friends, although the courts have long held that police have a legal obligation to protect not individuals, but society as a whole. When Clinton or Obama want protection, they use the Secret Service—at taxpayer expense—and they are not shy about using the very guns Obama and Speaker Pelosi want to ban first.

Today's progressives, like Clinton and Obama, also seem to believe we would all be living in a utopia if firearms could be abolished. They resist blam-ing criminals for crime. When someone picks up a gun to rob a convenience store, the gun, an inanimate object without volition of its own, is to blame, rather than the criminal. Progressive mayors from former Mayor Bloomberg of New York to former Obama Chief of Staff Rahm Emanuel, now Mayor of Chicago, refuse to blame their cities' criminals for violent crime. Instead, they blame the availability of guns in their cities, or elsewhere, as if the mere exis-tence of guns hundreds of miles away seduces otherwise peaceful residents to commit violent crimes.

Blaming guns for crime is a modern domestic version of the tendency of progressives in the 1960s and '70s to blame the world's troubles on the existence of nuclear weapons rather than on an aggressive Soviet Union. The cry then was for unilateral disarmament, which would, it was hoped, induce the tyrants of that era to beat their swords into plowshares. Today's spin on that theory is that denying guns to the law-abiding will force criminals to lay down their arms.

Opposition to the private ownership of firearms has become an almost religious tenet among progressives. The assertion that gun control or firearms confiscation will eliminate or significantly reduce homicide and violent crime cannot, in the progressive mind, be refuted by factual evidence to the contrary. Empirical study after empirical study have demonstrated that the availability of firearms and the propensity of people to engage in violence are unrelated in the real world. But these facts make no impression on today's progressives, who continue to insist that, if we could just restrict firearms ownership or register or confiscate the darned things, society would be safer.

President Obama and Hillary Clinton have embraced these tenets and are dedicated to eliminating the private ownership of firearms. The cautious talk about "common sense" regulations "consistent with the Second Amendment" has given way to praise for countries that have confiscated privately owned firearms and promises to appoint Supreme Court Justices who will overturn the recent Supreme Court confirmation that the Second Amendment, as well as the rest of the Bill of Rights, were about individual rights. And so it is and remains an all-out assault on firearms ownership.

The full text of the Second Amendment states:

> *A well regulated Militia, being necessary to the security of a free State, the right of the people to keep and bear Arms, shall not be infringed.*

The Second Amendment has often been deconstructed by those who want it to mean something other than what the Founders and the Supreme Court have found it to mean. Some would abolish the Second Amendment entirely, while others would twist it to restrict, rather than guarantee, the right to keep and bear arms. This book, however, is about four words of the Second Amendment too often ignored: *shall not be infringed.*

In Part I, we will examine the political history of the domestic gun-control movement and the evidence as to whether the most often suggested restrictions on firearms ownership work. We will examine how often guns are used in crimes, what measures have and have not been effective in dealing with gun crime, as well as how often and how important guns are in the prevention of crime and violence. We will review the ways in which the public perception of gun ownership has changed over the years and how public support for the Second Amendment has actually increased in spite of a decades-long effort by anti-firearms advocates and politicians to undermine that support.

Failing in the legislative arena, the gun fight switched to the courts. This election must be about the makeup of Supreme Court pursuant to the death of Antonin Scalia. Hillary Clinton has said that the *Heller* decision, which has been key to the question of what our country's Founders intended when they drafted the Second Amendment as part of the Bill of Rights, was wrongly decided.

The 2016 Presidential outcome could be crucial. The next president will have an opportunity to change the makeup of the United States Supreme Court. Associate Justice Ruth Bader Ginsburg is the most outspokenly liberal member of the current court. She, like Hillary Clinton, has said *Heller* was wrongly decided, is convinced the Founders never intended to protect the private ownership of firearms, and has said she hopes to cast a vote to overturn *Heller* before she retires. Published July 10, 2016, in an interview with the *New York Times*, Justice Ginsburg could not resist looking forward to the liberal court majority that Mrs. Clinton would create if she wins the White House and specifically singled out *Heller* as a "very bad decision" such a court could and should reconsider. (You can read more about this here: http://www.nytimes.com/2016/07/11/us/politics/ruth-bader-ginsburg-no-fan-of-donald-trump-critiques-latest-term.html.) She "cannot imagine what the country would be like" if Trump is elected and suggested that it would be time to move to New Zealand. The statement was roundly condemned by conservative and liberal court watchers alike, and the newspaper to which she gave her interview even led its editorial page in condemning the propriety, if not the substance, of her remarks, with the headline "Donald Trump was Right." The paper's editors might just as well have headed it "The NRA Is Right About Ruth Bader Ginsberg" (www.nytimes.com/2016/07/13/opinion/donald-trump-is-right-about-justice-ruth-bader-ginsburg.html), because, like the NRA leadership, Justice Ginsburg knows everything is on the table. For the future of the Second Amendment, the November vote will be the most important of our lifetimes.

Anyone who had any lingering doubts about whether Hillary Clinton was ready to double down on her opposition to the right of Americans to own firearms to protect themselves, their homes, and their families had only to tune into day three of the 2016 Democratic National Convention in Philadelphia in July 2016. The party and its nominee were ready, willing, and eager to make opposition to the Second Amendment rights of Americans a centerpiece of the 2016 campaign.

That evening's "festivities" included speeches by the parents of victims of children killed in the 2012 shootings at a Newtown, Connecticut, elementary school by a mentally deranged shooter; the parents of a victim of the 2016 attack on customers at an Orlando nightclub catering to gays by a committed jihadist; and former Congresswoman Gabby Giffords who was wounded by a shooter in Arizona and has become a spokesperson for one of the many anti-gun groups financed by former New York City Mayor Michael Bloomberg. Mr. Bloomberg also spoke.

Time magazine reported in the wake of the anti-gun fusillade that Democrats "embraced gun control at their convention." Democratic strategists would probably have preferred that the reporter use a phrase other than gun control after being cautioned by pollster Anna Greenberg to use words less likely to raise the hackles of Second Amendment supporters and gun owners. She advises Democrats to focus on phrases like "common sense restrictions" and in a memo available to Democratic delegates in Philadelphia to "talk about the 'gun lobby,' but not the National Rifle Association . . . about closing loopholes, not about stricter gun laws . . . about background checks, not a national gun registry. And, never . . . use the loaded phrase 'gun control.'"

Softer, more cautious language did little to hide the fact that for the first time in decades, a Democratic Presidential candidate is going to run *against* the Second Amendment. Connecticut Senator Chris Murphy, who unsuccessfully led a Senate filibuster in early July to force a Senate vote on gun control measures, was in Philadelphia and put the matter to reporters this way: "If Hillary Clinton wins, she wins with a mandate on this issue."

When Mrs. Clinton spoke to the delegates the next evening, she echoed President Obama as she vowed to fight for "reasonable" or "common sense" restrictions on guns but hastened to reassure the public that she is really a Second Amendment supporter. "I'm not here to repeal the Second Amendment," she declared, "I'm not here to take away your guns." The words *sounded* good only if one did not have any sense of what had come before.

Last fall, Mrs. Clinton told supporters and donors in New York City that she believes the *Heller* and *McDonald* cases, in which the Supreme Court held that individual Americans have a right to own and keep firearms in their homes for self-defense, were "wrongly decided." Yet her Republican opponent, Donald Trump, declared that in his opinion she would "abolish" the Second Amendment if she ever makes it to the White House." Her supporters immediately attacked Trump for the remark, arguing, as Politifact put it, that she has never said so "verbatim" or suggested "explicitly" a desire to abolish the Second Amendment.

To reach that conclusion, the fact checkers ignored the one question the Supreme Court was asked to answer in the *Heller* case—or they listened to the Democratic pollster on what to say and not to say. The *Heller* question was asked in light of a handgun ban in the District of Columbia that included a ban on a homeowner acquiring a firearm, even if registered, to keep in his or her home for self-protection. The court said the Second Amendment guarantees just such a right; Mrs. Clinton, in arguing that the Court was wrong, answered that very same question in the negative. If a court including a Clinton appointee reverses *Heller*, that court would in effect be abolishing the Second Amendment.

The Second Amendment would not be stricken from the text of the Bill of Rights, but it would remain an artifact just like the 18th amendment outlawing the importation and sale of alcohol that ushered in prohibition in the twenties with little or no interest except to historians. Voters should realize that what Mrs. Clinton has said and continues to believe is that there is no constitutionally protected right in this country to own any firearm even for the purpose of defending oneself, one's family, and one's home. That is her position and the position of those who try to use softer language to obscure a harsh truth.

Since the late sixties, many national Democratic Party leaders have been moving their party in the direction Mrs. Clinton embraces. Millions of Democrats at the grassroots level disagree with their party's direction, but the grassroots has little say within the national councils of the party. In past decades, many Democratic Members of Congress have been staunch Second Amendment supporters, but they are today a vanishing breed.

Anti-Second Amendment activists and donors like Michael Bloomberg have mounted a concerted effort to require as a matter of political correctness that all Democrats embrace the policies that Mrs. Clinton champions. It is becoming as unacceptable within the ranks of Mrs. Clinton's party to oppose the latest gun control scheme as it is to question party orthodoxy on issues like abortion.

Ambitious politicians have a habit of adjusting to reality within their own parties—witness the rabid anti-Second Amendment rhetoric from Mrs. Clinton's running mate. Former Virginia Governor Tim Kaine is today described as a fierce opponent of the NRA and an advocate of "common sense" firearms restrictions, but this is new.

When Mr. Kaine ran for Governor in Virginia in 2005, he ran as a moderate and a Second Amendment supporter. He positioned himself as a champion of the NRA-supported effort to get law enforcement to use existing federal laws to prosecute gun crime. When Richmond, Virginia, was the "murder capitol" of the country and the NRA developed "Project Exile," Kaine was the mayor cooperating with local and federal law enforcement to let gun criminals know they would be held accountable for their illegal use of guns. The project will be described later.

In 2005, candidate Kaine posted his position on the Second Amendment and gun control on his website:

> Tim Kaine strongly supports the Second Amendment. As the next Governor of Virginia, he will not propose any new gun laws. Instead, Tim Kaine will guarantee strict enforcement of our existing criminal laws. He will also expand the use of such enforcement strategies as Project Exile that target criminals who use guns rather than law-abiding gun owners.

The Tim Kaine who served as Chairman of the Democratic Party and addressed the Philadelphia Convention claims he changed his views because of what happened at Virginia Tech in 2007. Mrs. Clinton's managers have argued that one of the reasons she chose him as her running mate was because of his current support for firearms restriction.

Understand this: If Hillary Clinton becomes President and the *Heller* ruling is overturned, Americans will have no legal recourse against gun confiscation, because they will lose their individual right to keep and bear arms.

With *Heller* and other decisions, gun-control advocates have tried, so far unsuccessfully, to persuade the courts that reinterpreting the Second Amendment would be what the Founders wanted (or the latest spin, that the Founders were simply racist and wanted their guns only to shoot runaway slaves in the back). We will examine the current state of the law and efforts both in the courts and in changing the courts themselves to render the Second Amendment meaningless.

In Part II, we will analyze how the United Nations became so anti-gun and the dangers inherent in the international offensive being mounted by gun-controllers to use the U.N. and international treaties to undermine American constitutional rights in ways they have not been previously able to accomplish politically, culturally, or through the courts of the United States. This will include the story of how the Obama Administration and the President's Secretary of State, Hillary Clinton, worked with gun-control advocates here and abroad to help draft a treaty that could have serious consequences in their efforts to undermine the rights of gun owners in this country. (And, while she was at it, Clinton helped organizations that helped fund the Clinton Foundation, its own thorn in the side of gun-rights advocates.)

Finally, in Part III, we will look to the ways in which these challenges to traditional American freedoms can best be countered in the courts, Congress, and at the ballot box; and it will include specific actions that readers can take to protect these vital freedoms.

It is a sordid story—but one worth telling.

—David Keene and Tom Mason

PART I

The Arms Trade Treaty: Trouble on the Home Front

CHAPTER 1

The Players

The battle between gun-control advocates and Second Amendment supporters has raged for decades. In the late 1960s, crime spiked, riots raged in many U.S. cities, and the assassinations of Robert F. Kennedy and the Reverend Martin Luther King, Jr., focused attention on gun crime.

The advent of the so-called "culture wars" gave a growing number of liberal, anti-Second Amendment activists the opportunity to exploit concerns about increasing crime rates. Politicians of both parties responded by advocating for more restrictive gun-control laws. Gun-control measures that would never have even been seriously considered, let alone proposed, a decade earlier became a real possibility at both the state and federal levels.

These efforts were supported by poll figures at the time reflecting what appeared to be strong public support for gun control. In 1968, President Lyndon B. Johnson and the Democratic Congress enacted the Gun Control Act of 1968, the most restrictive anti-firearms legislation ever passed. In 1973, President Richard Nixon's Attorney General, Elliott Richardson welcomed the results of a two-year Justice Department study by a 22-member National Advisory Commission on Criminal Justice Standards and Goals. The Commission on August 9, 1973, issued a 318-page report in which it recommended "no later than January 1, 1983, all states should prohibit the possession, sale, manufacture and importation of handguns except for military and law enforcement officials." Attorney General Richardson accepted the report claiming "it may be the most important report, on crime control ever compiled in this country."

The Gun Control Act of 1968 was seen by many, including young Massachusetts Senator Edward M. Kennedy, as a "good first step" toward the new liberal goal of banning the private ownership and possession of firearms. Gun owners and Second Amendment advocates reeled, unprepared for what seemed an abrupt reversal of public, Congressional, and Presidential support for the Second Amendment: just 10 years before, liberals like President John F. Kennedy and Minnesota Senator Hubert Humphrey had been card-carrying National Rifle Association (NRA) members.

These measures and proposals awoke a sleeping giant, as gun owners and Second Amendment supporters began organizing a substantive debate on the wisdom of what had been enacted and ignited a backlash that was to change public opinion and create pro-Second Amendment majorities not only in Congress, but in most state legislatures. This book will touch on this history, but its primary focus will be on the battles that have ensued in Congress, the courts, the media, and the United Nations (U.N.) since the 1990s. The opposition to firearms freedom during this period has been led almost exclusively by liberal Democrats driven either by the belief that their measures might actually reduce violence, by an ideological hostility to the private ownership of firearms, or by what has thus far proven to be a mistaken belief that gun control will help them politically.

Bad Tydings

By David Keene

Maryland Senator Joe Tydings was considered a sure bet for re-election in 1970, but his support of President Johnson's gun-control legislation in 1968, as well as a bill he introduced calling for the registration all firearms, proved his undoing. The NRA was changing, and so was the willingness of gun owners to vote their values. The polls Tydings surveyed as the election approached showed strong support for his stance, and so he decided to ignore the warning signs that such support might be "a mile wide and an inch deep."

I was working in the Nixon White House at the time, and while we did not have all the sophisticated techniques and exit polls that allow people today to monitor voting in real time, we had friends in Maryland who were watching voters coming and going from the polls. Mid-afternoon on Election Day, a number of us were gathered in Nixon aide Chuck Colson's office, when someone wondered how things were going in Maryland. We called one of our people there, who reported that he did not know whether Tydings would be defeated but said there were "lines of pickup trucks at the polling places outside Washington's liberal suburbs and Baltimore, and most have gun racks in the back window."

When the votes were counted, Tydings had lost and became the first of many whose careers ended because they underestimated the power of the emerging gun lobby. His defeat persuaded those who were transforming the NRA into a powerful political force that they were on the right track.

The historic divide between anti- and pro-gun politicians has existed between those who represent urban areas with few firearms owners and those from more rural areas where the so-called "gun culture" is a part of everyone's lives.

This is ironic, because the assault on the Second Amendment that was kicked off in the mid-'90s had actually found staunch allies in states where firearms ownership enjoys widespread and strong public support. By the time a former Arkansas Governor and his Tennessee-bred running mate led the anti-gun forces of the 1990s, fights over gun ownership were increasingly ideological.

It was then that Charlton Heston—who played Moses in the *Ten Commandments* (1956) and starred in *Touch of Evil* (1958) with Orson Welles, *Ben-Hur* (1959), *El Cid* (1961), and *Planet of the Apes* (1968) before becoming the President of the NRA in 1998—famously said that the fight was less about guns than freedom. The Second Amendment had come to symbolize much more than in earlier decades, and it became a fight that was, in the eyes of both its strongest advocates and its strongest detractors, about an America and a set of values that were at the center of what came to be called a "culture war" that would pit liberals and conservatives against each other on a variety of fronts.

Clinton-Gore

William Jefferson Clinton was an Arkansas boy but was educated in the East and at Oxford. His values more resembled those held by others who have graduated from Yale than the University of Arkansas; and his wife, Hillary Rodham, was an upper middle-class product of Chicago's wealthy suburbs who had come to admire the chic radicals of the era like Saul Alinsky, a founder of modern community organizing who wrote *Rules for Radicals*, a left-wing manifesto to which quotes such as "Power is not only what you have but what the enemy thinks you have" and "Last guys don't finish nice" are attributed.

Clinton's Arkansas background helped him when he ran for the Presidency in 1992 but had less influence once he got to Washington than his liberal friends and his wife, all strong supporters of more restrictive firearms laws.

Clinton's Vice President, the former Senator Al Gore of Tennessee, was raised in Washington, D.C., where his father before him had represented Tennessee first as a Congressman and then as a Senator. Gore shared Clinton's prejudices on guns and signed on to his crusade against Second Amendment rights with an enthusiasm that ended his own career, when he ran to succeed Clinton, in 2000.

Not Interested

By David Keene

I used to attend the conference where Chelsea Clinton met her husband. Bill and Hillary chose nine of 11 Cabinet members from the attendees. Bill is a persuader, and as Arkansas' Governor, he used to bird-dog me, trying to persuade me and others to change our views on a variety of topics, or tried all he could to get us to declare ourselves in basic agreement with him, even when we were not. I quit attending those conferences until his Presidency ended.

President Clinton's assault weapons ban persuaded voters that their President was anti-Second Amendment and sparked an NRA campaign that contributed heavily to the Democratic Congressional losses in 1994 and gave Republicans control of the House of Representatives for the first time in 40 years. Jody Powell, White House Press Secretary to President Jimmy Carter and a Southerner, saw what was coming and urged Clinton to ease up on his crusade for gun control. He drafted a memorandum on guns and forwarded it to the new President through George Stephanopoulos, who was, at the time, one of President Clinton's closest advisors. In the memo, Powell pointed out that none of the restrictions and bans the President was supporting would do anything to reduce the crime he said he was fighting through these propositions, and, just as important, most gun owners knew this and concluded, not illogically, that these proposals were aimed not at reducing crime, but at reducing their rights. This, concluded Powell, might fuel a backlash that could cost Democrats dearly at the polls in 1994 and beyond. Stephanopoulos forwarded the Powell memo to President Clinton, after noting in the margin, "I agree with Jody."

President Clinton and Vice President Gore stuck with their liberal elitist friends and refused to back down, and Mr. Gore seemed to welcome a debate over his position on firearms restrictions, when he ran against former Texas Governor George W. Bush for the Presidency, in 2000. Clinton acknowledged, after the election results were in and the experts were counting chads in Florida, that their position on guns had cost his Vice President five states, including Mr. Gore's home state of Tennessee, which he lost to Bush by a 3.87-percent margin. In politics, that is decisive. (You can read more about this at http://prospect.org/article/bill-clinton-still-wrong-about-guns; and here http://uselectionatlas.org/RESULTS/state.php?year=2000&fips=47&f=0&off=0&elect=0.)

For a time, the sobering thought that their embrace of gun-control measures lacked public support and had cost them the White House forced Democrats to reexamine not their desire to restrict gun rights, but the wisdom of talking about that desire during political campaigns. Following their losses in 2000, many liberal Democratic candidates who actually favored more restrictive firearms laws began appearing in public with guns, bragging that they were ardent hunters and shooters. They wanted to take the gun debate off the table, and, for a while, the strategy worked. In time, the Democrats began to talk themselves into believing that, argued wisely, gun control would help them win elections.

President Obama

The freshman Illinois Senator who was to win back the White House for his party in 2008 absorbed the lessons of 2000 and was careful during his first Presidential campaign to downplay a lifetime of anti-gun advocacy in the interests of winning. During his community-organizing days in Chicago, Mr. Obama had served as a member of the Board of Directors of the Joyce Foundation, which played a key role in the effort to build a case against the Second Amendment's protection of private firearms rights. That view held that the Second Amendment did not guarantee an individual right to keep and bear arms at all but merely endorsed the right of the states to arm organized state militias or, in today's world, the National Guard. It was this view that the United States Supreme Court would ultimately reject in *District of Columbia v. Heller*.[1]

While Obama was on its board from 1994 to 2001, the Joyce Foundation hatched and implemented a $2.7 million grants program and paid for the publication of a book titled *Every Handgun is Aimed at You: The Case for Banning Handguns*.[2] Grants from the Joyce Foundation went to legal "scholars" who would write and place articles in law reviews nationwide arguing what came to be known as the "collective rights view" of the Second Amendment.[3] This effort was undertaken because pro-gun and anti-gun groups alike realized that, at some point, a case like *Heller* clarifying the meaning of the Second Amendment would make it to the Supreme Court. If the collective right view was accepted by a Supreme Court majority, it would mark the end of the individual right of Americans to own firearms.

At the time, the overwhelming weight of historic and academic scholarship was on the side of the individual rights interpretation, and this scholarship would prove to be key to the Court's ultimate decision, as the Justices researched the history and law review articles. To counter this, the Joyce Foundation decided to push legal scholarship their way via a massive amount of money for law reviews and universities; at the time, a $5,000 grant for a law review article was unheard of, and so the money to build a body of support for the collective view went a long way.

In 1999, the Chicago-Kent College of Law held a program on the collective versus individual interpretation of the Second Amendment. The agenda was limited to those who favored the collective view. The organizer of the program, Professor Carl Bogus, said at the time, "No effort was made to include the individual right point of view . . . [because] . . . Full and robust public debate is not always served by having all viewpoints represented . . . ."[4]

The results of this symposium and the law review articles funded by the Joyce Foundation were cited in numerous amicus briefs submitted to the Supreme Court during *District of Columbia v. Heller* by supporters of the collective interpretation of the Founders' words.

Like most of those ideologically driven in their hostility toward firearms ownership, Obama was looking for a way to achieve his long-held goal. As an Illinois State Senator, Obama supported banning "the manufacture, sale and possession of handguns" and voted for a state ban on semiautomatic firearms so flawed it would have outlawed most semiautomatic and even double-barreled shotguns. U.S. Senator Obama found himself consistently on the side of firearms prohibitionists.

With the strong memory of the cost former Vice President Al Gore paid for his support of gun control, Mr. Obama, in 2008, portrayed himself as a Second Amendment supporter. Smoother than previous candidates like former Governor Michael Dukakis, who famously drove a tank in his bid for President in 1988, or Senator John Kerry, who strutted before the cameras in hunting garb with price tags still attached, Mr. Obama simply kept the Second Amendment off the table. Try as they might, gun groups could not get traction, as other issues dominated that year's campaign. (Mr. Obama did make one slip, which has haunted him since. At a San Francisco fund-raising group, he famously derided those who "cling to their bibles and guns.")

Fooled

By David Keene

Obama's avoidance of the gun issue in 2008 worked. On July 4 of that year, my wife and I were stopped in a Choteau, Montana, antique car show, where a cluster of middle-aged men were gathered talking politics under an awning to escape the sun, drinking lemonade, and enjoying the day. Their discussion was pro-Obama, and they were deriding the very idea that he would "take their guns." When my wife began to tell them about Senator Obama's voting record and what he might do to restrict firearms ownership should he win the election, they began to laugh. In their world, the very idea seemed ludicrous. They simply could not imagine anyone trying. When we described some of the laws gun owners must contend with in Illinois, New York, and Washington, D.C., they thought we were joking.

I encountered a similar reaction from many four years later, when the re-election campaign was running ads in some rural areas promising that Mr. Obama would never take anyone's guns. As President of the NRA, I received a couple hundred letters from NRA members suggesting that we were hyping a nonexistent threat in order to raise money, the same charge many in the press were making. I suspect they feel differently now.

Obama had promised to change America, but the media and a weak 2012 Presidential candidate on the Republican side, Senator John McCain of Arizona, never forced him to define the change he had in mind. Although supporters pressed for action against gun rights during his first term, President Obama was reluctant to navigate that particular political minefield, knowing he would be running again in 2012. Mr. Obama did allow his State Department to go ahead with negotiations on an anti-gun treaty at the United Nations and sought regulatory changes that would toughen our nation's gun laws, and though he worked to avoid any overt action until after the 2012 elections, he knew something would happen to give him the chance to implement the anti-gun agenda to which he has been wedded for decades.

Fast and Furious

Still, President Obama, even during his first term, could not resist setting the stage in preparation for the day he would begin implementing his gun-control agenda. The way the Administration tried to exploit the "Fast and Furious" gun-walking operation illustrates the depth of his Administration's hostility to the Second Amendment. Mr. Obama remained willing to go to any length to pursue an anti-gun agenda as long as he could work under the radar. Bad luck and the courage of a few Bureau of Alcohol, Tobacco, Firearms and Explosives (ATF) whistleblowers alerted the public and Congress to the Fast and Furious campaign.

Fast and Furious is the code name for a government-sanctioned program in which the U.S. Department of Justice's ATF directed gun shops along the U.S. and Mexico border to allow Mexican criminals buy guns even when they could never pass the background checks. Store owners were punished when they resisted breaking the law—and that is when those owners began to understand that the penalties for *not* breaking the law would be worse than for following the law. They reluctantly complied with the ATF.

Whether the Fast and Furious program was designed to generate public support for more restrictive gun-control legislation or regulations is impossible to know, but it might as well have been. Before we follow this thwarted logic and applaud the agents who put their careers on the line to report the program's failings to Congress, an explanation of the culture at ATF will help reveal why it started and was allowed to go so far before it was stopped.

During and since Fast and Furious, Mexico has stepped up its complaints against the U.S. gun policies, lockstep with the goals of Obama and Clinton.

First, the Obama Administration and the Mexican government argued to the American public early on that the violence in Mexico was largely the result of illicit gun smuggling into Mexico from the United States. Mexico's President Calderón even came to speak to a Joint Session of Congress for renewal of the Clinton-era Assault Weapons Ban, charging that what was going on in his country could not be resolved unless the United States adopted emergency measures to halt the importation of illicit firearms into Mexico.

The charge was ludicrous on its face, but President Obama, Hillary Clinton, and their minions stood before network cameras to reinforce the claims and appeared before Congress urging stricter U.S. gun laws based on the charges. Secretary of State Hillary Clinton and the President tried to back up the demand for stricter gun-control measures along our southern border by citing evidence that many of the firearms deployed in Mexico were coming from the United States via "straw" purchasers buying them from U.S. gun dealers and then smuggling them into Mexico. These assertions were never backed up with hard evidence.

Independent investigations of the charges and the factual basis for them demonstrate that very few guns were making their way south of the border. Too, the idea that fully automatic and heavier weapons were being shipped south was ludicrous, as such firearms simply are not readily available to retail purchasers or to anyone else in the United States; such firepower would have to have been stolen from the military. More doubt was cast when investigative journalists began reporting that the bulk of the weapons in Mexico were being shipped to the drug cartels not from the U.S., but from Russia, China, and other nations via international gun dealers able to procure almost anything the cartels wanted on the international market.

What Mr. Calderón was really doing was joining his friends in Washington, to help push their domestic anti-Second Amendment agenda; whatever incentives Mexico was promised, then lost due to the leaks and public outrage, have never been made public. However, Mexico continues to damn the U.S. at every turn on the world stage and to fight internationally through the Arms Trade Treaty (ATT) for gun control in the U.S. on the premise of battling the continued violence in Mexico, this despite the evidence that the United States is not the main supplier of weapons to the Mexican drug cartels. In fact, the embarrassment of its complicity in "Fast and Furious" seems to be one of the reasons Mexico works so tirelessly to punish the U.S. internationally; that the first major Arms Trade Treaty (ATT) negotiations were hosted in Cancun was no coincidence.

Caught Red-Handed

Interestingly, after Fast and Furious began, ATF agents in Mexico reported, with genuine alarm, that firearms from the Phoenix area were turning up in Mexico. In one raid, they reported they had recovered something like a dozen guns traceable to Phoenix and wondered how this could be.

These agents had no way of knowing that these firearms were in Mexico because of the actions of their superiors, and one wonders why so few guns upset them if, as the President charged, 90 percent of the tens or hundreds of thousands of guns being used by drug gangs in Mexico had come from the U.S. A dozen firearms would have been but a drop in the bucket, hardly reason to get upset or wonder what had gone wrong in Phoenix.

When a Border Patrol agent was murdered and outraged ATF agents leaked news of the operation to Congress, the White House at first tried to blame a few "rogue" agents in Arizona and demonize the whistleblowers, but it quickly became clear that the entire operation was being run from Washington and that White House officials were continually briefed on its progress.

Blame Bush

Next, the Obama Administration tried to "blame it on Bush," with mixed success. President George W. Bush had developed a small, somewhat similar program. "Wide Receiver" was dreamed up by William Newell, ATF's Special Agent in Charge (SAC) of the Phoenix Field Division during the second Bush's Administration. In this operation, agents were supposed to follow the guns and apprehend the bad guys before the guns vanished, but the program was shut down almost immediately because of fear that the guns might "walk." William Hoover, ATF's Assistant Director for the Office of Field Operations at the time, shut down the program within two weeks of its implementation, as soon as Bush Administration Justice Department officials learned that ATF was running amok and guns were being lost.

A slow learner but with a new boss, Newell then initiated and ran Mr. Obama's Fast and Furious, where guns were never tracked at all—one way to solve the bureaucratic snafu of losing guns.

Justice Department officials were still blaming Bush months after Mr. Obama's Attorney General Eric Holder admitted, in responding to a direct question from California Congressman Darrel Issa, Chairman of the House Oversight Committee, that the two programs were not comparable. That did not stop the Sunday television news show talking heads from repeating the same blatantly false "Bush did it first" charge, even as on June 28, 2012, Holder, having failed to disclose internal Justice Department documents relating to the program in response to a subpoena, became the first Cabinet Member to be held in contempt in the history of our country.

Changing the culture of ATF is not achieved in one Congressional hearing. During the Fast and Furious scandal, Deputy Assistant ATF Director William McMahon, who oversaw the agency's Western region during the program's operation, had been receiving two salaries simultaneously. He also received permission to stay on paid leave while Fast and Furious was being investigated while at the same time receiving a six-figure salary as an official in the ATF Office of Professional Responsibility and a full salary at J.P. Morgan as Executive Director of Global Security and Investigations in the Philippines. Representative Issa (R-Calif.) and Senator Charles E. Grassley (R-Iowa) wrote in a letter to B. Todd Jones, the acting ATF Director, that "ATF has essentially facilitated

McMahon's early retirement and ability to double dip for nearly half a year by receiving two full-time paychecks—one from the taxpayer and one from the private sector."

ATF spokesman Mike Campbell said the agency was reviewing the letter. "Due to Privacy Act considerations, all we can confirm is that Bill McMahon is still currently employed by ATF," Campbell said. The letter Issa and Grassley wrote was provided to the *Washington Post* for an August 31, 2011, story titled "New ATF Chief B. Todd Jones Joins an Agency Shaken by Guns Scandal." (The story can be read at this link: https://www.washingtonpost.com/politics/new-atf-chief-b-todd-jones-joins-an-agency-shaken-by-guns-scandal/2011/08/31/gIQASxzauJ_story.html.)

McMahon was one of five ATF officials singled out in the Congressional Oversight Report named "Fast and Furious: The Anatomy of a Failed Operation." The report alleged that McMahon knew that no safeguards were in place to prevent a large number of guns from getting into Mexico and made no effort to stop them. McMahon testified before the House Committee on Oversight and Government Reform in July 2011, issuing this lackluster apology:

> However good our intentions, regardless of our resource challenges, and notwithstanding the difficult legal hurdles we face in fighting firearms traffickers, we made mistakes . . . . And for that I apologize.

No one seems to remember what the end game and good intentions were. During the two-year Fast and Furious operation, ATF agents watched as hundreds of firearms were purchased by gun-trafficking suspects. Some agents testified that they were ordered to let the guns "walk," so that the agency could trace the weapons to a firearms-trafficking ring. Several supervisors denied responsibility for what happened, arguing that they would have never allowed gun walking, but were told by the U.S. attorney's office in Phoenix that they did not have enough evidence to seize the guns being trafficked. When told the guns would eventually turn up at various crime scenes, Attorney General Holder and his crew thought this seemed like a good idea, with resulting publicity able to be used to push for more stringent gun-control laws in the U.S.

Fast and Furious was not shut down until late 2010, after the deaths of hundreds of Mexicans, U.S. Border Patrol Agent Brian Terry, and a U.S Immigration and Customs (ICE) officer. In the face of subpoenas and Congressional hearings, President Obama resisted turning over documents and e-mails generated during Fast and Furious, citing executive privilege. But there is no way the Justice Department and the White House should take all the blame—Secretary of State Clinton would have or should have known about something affecting Mexico.

The end game of Fast and Furious was clear: achieving gun control regardless of the costs in lives and property. Had the Fast and Furious scandal not leaked, it would have provided Obama-Clinton "proof" that guns were crossing the southern U.S. border and that U.S. firearms dealers were to blame for the illegal sales and any ensuing violence.

During Bill Clinton's presidency, Hillary was often accused of acting as co-President. Yet the regulatory and legislative efforts of the Clintons in the 1990s failed, so Obama switched to marketing police and mass shooter tragedies and, when additional legislation failed, to Fast and Furious and other scandals too numerous to mention. Ultimately, he has resorted to executive orders.

Bloomberg

In 2012, the gun-control lobby was also preparing for Mr. Obama's second term. The leading financial backer of the movement was then-New York City Mayor Michael Bloomberg. Mr. Bloomberg, a billionaire with a willingness to spend his money to achieve his personal goals, said he was ready to spend whatever it took to rein in firearms ownership. He then provided the funds behind most of the recent leading anti-gun advocacy groups and employed political strategists to prepare for a moment in which they could move in unison to restrict private firearms ownership.

The President's chance to fully embrace gun control in his second term came in the aftermath of the shootings at the Sandy Hook Elementary School in Newtown, Connecticut, December 14, 2012. In that tragedy, 26 students and teachers were shot dead—and as 2013 dawned just weeks later, American gun owners and Second Amendment supporters finally realized they had a real fight on their hands.

The Obama Administration, Bloomberg, and those in Congress and the media hostile to gun rights believed the tragic killing of students and school employees gave them the opportunity they had been looking for to mobilize public support for new gun-control laws. President Obama's first White House Chief of Staff, Rahm Emmanuel, famously bragged that every crisis could be exploited; the Obama Administration was prepared to exploit Sandy Hook for all it was worth.

Mass shootings are tragic, but one cannot tell from the worldwide press that they are also statistically quite rare. In a perfect world, no innocents would die by gunshot (or in other ways), but we do not live in a perfect world. In spite of the impression one might get from listening to anti-gun politicians, both gun crime and firearms-related homicides have been declining dramatically since the 1970s, even as firearms ownership has been skyrocketing.

In the United States Senate, California Senator Dianne Feinstein, who authored the Clinton-era "assault weapons" ban, bragged she had an updated ban in her drawer just waiting to be introduced. Within days of the Sandy Hook killings, she reached into her drawer and offered a new "assault weapons ban" to her colleagues, while the Obama Administration launched a campaign to impose other gun-control measures that many liberals had long sought.

While Senator Feinstein once again sought to ban guns based on their cosmetic appearance, in the wake of Sandy Hook she faced another problem. In the 1990s, the era of the Clinton assault weapons ban, few Americans owned the AR-15, the semiautomatic civilian version (now more commonly referred to as a Modern Sporting Rifle or MSR) of the automatic rifle carried by the U.S. military. By 2008, more than a million of AR-15s were in private hands; and the Supreme Court, in its *Heller* decision, seemed to say that a firearm so widely owned and commonly employed for lawful purposes could not be banned. Feinstein introduced her legislation as she had promised (or threatened), but the Democratic leadership, even in the post-Sandy Hook atmosphere, would not bring it to the Senate floor for a vote. There was no sit-in when the Democrats failed to bring gun legislation to the House Floor, as there was in the summer of 2016 under Republican leadership.

Still, the anti-gun lobbies were not about to let this latest crisis go unexploited; it was as if everyone had grabbed every gun-control measure ever proposed and offered it up as a solution to gun violence. Within days, new groups demanding action sprung up around the country, all with peace-loving or otherwise innocuous names. The President spoke to the nation, and Democratic Senate leaders promised action, with liberals at the state level following suit.

Many of these new groups were financed by billionaire Republican Mayor Michael Bloomberg, who said he was ready to spend whatever it took to rein in firearms ownership. The President kept asking for what he liked to call "common sense" restrictions on firearms ownership, including a renewal of the "assault weapons" ban and outlawing "high-capacity magazines," as well as a new series of "universal" background check requirements.

After Sandy Hook, the President actually defined what he meant when he referred to "common sense" restrictions–emphasizing that the only countries that had a good solution to gun control were England and Australia. They are, of course, two countries in which the private ownership of firearms and the right to defend oneself have been virtually outlawed by governments that have set out to confiscate those guns owned by their citizenry.

The National Rifle Association

President Obama, Mayor Bloomberg, and anti-gun advocates in the media knew from the beginning of their campaign that to win they were going to have to crush, demonize, or find some way around the NRA, other pro-gun groups, and the tens of millions of gun owners who looked to them for leadership.

The NRA was formed in 1871 in New York by a group of Union officers who were afraid, even then, that their fellow citizens were losing touch with the firearms traditions so important to the Founders and so critical to the birth of the American Republic. Their fears were born of their just-ended American Civil War experience, in which the still-young country's armies drawn from the newly industrializing cities of the Northeast found themselves at a disadvantage against those from the Confederate South. The Confederate soldiers had been recruited from the rural South, where young men grew up with firearms and knew how to handle them. The Union Armies, conversely, were drawn from the immigrant populations of Boston, New York, Philadelphia, and other newly industrializing cities along the Eastern Seaboard. Most of these first-generation Americans had come here from Europe and knew little about guns. As the Union Army grew, many recruits received little real training and had to face a skilled enemy with guns they barely knew. With ammunition in short supply, many barely teen recruits took their first shots not during training, but on the battlefield. They did not fare well.

The saying at the time was that a Confederate infantryman was worth three of his Union counterparts. The problem the South faced was that for every Confederate there were five Union soldiers. Eventually, resources and numbers proved decisive, but the consensus view among many northern officers was that the war went on far longer than it should have simply because their recruits had lost or never acquired a familiarity with the weapons of the day, firearms that were second nature to many southerners and earlier generations of Americans.

Although it is seldom stated, today's underlying aversion to the necessity of war and the outgrowth of the anti-war Left of the 1960-1970 generation may be a large part of the Left's current anti-gun stance, especially at the U.N. (which we will cover in Part II). In addition, the urbanization of the mostly northern and coastal parts of the United States is what comprises today's Democratic Party strongholds, places where guns are used by criminals, not by hunters and sportsmen.

General George W. Wingate, who had authored the Union Army's manual on rifle marksmanship and training, was one of those most concerned about the need for marksmanship training, because of what he witnessed during the war. He and several other Union veterans formed the NRA because:

*The general ignorance concerning marksmanship which I found among our sol-
diers during the Civil War appalled me, and I hoped that I might better the
situation. I believed that if I could help to dispel the prevalent ignorance about
rifle shooting I might bring our American riflemen nearer in actuality to his
legendary stance.*

Wingate served as President of the NRA just long enough to establish the
new organization and kick off a series of national and international competitive shooting events that helped popularize the shooting sports during their
early days and survive to this day. As the NRA grew in influence during the
next few decades, the association's presidents included Civil War heroes General Winfield Scott Hancock, former Commander-in-Chief of the Army Philip
Sheridan, and former General and President Ulysses S. Grant.

In its beginning, the NRA focused almost exclusively on working with the
government to encourage and facilitate marksmanship within the military. By
the early 20th century, though, the focus had shifted to civilian marksmanship,
gun safety, law enforcement training, and educating young people. By 1911,
the Boy Scouts of America required the NRA training and safety regimen as a
prerequisite for Scouts seeking a merit badge in marksmanship. That badge was
discontinued in 2012, but Rifle Shooting and Shotgun Shooting merit badges
continue to be maintained.

During World War I, military leaders and common soldiers returning from
Europe encouraged the NRA to do more to expand its activities encouraging
young Americans to become proficient in the shooting sports. While the Civil
War persuaded Generals Ulysses S. Grant and Phil Sheridan of the need for an
organization like the NRA, the First Great War made General John J. Persh-
ing a true believer and lifelong NRA supporter. After World War II, President
Harry S. Truman wrote, "I hope that the splendid program which the National
Rifle Association has followed during the past three-quarters of a century will
be continued. It is a program that is good for a free America."

There were always some who disagreed, but most Americans supported the
Second Amendment and the goals of the NRA. NRA supporters and members included corporate presidents, law enforcement officers, working men and
women, farmers, and soldiers, as well as Democrats and Republicans. Even
today, about one in three NRA members is a Democrat. Youngsters looked
forward to getting their first rifle, usually at Christmas; fathers took their sons
hunting; and high schools and colleges fielded shooting teams from one end of
the country to the other. In the 1940s and '50s, children played with cap guns;
and Western-themed hats, toys, curtains, sheets, and bedspreads were mainstays
of childhood, as they played Cowboys and Indians and dreamed of growing up
to be a prospector, cowboy, or soldier.

Opening Day
By David Keene

I was raised in Illinois and Wisconsin, and a rite of passage was buying a used car or truck you probably worked to afford. I had a Model A and, like most kids, threw the rifle in the car during hunting season so I did not need to go home after school before I went hunting deer at dusk. Opening Day was what they would now call "liberal leave" day, since "colds" were so common the first few days of hunting season. Even the teachers caught colds.

Until President Johnson came to office, the NRA had drawn its support from all over the country and across the political spectrum, but it had been only tangentially involved in politics. The organization employed no lobbyists, the NRA did not endorse candidates, and the NRA Board included few politically experienced leaders. At first, many leaders of the organization vehemently wanted to avoid any political involvement and even urged that the NRA headquarters be moved away from the Washington, D.C., area, in order to avoid being pulled into the rancorous debates developing in Congress and in the media.

The Modern NRA

In the late 1960s and early '70s, polls showed massive public support for gun control, and politicians of both parties vied with one another to come up with more and more draconian measures to demonize gun owners and destroy what they began calling "America's gun culture." Finally, enough NRA members and firearms advocates recognized the imminent threat and joined forces to demand that the NRA take the lead in the fight to save the Second Amendment. Among those calling on the NRA to engage as the preferred defender of America's Second Amendment rights was a leading Democrat, John Dingell, Michigan Congressman and a member of the NRA Board. Dingell made it clear that if the NRA was not willing to lead the fight, all would be lost.

At an NRA Board meeting in 1975, after a contentious 18-hour debate in which deliberations and voting carried on through the night and members blocked the doors even to bathroom breaks, the NRA decided to become more politically active. They later created its Institute for Legislative Action (ILA) with strict rules on whom it endorsed and what the new entity could do. ILA quickly mobilized and led American gun owners in their fight to protect their Constitutional rights, elect officials friendly to the shooting sports, and maintain a visible and highly effective lobbying staff to work with Members of Congress and the various states. With this shift, the modern NRA was born, and its leaders vowed to do everything in their power to restore those rights already lost and to make sure that future generations of Americans would be able to own firearms for self-defense and to enjoy the shooting sports. Although these political efforts represent a mere 8 percent of the overall NRA budget, even in election years, all the training, competitions, youth sports, and safety programs like Eddie Eagle (GunSafe©) combined never receive the press this 8 percent gets.

Over the years, the NRA has proved itself a formidable defender of firearms rights. Candidates for public office seek its support; according to Gallup polls, 40 million Americans look to the organization for leadership on firearms issues, and Capitol Hill magazines consistently rank its cadre of lobbyists as one of the single most effective advocacy groups in the country and in Washington. Faced with the effectiveness of the NRA, many anti-gun activists wishing to accomplish their goals have been persuaded to find some way around the Congress, and then, when that did not work, around courts, and when that did not work, around the Constitution and the sovereignty of every government in the world.

A Shill? Don't Think So!

By David Keene

During the 2012 fight for new firearms regulations in the wake of Newtown, the four million-member National Rifle Association of America was seen by the President of the United States Barack Obama as the principal obstacle to passing the restrictions the Democratic Congress sought. A major effort was launched to demonize the organization and render it irrelevant. The President and his supporters alleged that, while the NRA might once have represented hunters and competitive shooters, by 2013 the NRA had become little more than a shill for a greedy firearms industry. "Not your father's NRA" was what they trotted out. As President of the NRA, I asked just how much of our budget was attributable to "industry" contributions, and it turned out to be about 4 percent of the total, with most of that going to traditional nonpolitical activities through the NRA Foundation.

The NRA's 76-member Board is elected by its membership and, in turn, elects the organization's officers. The regular officers (President and the First and Second Vice Presidents) are unpaid volunteers, while the full-time Executive Vice President, Wayne LaPierre, is the top staffer, or CEO. The other officers are the Executive Director of NRA-ILA, the Director of General Operations, NRA's Treasurer, and the NRA Secretary, who also serves as General Counsel.

NRA Leadership Today

NRA Executive Vice President Wayne LaPierre was raised in Virginia, near the Kentucky-Tennessee border, and became a teacher. He joined the NRA and rose through the ranks to become head of ILA and was named Executive Vice

President of the NRA three decades ago. The modern, powerful NRA is, in many ways, a creation of LaPierre. He is the public face of the NRA and takes the hits in the press.

In 2013, then-NRA President Keene, LaPierre, and Chris Cox, ILA's Director, took to the road to fight the Obama Administration's newly introduced gun restrictions. During his two years as NRA President, Keene was on the road nearly 250 days, speaking at NRA meetings and pro-Second Amendment rallies all over the country and sitting for hundreds of print and broadcast interviews. All the other NRA officers also spent weeks on the road in an exhausting, but crucial, time, and it quickly became apparent that the NRA had a far better chance of winning the public and political debates than its critics believed in the days immediately following the Sandy Hook shootings.

Chris Cox grew up in Tennessee and came to Washington to work for a Democratic "blue dog," Tennessee Representative John Tanner. By the time Cox left the Hill, in 1995, to work for the NRA, Tanner was one of a vanishing breed of Democrats who staunchly supported the Second Amendment rights of his constituents.

Cox moved up the ranks of ILA, which he now heads. In partnership with LaPierre, he has the principal responsibility within the organization of directing NRA's federal and state lobbying efforts and of devising and implementing its election strategy. ILA is consistently ranked as one of the most effective lobbying operations in Washington, and Cox has reshaped the electoral strategy and ability of the organization to identify and reach gun-friendly voters in the states' ILA targets.

Other Gun Groups

The NRA is not the only pro-gun group in the country, nor is it an umbrella organization. The veterans' organizations, including the 22 congressionally mandated groups, have a significant say in our gun culture. The World Forum on Shooting Activities (www.wfsa.net/) is made up of 43 gun organizations and keeps a watchful eye on the international realm. Specialty groups like the National Muzzle Loading Rifle Association (www.nmlra.org/) maintain social and informative membership organizations. The National Shooting Sports Foundation (www.nssf.org) is the firearms industry trade association and works tirelessly to help protect shooting and hunting. Shooting ranges, gun stores, and private citizens donating their time at gun shows across the country pass the sport and safety along to our young every weekend of the year, including events like the annual National Matches at Camp Perry in Ohio, where families bring together several generations of shooters to compete, spending weeks in the grounds' acres of tents and mobile homes and filling the hotels for miles.

After the Newtown tragedy, 24-year-old Maria Butina founded the Right to Keep and Bear Arms in Russia, saying, "The murderer planned this knowing that no one would be armed." The Safari Club and the St. Hubertus Society also help maintain international standards and professionalism and guide regulations in countries whose economies depend on hunting.

Rather than list the hundreds of other organizations that support Second Amendment issues, this book will shortcut references under the monikers NRA or "pro-gun groups." Be assured that not naming all the national, state, and international organizations at this time or throughout the book does not negate our respect for—and often membership in—these organizations.

The Media and Gun Policy Today

A national press corps willing to report every accusation as an actual fact, whether true or not, enthusiastically supported the recent anti-NRA campaign. Liberal pundit Mark Shields, appearing on Public Broadcasting System's *The News Hour* the day the President spoke to the public after Sandy Hook, claimed the NRA was imploding, that members were leaving the NRA "in droves," because most NRA members agreed not with the organization's leadership, but with President Obama's demand for new gun laws.

Meanwhile, during Mr. Obama's speech, more than 58,000 people called the NRA to join; estimates point to more than twice as many hanging up because they could not get the busy NRA staff to pick up the phone fast enough to let them join. The effort to demonize the NRA having failed, the organization went on to lead the fight to defeat the Obama anti-gun campaign—but it was not easy. Mr. LaPierre, Mr. Keene, and other top staff and leading volunteers received hundreds of death threats. NRA president Keene even had an Internet game named, touchingly, "Kill David Keene."

By the time the Senate rejected an amendment requiring a so-called universal background check, NRA membership had skyrocketed from four million members to more than five million, and since then NRA membership has continued to climb.

NRA members, along with millions of other Americans who value the Second Amendment rights guaranteed by the Constitution, prevailed. Reason trumped emotion, as the public and lawmakers alike concluded that none of the proposals the President described as "common sense" reforms would have prevented the tragedy that was exploited to pass these gun restrictions.

In the year-end reviews of 2013, Shields, not a bad man, just a very liberal one, claimed he had thought that surely the shooting deaths of elementary school students would allow Americans to outlaw guns, but he was mistaken. In other words, our Constitution trumped immediate moral outrage, and the attempt to exploit tragedy failed.

America's gun owners had once again demonstrated their unity in opposing measures that would restrict their Constitutional rights. They signed petitions, called and visited their Senators and Representatives, and attended demonstrations around the country that in total brought out hundreds of thousands of men and women willing to let their elected officials know that they opposed what the President and Mayor Bloomberg sought.

But the battle is just a battle, not the war.

Media Bias

While the "players" in the continuing drama may include President Obama and Mrs. Clinton, along with Michael Bloomberg and anti-gun Senators, on the one side against pro-Second Amendment groups on the other, there is one other major entity that sides almost exclusively with those favoring gun control. The major media, both print and broadcast, is, essentially, "in the tank" with the gun-control lobby. Over the years, they have favored virtually every attempt to restrict firearms rights, misrepresented the positions of the two sides on important issues, and done whatever else they could to assist the forces seeking to restrict firearms rights. In the 1990s, they purposely aired reports designed to lead the public to believe that fully automatic machine guns were the target of the Clinton "assault weapons" ban, when they knew (or should have known) that the ban was designed to prevent the sale of *semi*automatic firearms. Katie Couric's misleading segments in her televised gun special that aired in the summer of 2016, segments for which she had to apologize, are common. (And the apology is remarkably uncommon.)

This is the same American media that has allowed the international community to work in silence on an anti-gun treaty to take away the right to bear arms from all citizens of the world—with the governments of half the world's population objecting. The story of this travesty by the United Nations over the objections of China, Russia, and others will be detailed in Part II.

When the antigun lobby wanted to ban firearms sales to anyone on the government's "no fly" and "watch" lists, they promoted the narrative that those on the lists can now walk into a gun store without the FBI being alerted to any attempt they make to buy a gun. This has also been the claim of politicians like Mrs. Clinton who know better, as the NICS background check run by gun dealers on all purchasers is run by the FBI, and those on the lists get special scrutiny. Not only was the Orlando shooter fully cleared by the FBI to purchase a gun, he was cleared to work for the government. No new law will stop incompetence.

The Media Research Center (MRC) is a media watchdog on the conservative Right. MRC noted that the major broadcast media channels (ABC, NBC, and CBS) devoted extraordinary time in 2015 to the allegedly illegal killing of

Cecil the Lion in Zimbabwe. MRC might also have pointed out that while it is estimated that more than a million times a year American citizens with legally owned firearms thwart violent criminals intent upon murder, rape, or robbery, rarely are such often dramatic instances in which lives are saved by "good guys with guns" reported.

The media used the largely misleading accounts of how the Zimbabwean lion died to attempt to discredit hunting, particularly African hunting. In fact, many African governments support and promote trophy hunting, not only because the trophy fees benefit local villagers and serve as an incentive to keep them from killing the animals as nuisances, but because controlled hunting is used as a wildlife management technique lest the species overcrowd and starve. The meat from such hunts goes to feed the villages. A typical African guide will not field dress (take out the entrails immediately, in the field, so the meat does not spoil) because he is certain to find some human remains in the stomach—as in tiny tennis shoes that have not been digested. This is not an old wives' tale or a myth, this is fact. As an African tribesman said, "why are the Americans so worried about elephants and lions and not about all of the villagers who have been killed by elephants and lions?" An African student spoke out in typical fashion in the *New York Times:* "the village boy inside me instinctively cheered: One lion fewer to menace families like mine." (Read the full article at this link: http://www.nytimes.com/2015/08/05/opinion/in-zimbabwe-we-dont-cry-for-lions.html?_r=0.)

Partisanship

President Obama and his allies knew that to win their war on American gun ownership, they were going to have to get the NRA either to fold or stand aside, because they were not going to be able to roll over the organization as they had initially believed possible. The bipartisan sponsors of the President's proposal for "universal background checks" were two Senators considered friendly to the NRA.

One was Republican Senator Pat Toomey of Pennsylvania. More NRA members live in Pennsylvania than in any other state, including Texas. Pennsylvania also sells more hunting licenses than any other state, and even Toomey's liberal Republican-turned-Democrat predecessor, Arlen Specter, had usually voted in the Senate with the NRA. Toomey either did not realize this or believed he could withstand what he hoped would be temporary hostility from the state's gun owners if, in return, he earned the gratitude of establishment liberals and moderates in Philadelphia and Pittsburgh.

West Virginia Democratic Senator Joe Manchin also hailed from a gun-friendly state and famously won his seat with the help of television ads showing him shooting a rifle. But he quickly threw in with the Democratic Senate leadership and became the public face of the effort to impose the expanded background checks the Obama Administration was seeking. Manchin has a fairly conservative voting record for a Democratic Senator, but his actions infuriated Second Amendment supporters in his home state. A former Governor, Manchin was an NRA member and, apparently, believed he could somehow persuade the NRA leadership to stand aside as his amendment moved toward a Senate Floor vote. (More about the Manchin-Toomey Amendment is in the Universal Background Checks chapter.)

Fish On!

By David Keene

I had finished a speech in Colorado, and took a rare day off to float the Missouri River in Montana, in search of early season trout. I have owned a second house in the West Virginia highlands for 30 years, and Virginia's Senator Joe Manchin lobbied me hard in seeking NRA's support, or at least neutrality, for the Manchin-Toomey gun proposal. Mr. Manchin rang my cell phone with a final plea, as the Senate neared a vote. He realized that unless he could get the NRA to give it a pass, the amendment was doomed. He asked the NRA to accept this "common sense" compromise, which the Senator argued avoided harsher restrictions that might be triggered if the Amendment did not pass.

I told Mr. Manchin that his West Virginia rural constituents may not welcome the idea that their Senator had written the bill that would make them drive to the nearest big town and get permission to loan their son a gun. I also told him I was fishing, a simple enough reason not to talk, and that compromise was not even a possibility. Mr. Manchin persisted until I told him I was sorry, but I had a trout on the line and broke the connection.

Texas Republican Senator Ted Cruz, a strong Second Amendment supporter and friend of the NRA, was convinced there were not enough votes to defeat the Manchin-Toomey Amendment and wondered about the possibility of the NRA "scoring" the Senate vote to gauge support for Cruz's proposed filibuster. "Scoring" means counting the vote in grading members of the Senate when the NRA decides whom to endorse, thereby enabling pro-gun forces to prevent a vote. A filibuster calls for more than a simple majority vote to pass legislation. Meanwhile, ILA Director Chris Cox and NRA President Keene were receiving calls from NRA-friendly Senators who claimed to have the votes to defeat the Manchin-Toomey outright and wondered why anybody would want to prevent putting the "bad guys" on the record. Ultimately, it was decided that the NRA would not score the proposed filibuster. Cruz's gambit collapsed, but, fortunately, on April 17, 2013, the full Senate voted on and rejected the Amendment.

More restrictive proposals like California Senator Dianne Feinstein's attempt to resurrect the Clinton-era "assault weapons" ban did not make it to the Democrat-led Senate floor for a vote. Firearms owners were ecstatic, but a closer look at what was going on that spring makes one wonder if they should have been.

The States

The high-water mark for those seeking to restrict or, ultimately, ban the private ownership of firearms had passed when politicians in the 1960s through the early '90s had embraced gun control as an issue. Now, post-Sandy Hook, the public, particularly the voting public, was not with them.

For more than a decade, the gun-control movement had attacked firearms on multiple fronts. Rebuffed on most fronts, a few states with virtual one-party rule, such as New York, Maryland, and Colorado, and the District of Columbia, rammed through additional firearms restrictions. But far more states actually liberalized their laws while the battle for further restrictions waged in the media and in the Senate.

States that adopted gun restrictions drove jobs away. Remington moved most of its production to Alabama, although New York's anti-gun Democratic Governor Andrew Cuomo actually called Remington officials promising tax breaks if they would stay, even as he was attacking them in the press. Southern Maryland also felt the economic effects, as the 600-year-old Italian company Beretta, with 1,100 jobs in Accokeek, Maryland, moved to Gallatin, Tennessee. Texas, the Carolinas, and Tennessee saw jobs flow their way in the middle of a long, stimulus-drained recession, thanks to governors and state legislatures that turned on manufacturers.

The battles are never over. Virginia's current Governor, Terry McAuliffe, a friend of the Clintons, decided that, like President Obama, he and his Administration could take "executive actions" to bypass the legislature and impose additional restrictions on firearms. In December 2015, McAuliffe's Attorney General announced that Virginia would no longer provide reciprocity for citizens of 25 states holding concealed carry permits issued by their home states. This "executive order" is much like President Obama's many orders to overturn the will of Congress and the people. Had this gone unchallenged in Virginia, no state would be safe from an executive willing to ignore his or her legislature. The Virginia legislature resisted, thankfully, and forced the Governor to a compromise that, while far from perfect, protected the rights of Virginia gun owners.

The Good in Blue
By David Keene

In the midst of the battle over President Obama's post-Sandy Hook gun-control campaign, I was invited to a televised interview in Cambridge by Harvard's Institute of Politics. I had been an Institute Fellow in the 1970s. CNN's John King interviewed me, followed by a lengthy question-and-answer session with several hundred students. King was aggressive but fair, and the students listened attentively. Most of their questions were probing and marginally hostile, but we had a good exchange that I enjoyed.

The organizers must have feared the worst, because in addition to a gaggle of reporters, several dozen well-armed Harvard, Cambridge, and Boston police ringed the room; gun rights advocates and NRA Officers are not as highly regarded or as warmly received in Massachusetts as they might be in the South. Similar to the audiences at places like England's Oxford, the bulk of the audience in Cambridge favored stronger gun-control measures because that is what they'd been told and taught is necessary and right and what their culture unquestioningly believes. They tended to blame gun crime and mass shootings more on the firearms than on those using them, rejected the idea that guns in private hands might actually reduce crime, and believe our streets, homes, and schools would be far safer places if gun ownership could be eliminated or severely restricted.

The law enforcement officers at that interview were there to protect me from the audience (or maybe the audience from me, as some of them likely viewed it). Imagine the students' surprise when the program ended, and, as the audience of young adults milled around congratulating one another on the rightness of their views, their protectors lined up to shake hands with or have their pictures taken with the President of the NRA. What the students did not realize is that many law enforcement officers—even in places like Cambridge and Boston—are often NRA members and certified instructors who do not buy the arguments Misters Obama and Bloomberg peddle.

As I was leaving, a senior officer introduced himself as an NRA member, then thanked me for my service and "for coming up here to try to talk some common sense to these kids." He was not one of Bloomberg's guys, although his mayor and Bloomberg demanded more gun control in the name of crime reduction. Cops know gun control does not make sense, just as they know it may actually prove counterproductive.

Big-city police chiefs, however, are beholden to big-city mayors, who are almost exclusively liberal Democrats. Like those Harvard students, these mayors believe, as an article of faith, that gun control and higher taxes are good. America's sheriffs are a different story. They are elected and, so, more accurately reflect the views of their constituents. There are some who are liberal and agree with Bloomberg, but most are prone to saying what they believe, rather than what some other politician wants them to. And like the street cop colleagues in bigger cities, sheriffs know their problems will never be solved by stricter gun-control measures, but by prosecuting and locking up criminals, providing treatment to the dangerously mentally ill, and protecting the rights of law-abiding private citizens to own firearms and learn how to use them should they ever need them to protect themselves, their homes, their businesses, and their families.

Law Enforcement's Role in Gun Politics

The image of a law enforcement community united in its opposition to the private ownership of firearms and marching in lockstep with politicians like former-Mayor Bloomberg, California Senator Diane Feinstein, and President Obama was never true and has been breaking down in recent years. In Wisconsin's Milwaukee County, for example, Democratic Sheriff David Clarke has publicly urged citizens to learn how to use firearms to protect themselves and their families:

> *There are certain situations—and I think most people get that—where 9-1-1 is going to be of no use. For instance, once the wolf is at the door, once the intruder is inside your home, once you're on the street and someone sticks a gun in your face to take your car or your wallet, you don't have the option of calling 9-1-1.*

Sheriff Clarke has emerged as one of the most outspoken and articulate law enforcement officers of our time, favoring the private ownership of firearms as a means of protection and crime control. For this, Mr. Bloomberg and anti-gun forces targeted him. Hundreds of thousands of dollars filled the coffers to relieve him of his office during recent elections—but Milwaukee voters felt otherwise.

On FOX's *Sean Hannity*, Sheriff Clarke said, "Look, if you want to reduce violence—and the President knows this—you target criminals. You do not target otherwise law-abiding citizens. And you don't make them have to go jump through hoops in a higher threshold to exercise their 2nd Amendment rights." (You can see the full interview here: http://www.cnsnews.com/blog/michael-w-chapman/sheriff-clarke-president-obama-and-mrs-bill-clinton-they-are-anti-gun-bigots.)

Clarke is not alone. Detroit's Police Chief James Craig suggested last year that what his city needs is more honest citizens with firearms and permits that will let them carry them concealed, to help his officers take the city back from the gangs and thugs. Yet, as the debate raged and California Senator Diane Feinstein announced that she "knew for a fact" that her gun-control efforts had unanimous law enforcement support, PoliceOne.com surveyed more than 15,000 active duty and retired cops nationwide. They represented large and small jurisdictions, with the average respondent serving in a police or sheriff's department having something like 500 officers. Seventy-one percent responded that Senator Feinstein's proposed ban on what she calls "assault weapons" would do nothing to improve officer safety, and another 20 percent thought the ban would make things worse. When asked what would work, they supported arresting and punishing gun crime over restricting firearms ownership by a large margin, and 76.6 percent agreed that trained and armed schoolteachers and administrators would help deter school shootings. (You can read more about this here: https://www.policeone.com/Gun-Legislation-Law-Enforcement/articles/6183787-PoliceOnes-Gun-Control-Survey-11-key-lessons-from-officers-perspectives/.)

The findings tell us more about the real feelings of the men and women who protect us than MSNBC, the *New York Times,* or the *Washington Post*.

The NRA counts more than 100,000 law enforcement officers among its membership and many distinguished police officers serve the local and national boards. Cops, in short, are far more likely to be found at an NRA event than to be sharing a stage with Mr. Bloomberg or his cronies.

The Brits and Harrisburg's Outdoor Show

Harrisburg, Pennsylvania, is the home of the nation's largest and most successful "outdoor show." For a week in February each year, as many as a million visitors flock to the city to walk the halls of a massive show that highlights firearms, hunting, fishing, boating, and other outdoor activities. It is cold in Harrisburg in February, and not always easy to get there.

In 2013, in the wake of the Sandy Hook tragedy, the British company that had been organizing the show for some years announced, just a few days before it was to open the doors, that vendors would no longer be able to display the sorts of firearms the President and his friends were trying to ban. Specifically, this meant the show was banning the display of the AR-15, the civilian semi-automatic version of the United States' military rifle. There are more than eight million AR-15s in civilian hands. It is the most used long arm and rifle used in competition, training and plinking, hunting, and self-defense. Variants are manufactured by dozens of companies.

Vendors began to walk out of the show when news of the ban spread. More than 300 vendors pulled out of the show within hours, as manufacturers of bow hunting and fishing equipment and other outdoor-related companies joined firearms manufacturers and dealers. The show collapsed and was cancelled within a day and a half. The fact that outdoor enthusiasts put up such a united front was not lost on politicians, symbolizing the utter failure of the anti-gunner's attempt to divide and conquer.

Tom Millner, the CEO of Cabela's, the nation's largest outfitter, remembers an assistant coming into his headquarters office in Sydney, Nebraska, the morning the ban at the Harrisburg show was announced to ask what they should do. "Pull the plug," he said, "Now!" Around the country and in Harrisburg, others were doing the same. After the show collapsed, Pennsylvania sought a new group to organize and bring back a week of tourism to the bankrupt capital city during its slow winter season. That contract went not to professional show organizers, but to the NRA, and it remains as successful today as ever.

Zenith Days

By Tom Mason

Before I finished law school, my shooting consisted of plinking with my 22 Colt Police Positive and my single-shot Winchester. By 1997, my best law school buddy, Jeff Campiche, was District Attorney for Pacific County on the Pacific Coast of Washington State. Jeff invited me to opening day of the bird season, a glorious, all-blue sky day around Wilapa Bay.

The ducks and Canada geese had not been shot at yet, so they came to our decoys without hesitation. We bagged our limit (meaning that government regulations and nature preservation rules limited our hunting, not the number of birds we could find). After lunch, we culled pheasants the Washington Fish and Game had planted on one of the Bay's islands, until we hit that limit.

That day was one of the zeniths in my long hunting career. It is those same days and others like them that have so many multi-generational families standing in the snows of Pennsylvania, in February.

After their voices were heard over the Harrisburg show debacle, firearms owners were ecstatic. But a closer look at what was going on later that spring makes one wonder if they should have been. Those seeking to ban or restrict firearms ownership in the United States have been losing battle after battle at the federal level and in most states, as well as in the courts. What many fighting to stave off Congressional and state-level attempts to gut the Second Amendment did not realize at the time, however, was that even as they were winning these battles, anti-gun forces were mobilizing in an entirely different forum to accomplish what they have thus far failed to accomplish through legislative and judicial action in this country.

The United Nations: The New Front to Gun Confiscation

In the wake of so many domestic setbacks, anti-gun forces began to rely on the United Nations and international treaties that might somehow allow them to accomplish some, or even all, of their goals without having to win political or judicial support in this country. For more than a decade, in fact, the gun-control movement had attacked firearms on multiple fronts, but, rebuffed on most, put more and more reliance on the United Nations and on international treaties that might somehow allow their organizers to accomplish some or even all of their goals without having to win political or judicial support in this country.

On April 2, 2013, just two weeks before the defeat of the Manchin-Toomey Amendment in the U.S. Senate and ending a battle begun in 1996, the U.N. General Assembly adopted the Arms Trade Treaty by a vote of 153 to 3. Until President Obama was sworn in and sent Mrs. Clinton to the State Department, the United States government had consistently argued that it would never get U.S. support unless the rights of our citizens were protected. The Obama Administration had dropped this requirement and voted with the majority.

Following the vote, a hundred or more anti-gun activists gathered on the U.N.'s East River esplanade in Manhattan, the most expensive real estate in the U.S., where its citizens pay for the U.N. to stay tax-free. Those in attendance broke out champagne and celebrated a historic victory in the war against the private ownership of firearms. They laughed, toasted one another, and traded rumors that some among them might be nominated for the Nobel Peace Prize as a result of their successful seven-year battle to establish an international gun-control regime.

The celebration was led by a group calling itself "Control Arms" and its director Anna MacDonald, who smiled as the rumor spread via Twitter and Facebook speculating that, if American anti-landmine activist Jody Williams could win a Nobel prize for her efforts, surely MacDonald would get one for what had been accomplished that day in the U.N. General Assembly.

They should have been toasting President Obama and Secretary of State Clinton, because it was their hostility to the Second Amendment that prompted them to reverse the long-time opposition to such a treaty and enable its passage. To suggest that by doing so they betrayed the oath they took, on assuming their high offices, to defend the Constitution against all enemies foreign and domestic is an understatement.

---

[1] *District of Columbia v. Heller, 554 U.S. 570 (2008), http://www.law .cornell.edu/supct/pdf/07-290P.ZO.*

[2] *Josh Sugarman Every Handgun is Aimed at You: The Case for Banning Handguns (New York: The New Press, 2002).*

[3] *The seminal law review article on the other side was Stanford Levinson, The Embarrassing Second Amendment, 96 Yale L.J. 637-659 (1989).*

[4] *Bogus is aptly named. More at Carl Bogus, "The History and Politics of Second Amendment Scholarship: A Primer," Chicago-Kent Law Review, 76, no. 1 (2000).*

CHAPTER 2

The Courts

Facts are stubborn things; and whatever our wishes, our inclinations, or the dictates of our passions, they cannot alter the state of facts and evidence.

—John Adams, U.S. President

The Judicial Front: *Heller, McDonald,* and the Post-Scalia Court

It used to be that most Americans who had studied the Second Amendment believed it was intended, from the time of its adoption, to protect the right of individual Americans, as the language of the Amendment put it, "to keep and bear arms." The United States Supreme Court did not specifically adopt that interpretation until June 6, 2008, when the Court announced, in a five-to-four vote, that it affirmed a decision of the D.C. Circuit Court of Appeals in *District of Columbia v. Heller*.[1] Written by the late Associate Justice Antonin Scalia, the case reflected the Court's endorsement of the Second Amendment's guarantee of an individual right. In a later decision, the Court applied the same reasoning not only to federal enclaves such as the District of Columbia, but also to the States.

The debate over the intent of the Founders in including an amendment on gun rights in the Constitution's Bill of Rights has been rancorous and disingenuous. Gun-control advocates have argued that the Second Amendment does not mean what it says or that the Founders did not intend it to guarantee the right of individual Americans to own firearms, much of it based on the Joyce Foundation papers. The Supreme Court found those arguments did not wash.

A more intellectually honest argument by the anti-gun groups would be that the Founders got it wrong and should never have guaranteed such a right in the first place. The problem with that approach is that it would require anti-gun groups to acknowledge the Second Amendment as a roadblock in the way of what they really want to do and force them to seek its outright repeal or modification. When the Constitution was amended to outlaw the consumption of alcohol, opponents of prohibition did not claim that the Amendment had not really meant to ban drinking. The voters who wanted the Amendment gone set about seeking its repeal and eventually got it repealed by persuading their fellow citizens that what its authors wanted was wrong. They won an honest debate, the sort of debate firearms prohibitionists have resisted seeking, as they instead argue that the Second Amendment simply does not mean what it says.

Gun-control advocates have avoided the honest debate, because it would be difficult to win. Most Americans are concerned about crime, violence, and terrorism and understand that these problems stem from the motives and acts of criminals, thugs and terrorists. Most Americans are not willing to ban firearms, even if they do not own one.

Democratic presidential candidates since Al Gore's defeat in 2000 have tended to downplay their hostility to the Second Amendment, and most liberal politicians, including President Barack Obama, in the days following the Supreme Court decision were cautious about attacking the decision itself. Attacking *Heller* would put them on record as opposed to the right of Americans to own firearms.

Hillary Clinton has taken the opposite tack, making gun control a central part of her 2016 campaign. But she, too, wants to have it both ways. When Donald Trump emphasized Clinton's aversion to guns and that she would, essentially, repeal the Second Amendment, she and campaign spokesmen charged him as a "liar"—and the name-calling began. (You can read more about this here: http://www.nola.com/politics/index.ssf/2016/06/hillary_clinton_condemns_donal.html.)

Anyone with doubts as to Mrs. Clinton's intentions has not been listening very carefully to what she has been saying. While her defenders in the media have claimed that the NRA and her critics overstate her opposition to the private ownership of firearms, in a leaked 2015 audio she herself has stated flatly that *District of Columbia v. Heller* was "wrongly decided." (Click here to hear the audio: http://freebeacon.com/politics/leaked-audio-clinton-says-supreme-court-is-wrong-on-second-amendment/.) Her advisor, Maya Harris Bloomberg, in May 2016 confirmed this position to Bloomberg. (See this link for the relevant article: http://www.bloomberg.com/politics/articles/2016-05-20/hillary-clinton-believes-pivotal-gun-rights-ruling-was-wrong-adviser-says.)

The Court in *Heller* was faced with only one question: does the Second Amendment protect the right of individuals to keep firearms in their home for self-protection? The Court decided that it does. The opposition, naturally, argued that no such individual right exists. Mrs. Clinton, if she becomes President of the United States, can be expected to appoint Supreme Court justices who agree with her and would be in a position to reverse *Heller*—thus rendering the Second Amendment meaningless.

In a semantic sense, the Clintons, who have so parsed the English language from Whitewater to Monica Lewinsky, can technically say that she does not seek to "abolish" the Second Amendment, as Donald Trump has charged. But she would render it meaningless, which amounts to the very same thing. (Former Congressman Bob Barr wrote about Bill Clinton's peculiar ability to twist and redefine words to meet his own purposes in his book *The Meaning of Is*. You can find the book at this link: https://books.google.com/books/about/The_Meaning_of_Is.html?id=cbEeOsgAd_wC&hl=en.)

The importance of what another President Clinton would do cannot be overstated. If *Heller* is reversed, that right guaranteed by its decision will no longer exist; the limbo that existed prior to *Heller,* in which advocates and opponents of the right argued and decisions were made simply on policy grounds, will be resurrected. Just as important, if *Heller* is reversed, things do not go back to the way they were. Instead, the federal government will have the right to regulate, register, or eliminate firearms ownership, and gun owners will have no recourse. It is that simple. If Mrs. Clinton is elected President and has her way, the right to private ownership of firearms will cease to exist.

By midsummer 2016, Mrs. Clinton began escalating her anti-gun rhetoric, while suggesting that, like President Obama, she merely favors "common sense" restrictions on gun rights that will make the nation safer. As she did so, she began singling out two nations that, in her opinion, have "done the right thing" in dealing with firearms ownership. Those nations are Great Britain and Australia, both of which ban the private ownership and possession of most firearms, and neither of which recognizes a citizen's right to defend themselves, their family, or their home.

Scalia Dies

The reality of what is at stake, in terms of the Supreme Court, was driven home to millions of Americans on February 13, 2016, when Supreme Court Justice Antonin Scalia died in Shafter, Texas.

Justice Scalia will go down in history as one of the most influential figures in the history of the Court. He was its most influential conservative and the intellectual leader and driving force behind many decisions, including *Heller*.

The next President will, because of the age of several justices, have the opportunity to alter the makeup of the Supreme Court. But Justice Scalia's death made that opportunity immediate and led Senate Majority Leader Mitch McConnell of Kentucky to announce, within hours of the Justice's passing, that the Senate would not even consider a replacement before the election. Leader McConnell understood immediately that the stakes are enormous and dug in, hoping that a Republican President will be elected in November so that the Court will not be lost for decades.

The appointment of a Justice who would create a liberal majority would doom more than just the Second Amendment. Many of President Obama's critics in the Senate and within the legal community believe that he has gone beyond any rational interpretation of his prerogatives as the nation's chief executive to, effectively, rule by fiat. Even as a closely divided Supreme Court has balked at a number of Mr. Obama's decisions, if the next President gets to break the tie that exists on some important issues by naming a liberal replacement for Justice Scalia, and follows that up with one or two more young liberal Justices as others on the Court retire, the Court could become little more than a rubber stamp for an imperial presidency. Gun owners focus on the impact such appointments would have on the Second Amendment rights they cherish, but First Amendment guarantees of free speech and religion, among others, would also be affected. A liberal Supreme Court majority could even begin enforcing portions of the U.N. Arms Trade Treaty (ATT), whether or not it is ratified by the Senate as required by the Constitution. Several members of the Court already believe that U.S. courts should look to international standards and foreign courts for guidance in rendering opinions affecting the American people, and that is an attitude that could lead the Court to redefine the meaning of the guarantees written into the Constitution itself. All these things combined underscores why so many believe the 2016 Presidential elections should be all about the Court.

That the Supreme Court would consider guidance from something other than our Constitution was scandalous and made international headlines when the Center for International Studies presented Republican-appointed Sandra Day O'Connor with its World Justice Award, in 2003. In her acceptance speech, Justice O'Connor claimed that U.S. courts should take foreign law and traditions into consideration when they make their rulings, arguing, "The impressions we create in this world are important, and they can leave their mark," according to the *Atlanta Journal-Constitution*. (You can read more here: http://www.rfcnet.org/pdfs/SupremeInternLaw.pdf.)

The battle over the private ownership of firearms has been and continues to be waged on many fronts. For decades, gun owners have fought local, state, and federal firearms restrictions; many proposed laws designed to "control" access to or ownership of guns represent violations of the Constitution's Second Amendment. These threats are real and the battle continues, but the ATT and the willingness of U.S. judges to bow to foreign precedent and opinions add a new threat.

Supreme Court Appointments

In Scalia's wake, the appointment of his successor is the single most important political development of the 2016 election cycle. Gun advocates were
unable to prevent the confirmation of President Obama's appointments of
Sonia Sotomayor and Elena Kagan as some expected, but neither threatened
the balance on the court. Appointing a liberal to Scalia's seat would change
the court for decades and could easily result in the reversal of *Heller* and other
crucial cases.

When President Obama's first two Supreme Court appointees testified
before the Senate prior to their confirmation, each reasoned that the *Heller*
decision answers the question of whether the Second Amendment protects an
individual, rather than a "collective" right. This was the question at the heart of
the case, and the liberal effort to persuade the Court to endorse the collective
interpretation of the Amendment was, as we shall see, crucial to the future of
individual firearms ownership. Both Sotomayor and Kagan testified that *Heller*
rendered the debate over which view was correct moot and enshrined the individual rights view as "settled law" that should be followed. The NRA and other
pro-Second Amendment groups doubted the sincerity of the two appointees,
and since their appointments, neither Justice has behaved on the Court as if
Heller were settled law, and, as a result, the NRA and other gun rights groups
will expect Senators to require more than simple assurances on the Second
Amendment from any future nominee.

At the time of the Kagan and Sotomayor appointments, Chris Cox, who
heads the NRA lobbying and political shop, warned that if the President tried
to replace a pro-Second Amendment Justice with one NRA would consider
opposed to gun rights, the NRA would fight it with everything at its disposal.
In March 2016, following the death of Justice Scalia, President Obama did
just that. Merrick Garland, Chief Judge of the D.C. Circuit, is not the most
liberal jurist the President could have named—except when it comes to Second Amendment questions. Garland's record shows him to be a consistent opponent of gun rights, and, as such, the NRA immediately declared him an
unacceptable threat to Second Amendment rights and asked its members to
support Senator McConnell's refusal to consider such an appointment prior to
the November elections.

The Freedom That Protects All Others

The Bill of Rights contains some pretty plain language. It was added to the
Constitution because many were concerned at the time of its creation that the
body of the Constitution failed to provide explicit protections for fundamental
rights. The words of the Second Amendment can be recited by most American

gun owners. They are emblazoned on virtually everything every pro-gun organization in the country distributes and have been described by former NRA President Charlton Heston, among others, as guaranteeing "the freedom that protects all others":

> *A well regulated Militia, being necessary to the security of a free State, the right of the people to keep and bear Arms, shall not be infringed.*

Gun owners have always believed that the Bill of Rights' Second Amendment protects an individual right, but, in the mid-1960s, revisionist legal experts recruited and paid handsomely to promote what came to be known as a "collective" interpretation of the Founders' words. They argued that the Second Amendment had nothing to do with individual rights but merely guaranteed the states the right to maintain a "well-regulated militia."

These few words were critically important to both sides of the debate. If the Amendment did not protect an individual right, "shall not be infringed" would be meaningless: policymakers and politicians could do whatever they wanted to restrict or even abolish "the right to keep and bear arms."

NRA leadership recognized the importance of this battle and encouraged historians and legal experts to examine and analyze the original intent of the Founders. In time, their work was recognized as definitive. Even experts such as Harvard University's Laurence Tribe, personally hostile to private firearms ownership, reluctantly concluded that the Second Amendment meant exactly what the Founders and the firearms community said it meant.

The opinions of scholars and legal experts do not necessarily affect policy makers when absent a definitive court ruling. The Supreme Court had never decided a case that required it to answer the basic question of whether Americans actually had a fundamental *individual* right under the Second Amendment to keep and bear arms. Both pro-gun and anti-gun advocates knew that one day the Court would be forced to answer that question and each prepared, but neither side expected it to come before a closely divided court as soon as it did.

Dick Heller

Historically, the District of Columbia has not just restricted firearms ownership, it outright banned the possession of handguns by its citizens, even in cases where residents living in some of the city's most crime-ridden neighborhoods argued they needed them in their own homes for self-defense.

In 2003, Dick Heller, a D.C. resident working as a security guard, sought permission to keep a handgun in his home for protection. Heller knew how to handle firearms and was permitted to carry one as part of his job, but the D.C. government refused to allow him to keep one at home.

Joined by five other D.C. residents who had been similarly denied permission to keep a gun in their homes for self-protection, Heller sued the District with the help of lawyers recruited by the Institute for Justice, a non-profit public interest organization, claiming the D.C. government was denying a fundamental constitutional right guaranteed by the Second Amendment.

In many ways, Heller was just the sort of plaintiff gun rights advocates hoped would bring such a case. The case would certainly require the federal courts and, perhaps, the Supreme Court itself to finally address the question of whether citizens had the individual right to "keep and bear arms," as gun advocates and millions of other Americans believed.

Both sides were nervous about the sitting Justices who would decide the case. The NRA believed it would be difficult to get the right decision out of a Court that included the likes of Stephen Breyer, Ruth Bader Ginsburg, and John Paul Stevens. The opposition was just as nervous knowing that John Roberts, Antonin Scalia, and Clarence Thomas would be in on the decision. Both sides could only wonder where Justice Anthony Kennedy would come down.

Heller's lawyers decided to take the risk, and the fight was on. Ultimately, the Supreme Court decided the case by a five-to-four vote, with Justice Scalia writing the majority opinion and Justice John Paul Stevens writing for the minority. As both sides predicted, Justice Anthony Kennedy cast the deciding vote—on the side of the individual rights interpretation of the Second Amendment.

The decision in *District of Columbia v. Heller* was a great victory, but it did not mean gun owners had won the legal war. Indeed, there were two problems with the decision.

Originally, the Bill of Rights applied only to the federal government, but, over time, most of the rights guaranteed by the Founders were extended to the states through judicial decisions using a doctrine known as "incorporation." But *Heller* as decided applied only to the District of Columbia, a federal enclave, rather than to a state. As a result, gun owners residing in the District after *Heller* theoretically enjoyed greater rights than their counterparts in New York, California, or Illinois. That was to change soon, however, as an African-American Chicagoan stepped up to the plate.

Otis McDonald was born to Louisiana sharecroppers, moved north during the Great Depression at the age of 14, ended up in Chicago, served in World War II, then returned to Chicago to work as a janitor with the city school system. He married, bought a house in what was then a pretty decent neighborhood, raised a family, earned his high school GED, and became active in his union.

By the time he retired, much as it had for the Clint Eastwood character in the 2008 movie *Gran Torino*, McDonald's neighborhood had deteriorated. Living amongst gangbangers, prostitutes, and drug dealers, McDonald went to sleep every night not knowing if his home would be broken into before morning or how he would defend himself and his wife if it were. Otis McDonald's American Dream was quickly turning into a nightmare, but he decided to act. Like Dick Heller in Washington, D.C., Otis McDonald sought and was refused permission under Chicago's gun laws to keep a gun in his home to defend himself. Like Heller, he decided to go to court.

Guns in Black America

As a U.S. military veteran, McDonald knew the history of gun control in America and said later that, as he sat in the Court listening to the arguments, he realized he was there not just for himself, but also for those African-Americans who had been denied the right to defend themselves since the days following the Civil War. The result was another five/four decision. *McDonald v. Chicago* [2] incorporated the protections of the Second Amendment and applied them to the states. Illinois and other states would soon discover that the courts would no longer simply accept the restrictions they might impose on the fundamental right of Americans to keep and bear arms.

Otis McDonald knew enough about the history of gun control and its imposition during reconstruction following the Civil War to know better than most that modern gun-control laws are directly descended from laws imposed to keep firearms out of the hands of newly freed slaves. And he knew that the possession of firearms was essential to the efforts of blacks in the South to protect themselves and their families from white supremacist terrorism during the last century. McDonald knew, too, of the fact that even civil rights leaders who preached non-violence were too often forced to rely on their right to bear arms for self-protection. The Reverend Martin Luther King, Jr., applied for a carry permit during the 1955 Montgomery Bus Boycott and, though he was turned down, filled his home with guns and welcomed armed neighbors volunteering to stand guard in protection of him and his family.

There are others.

Condoleezza Rice, former Secretary of State under George W. Bush, knew this history, as well, and she remembers the armed neighbors who surrounded her family's home to protect them from a Klan mob, facts that have led Rice to proclaim herself a Second Amendment "absolutist."

Roy Innis, who walked with Martin Luther King and is on the NRA Board, heads the Congress of Racial Equality (CORE). His son, Niger Innis, CORE's spokesman, said at a 2013 press conference, "For black Americans, we know that gun control has ultimately been about people control. It sprouts from racist soil; be it after the, or during the infamous Dred Scott case where black man's humanity was not recognized."

And there is Harry Alford, President of the Black Chamber of Commerce, who praised the National Rifle Association in his speech at the same event, saying, "The National Rifle Association was started, founded by religious leaders who wanted to protect free slaves from the Ku Klux Klan." (Read more of Mr. Alford's remarks here: http://dailycaller.com/2013/02/22/black-conserva tives-gun-control-has-racist-roots-video/#ixzz4Awp5P1TV.)

The Question of Scrutiny

The second problem with *Heller* was that, in its decision, the Court ruled that the Second Amendment is subject to reasonable restrictions but did not explicitly state that such restrictions would have to pass the "strict scrutiny" of the federal courts. In other words, the Court did not address the question of what *degree* of scrutiny would have to be applied by the courts to subsequent restrictions on the rights the Second Amendment guaranteed. Why? For the simple reason that they did not have to, as the only issue *Heller* presented the Court regarded an absolute ban on the private ownership of a handgun for home defense. The way in which federal courts will have to judge future restrictions on the fundamental right protected by the Second Amendment was left to be decided later.

No case addressing this all-important issue has yet to reach the Court, but one will, because lower court judges are applying differing standards in judging what gun restrictions are constitutional under *Heller*. Thus, the decision the Justices reach when those questions come before them will be every bit as important as those addressed by *Heller* and *McDonald*.

What Sorts of Restrictions Are Legitimate Under *Heller*?

In the majority opinion in *Heller*, Justice Scalia acknowledged that even a fundamental constitutionally protected right, such as the right to free speech or, in the immediate instance, the right to keep and bear arms, is subject to long-standing and reasonable restrictions. Most famously, one cannot yell "Fire!" in a crowded theater when there is no blaze and expect to be protected by the First Amendment. The level of scrutiny the courts will ultimately apply to the examination of such restrictions will decide which are "reasonable" under *Heller* and which comprise an unconstitutional violation of the Amendment's demand that the right to keep and bear arms "shall not be infringed." This language is stronger than in other parts of the Bill of Rights.

The Supreme Court ordinarily requires that restrictions on fundamental rights, such as the right to free speech, be subjected to "strict scrutiny," which means that they can only be upheld if they are "necessary to serve a compelling state interest and are narrowly drawn to achieve that end." This is language used in the 1998 landmark legal case *United States v. Corrigan* (a record of that case can be found here: http://caselaw.findlaw.com/us-11th-circuit/1455029.html) and dictates regulatory policy in many issues unrelated to firearms. To avoid the requirement to apply "strict scrutiny" to future firearms restrictions, the Court would have to decide that the guarantees of the Second Amendment are not "fundamental." Some lower courts are declaring the Second Amendment nonfundamental, in order to uphold restrictions that could never survive such scrutiny.

This will inevitably lead to conflicts among the various federal judicial circuits that will, at some point, require the Supreme Court to address the question. It is clear that several members of the Supreme Court are reluctant to take up such cases. The Court refused to grant certiorari (to take up the case by a higher court) in a case originating in Highland Park, Illinois, which banned both "high-capacity magazines" and "assault rifles." The Seventh Circuit upheld the Highland Park restrictions, limiting *Heller's* application to total bans on handguns.

Justices Scalia and Thomas urged their colleagues to take the case, writing that the lower court "ignores *Heller's* fundamental premise," and criticized their colleagues for their "refusal to review a decision that flouts two of our Second Amendment precedents." The Seventh Circuit never came close to applying "strict scrutiny" to the Highland Park restriction, arguing that even if it could not be shown that the restrictions enhanced public safety, it was enough that they "may increase the public's sense of safety." Such a finding, if allowed to stand, would eventually render the *Heller* decision meaningless, a fact that Justice Thomas highlighted, saying, "If a broad ban on firearms can be upheld based on conjecture that the public might feel safer (while being no safer at all), then the Second Amendment guarantees nothing."

Prior to *Heller,* the question of what restrictions might be imposed on gun ownership had been decided on a purely political basis, as most politicians and policymakers assumed gun ownership was a privilege, rather than a right. After the 1968 Kennedy and King assassinations, the country was in the mood for the gun restrictions. The riots of that summer and the spike in street crime and violence that characterized the era led to a widely held assumption among policymakers that they could do what they pleased in the name of controlling crime and violence, by treating firearms ownership not as a right, but a privilege to be granted, conditioned, or even denied by government. Regulations and laws restricting firearms ownership and use were seen as constitutionally acceptable, regardless of how far they went. This assumption led jurisdictions like the District of Columbia to ban guns, even for self-defense. After *Heller* and *McDonald,* the courts and those who make and administer our laws have to look at the matter differently. The restrictions government can impose on a *privilege* are far different from those that can be imposed on a constitutionally protected *fundamental right.*

In many ways, the state of the law regarding the legitimacy of such restrictions is similar to the state of the law regarding speech restrictions a half-century or more ago. In the next few years, the federal courts will render decisions on the lengths to which policymakers can go in circumscribing or limiting the right to keep and bear arms, as guaranteed by the Founders, beyond the restrictions on the machine guns and short-barreled rifles and shotguns "grandfathered" by *Heller*.

Some jurisdictions have sought restrictions that fall short of outright bans but put so many obstacles in the way of possessing or buying a firearm as to make real-world ownership almost impossible. The District of Columbia, after *Heller*, decided to require residents to first obtain their guns in the D.C.—when there was no licensed dealer serving the public. Those seeking to purchase a gun also faced an incredible maze of forms and regulations. One of the tales of this travail is told in the *Washington Times'* former reporter Emily Miller's book, *How Emily Got Her Gun.*[3]

(These restrictions were somewhat eased, as the District faced another lawsuit charging that the scheme was an attempt to impose a de facto ban, when an outright ban could not survive constitutional scrutiny.) Other jurisdictions impose special taxes on firearms purchases or on ammunition.

The question of when such a tax becomes not a tax, but an unconstitutional burden on a fundamental right, will ultimately be decided in the courts. These decisions will be analogous to those rendered on the once-conditioned "poll tax" for the right to vote. The point is that the courts will continue to be a major battleground in the fight to preserve the rights of Americans under the Second Amendment, even if the Supreme Court eventually imposes a requirement that the lower courts examine such burdens with strict scrutiny. After *Heller* and *McDonald*, the courts will take on cases knowing that there is a right to be protected, but with the power to decide whether specific restrictions are reasonable or not.

Another Way *Heller* and *McDonald* Could Be Rendered Meaningless

The makeup of the Supreme Court matters. This Court has a powerful effect on law, simply by treating lower court decisions with benign neglect. The Supreme Court can refuse to hear cases that require hard answers. Thus, as in the Highland Park case, the Supreme Court has so far refused to hear cases questioning whether and to what extent the states can limit or deny concealed carry permits, even though there are already lower court decisions in clear conflict on the issue. Even worse, by simply refusing to review the decisions of liberal lower courts, the court is severely restricting the scope of Second Amendment guarantees and seemingly violating the letter and spirit of *Heller*. In this way, a future Supreme Court could, even without actually reversing *Heller* and *McDonald*, turn victory into defeat for America's gun owners.

Justice Kennedy was the deciding vote in *Heller* and *McDonald,* and experts assume Justice Kennedy will continue to be the deciding vote in future Second Amendment cases, so an understanding of how he might address future restrictions on the Second Amendment is crucial. It is, of course, impossible to be sure of any predictions, but Justice Kennedy's belief in the importance of foreign court decisions, international opinion, and treaties in interpreting the Constitution is troubling. It is possible, after all, to believe, as he does, in the meaning of the Second Amendment as guaranteeing individual gun ownership, while at the same time finding severe restrictions on that right are "reasonable."

The leading public advocate of taking into consideration foreign court decisions, public attitudes, and even treaties to which the United States is not a party when deciding cases is sitting Supreme Court Justice Stephen Breyer, who wrote a book on the subject in 2015, *The Court and the World: American Law and the New Global Realities.*[4] Justice Kennedy is more inclined to take foreign court decisions and world opinion into account in rendering decisions than any other Justice save Breyer. His attitude that American law can and should be affected by prevailing world opinion is particularly troubling when it comes to gun rights, because our laws and rights are unique and our Founders' views on the private ownership of firearms are opposed by most foreign governments, courts, and political leaders.

Most foreign governments and the United Nations reject the very idea that individuals have a right to defend themselves or their families. That argument makes little sense in a historic context—and seems farfetched to American gun owners—but might well find traction among jurists willing to give deference to foreign practices and beliefs.

The U.S. in the Minority

In this context, the Arms Trade Treaty (ATT), which we will discuss further in Part II, and the regulations called for under its terms and definitions that have yet to be written could impact domestic U.S. court decisions in future years. Justice Kennedy voted with the majority in *Heller* and *McDonald* but given his willingness to defer to foreign practices might well vote with the liberal bloc in a case that turns on the "reasonableness" of various restrictions on firearms ownership.

The United Nations and ATT supporters reject the idea that individuals have a right to defend themselves or their families, arguing that this is a job for the government. Most foreign firearms laws include stringent licensing requirements and prohibitions on far more firearms than most U.S. jurisdictions, and most require a detailed gun registry that allows the government to locate guns and their owners should they decide on confiscation as part of their firearms policy. The list of favored restrictions under the ATT includes prohibitions on the ownership of so-called "assault weapons" and "high-capacity magazines," as well as other items on the Obama-Clinton wish list of restrictions those two would like to impose here.

Should one of these restrictions enacted by legislators in this country make it to the Supreme Court, the argument will be raised that world opinion and world courts, as well as lawmakers in other nations, consider such restrictions legitimate and that, as part of the world community, so should we. That is an argument that makes little sense in a historic context and seems farfetched to American gun owners, but might well find traction with some members of the current Court, including Justice Kennedy.

The point of this discussion is to emphasize that the Court's debate over gun control is not going away. During the next decade, as anti-gun legislators and policy makers in various jurisdictions come up with new and, perhaps, innovative ways to further restrict firearms availability, numerous cases will make their way up through the lower courts, and then the Supreme Court is going to end up determining whether such restrictions will have to undergo strict scrutiny and what the Court as it current stands actually meant in *Heller* in its endorsement of reasonable restrictions on our Second Amendment rights.

The recognition of this basic and potentially dangerous reality motivates gun-owner groups like the NRA in the maintenance of a strong legal arm as an essential part of any attempt to protect the rights of America's gun owners. But all of NRA's successes in Congress and at the ballot box could be undone by a hostile Court that decides to rewrite the Constitution and Bill of Rights. It was, perhaps, the NRA's continued focus not just on the legislature, but the courts, that led liberal Georgetown University Law Professor David Cole to conclude in his 2016 book *Engines of Liberty: The Power of Citizen Activists to Make Constitutional Law*[5] that "The NRA, more so than any court, is the Second Amendment's best protector."

[1] *District of Columbia v. Heller, 554 U.S. 570 (2008), available at http://www.law.cornell.edu/supct/pdf/07-290P.ZO.*

[2] *McDonald v. Chicago, 561 U.S. ___, 130 S.Ct. 3020 (2010), available at http://www.law.cornell.edu/supct/pdf/08-1521P.ZO.*

[3] *Emily Miller, How Emily Got Her Gun (Washington, DC: Regnery, 2013).*

[4] *Stephen Breyer, The Court and the World: American Law and the New Global Realities (New York: Alfred Knopf, 2015).*

[5] *David Cole, Engines of Liberty: The Power of Citizen Activists to Make Constitutional Law (New York: Basic Books, 2016).*

CHAPTER 3

"Change the Culture"

M any of those who support one gun-control measure or another actually believe restrictions on gun ownership will reduce crime and violence. Those ideologically opposed to firearms ownership tout measures that sound reasonable initially. They run into difficulty, however, when policymakers and the public actually focus on how those measures would be implemented and begin to assess whether the laws or regulations would make any real difference.

The debate over the meaning of the Second Amendment centers on the question of whether individual Americans do or should have a constitutionally protected right to own and use firearms for lawful purposes. That question has been answered for now, but the questions of what "reasonable restrictions" might be both lawful and further the goals of reducing crime and violence in society remain.

Much of the gun debate focuses on symbolic and sometimes nonexistent problems and "solutions" that would do little, if anything, to reduce gun violence or gun crime. For instance, on his Town Hall Tour in the summer of 2016, President Obama tried to make the case that individuals on the federal no-fly list should not be allowed to buy guns. A quick analysis in this chapter will show that the refusal by Congress and the NRA and other pro-gun groups—a refusal viewed as "outrageous" by many on the gun-control side—to include the government's terrorist watch list and no-fly list individuals into the National Instant Check System (NICS) in an attempt to keep them from buying guns is a valid refusal.

During any campaign season, a lot of talk centers around some sort of "clean air bill," a "safe transportation bill," or something else that makes a good sound bite. This season it is "no-fly list." But giving a bill a superficially appealing name does not mean the proposed legislation will actually achieve its lofty goals. The various proposals to require "universal background checks" for all firearms transfers and other regulations sound good (to many) but in actuality would cause more problems than they would solve.

Most such proposals are more about politics than substance, and those advanced in 2016 promise to be no different. Candidates complain about the so-called "gun show loophole," the ability of felons to buy guns, including machine guns over the Internet or from private sellers hiding in the shadows, and the need to prevent those who have concealed carry permits from one state from using them to carry concealed in others. In this chapter, we take a closer look at the effectiveness of such proposals and the motives of those who make the case for them, knowing full well that these "solutions" would make little difference beyond imposing even greater burdens on families and individuals who enjoy the shooting sports or need a firearm for protection.

Gun owners have come to accept that they are the real targets, that those who want to restrict Second Amendment rights are more interested in targeting gun owners than they are in reducing crime, keeping firearms out of the hands of the dangerously mentally ill, or developing measures that might help accomplish these goals. It has been said that even the paranoid have enemies, and the evidence suggests strongly that Second Amendment supporters who see themselves and their values as the real targets of the gun-controllers have a point. The evidence also suggests that gun owners are at least partially correct about the targeting and not paranoid.

Change the Culture

The real goal of the gun-control advocacy community and the politicians they support is to change what they like to call the "American gun culture." They want to make the shooting sports, self-defense, and gun ownership as socially unacceptable as smoking. Sometimes they even admit this is their real goal.

In 1995, while former U.S. Attorney General Eric Holder was serving as U.S. Attorney for the District of Columbia, he spoke to the Women's National Democratic Club. CSPAN 2's tape of this event shows Holder marveling at the change in attitudes toward smoking that has been engineered over the years and urging gun-controllers to learn about how that change occurred. "You know, when I was growing up, people smoked all the time. Both my parents did. But, over time, we changed the way that people thought about smoking, so now we have people who cower outside of buildings and kind of smoke in private and don't want to admit it."

Mr. Holder said what worked with smokers could work with gun owners, if we "really brainwash people to think about guns in a vastly different way." He said the goal had to be to make people "ashamed" to own guns. Speaking about a legal activity and as an attorney for the law, the future Attorney General asserted, "What we need to do is change the way in which people think about guns, especially young people, and make it something that's not cool, that's not acceptable. It's not hip to carry a gun anymore, in the way in which we've changed our attitudes about cigarettes." (www.youtube.com/watch?v=RXwo9lARAgg)

On December 22, 2015, Virginia Attorney General Mark Herring, a leading legislative gun-control advocate even before his election as the Commonwealth's Attorney General, announced that he was cancelling Virginia's reciprocity agreements with some twenty-five other states on the grounds that their concealed carry permit requirements were not as tough as those imposed by the Commonwealth. Herring even admitted at the time that this was part of a national effort to find ways to bypass the legislature's hostility to gun-control measures. This change, had it been implemented, would have made it illegal for some 6.3-million citizens from the affected states to visit or travel through Virginia with a concealed firearm. South Dakota, Tennessee, Washington, Wisconsin, and Wyoming immediately announced, in retaliation, that they would no longer honor Virginia's 420,000 concealed carry permits.

At the press conference announcing his decision, Mr. Herring was asked by a *Washington Post* reporter if he or his office could name a single crime committed in Virginia, by an out-of-state concealed carry permit holder, that would have been prevented had he acted earlier. The answer: a simple "No." The Commonwealth of Virginia's top elected law enforcement official was announcing a "solution" to a nonexistent problem and was willing, in the process, to impose a burden on almost seven million American gun owners. His announcement had far less to do with a concern for the safety of Virginia citizens than it did with his hostility to gun ownership and desire to help "change the culture."

Mr. Herring's order, had it gone through, would have made Virginia less safe for its residents and visitors. Crimes involving concealed carry permit holders are extremely rare, as the men and women granted such permits in any state undergo a more thorough background check and gun handling and safety training than anyone without a permit. *Every* jurisdiction that allows citizens to carry concealed has experienced a drop in violent crime. Reducing the number of good guys with guns reduces, rather than enhances, public safety.

The political backlash and the intervention of the state legislature following Mr. Herring's action led to negotiations to stop the travesty between the Republican Virginia Senate and Virginia Governor Terry McAuliffe, former Chairman of the Democratic National Committee, Co-chairman of President Bill Clinton's 1996 re-election campaign, and Chairman of Hillary Clinton's 2008 presidential campaign. When the smoke cleared in a compromise in early 2016, gun-control advocates were outraged that one of their own was forced to back down from another chance to punish and demonize gun owners.

The fact that the Herring proposal would have done nothing to reduce gun crime in Virginia did not bother Michael Bloomberg's Everytown for Gun

Safety Research Director Ted Alcorn, because reducing crime was never the point. When asked, Mr. Alcorn said that "setting cultural norms" is more important and "something that laws do."

This drive to "change the culture" has led gun-control advocates to target gun owners and Second Amendment rights advocates and has destroyed any good will between Second Amendment supporters and government regulators. American firearms enthusiasts have been derided, in recent years, as dumb, reckless, and criminal by those who, overwhelmingly, have never been hunting, shot or owned a gun, or even known anyone who has. Many of the most ardent gun-controllers among us have never been to a rifle or shotgun range, often do not like police, and have never visited a National Park or been in the woods since childhood, if then. In comparison, Germany, while no hotbed of gun freedoms, has its preschoolers spend one day a month in the woods, vastly unsupervised compared to American children. The German education system, and that of many others, reflects first its country's culture and *then* its policies. It should not be hard to connect the dots here and understand that time in the woods for many Americans would go a long way toward supporting the gun community in retaining their freedoms and increasing what should be a curiosity for the truth.

Gun Shows

The "gun show loophole," so often attacked by liberal politicians and the media, is actually more myth than reality. To hear politicians like current and former New York Democratic Senators Chuck Schumer and Hillary Clinton, one would think that an American gun show most resembles a Pakistani arms bazaar, where criminals and terrorists can buy just about anything and with no questions asked.

This is most decidedly not the case.

More than 90 percent of the guns sold at any gun show are purchased through Federal Firearms Licensed (FFL) dealers who run a Federal Bureau of Investigations (FBI) National Instant Criminal Background Check System (NICS) check on the purchaser before completing the sale.

Private sales are the exception, because, generally, a private party can attend a gun show and sell a gun to another private party without requiring the purchaser to undergo a background check. The two would have the same right to buy and sell their guns in this way at their homes. Even with that private sale, however, federal law prohibits anyone who cannot pass a NICS check from buying a gun even from a private party, *and that makes it a felony for one private party to sell a gun to a prospective purchaser if he or she knows or has reason to suspect that person is prohibited from making such a purchase.*

No Takers

By David Keene

During the brouhaha following Sandy Hook, I agreed to be interviewed about various "common sense" gun-control proposals at a Monitor Breakfast. A prestigious event hosted by the *Christian Science Monitor,* it is organized so that about 50 broadcast and print reporters can question a "newsmaker" on issues for which they report. After several questions about the so-called "gun show loophole," I asked for a show of hands to see how many of these reporters had ever attended a gun show. No hands went up. I proposed that the moderator pass around a sign-up sheet for those interested in attending Washington, D.C.'s largest gun show the next weekend. I offered to attend with any interested journalist, arrange meetings with the show organizers, and provide a private tour of the NRA's National Firearms Museum. Attendees could sign up or call the moderator.

The next morning, the breakfast event's moderator called to say that not one reporter was interested in actually attending a gun show!

A suspicious purchaser who wanders around a gun show seeking a seller who is unlikely to require a background check raises red flags in most prospective sellers' minds. Most shy away from such buyers. Too, most sellers will require the buyer to go to a friendly dealer for a NICS check as a condition of the sale, but especially if someone is acting oddly. The Orlando shooter was acting oddly in June 2016 when he wanted to purchase a gun, and was subsequently turned down and reported to the FBI.

A handful of companies organize almost all of this country's gun shows. At one point, as the debate raged over closing the so-called "gun show loophole," it was suggested that, even under existing law, the Bureau of Alcohol, Tobacco, Firearms and Explosives (ATF) could set up a booth that would allow private sellers access to NICS, and the show organizers would then require NICS to check for all on-premises sales.

ATF was not interested.

In other words, when the government had an opportunity to fix the "gun-show loophole" it refused—in favor of having a political issue.

In reality, the private sale of most firearms is not much different from the private sale of almost anything else that can be legally and privately owned. Such sales are particularly analogous to the private sale of an automobile. Automobile dealers are licensed and regulated, and they sell most of the cars in the U.S. However, if you want to sell a car or buy one from another private party, dealer regulations do not apply. Now, most car dealers probably would not mind outlawing private auto sales, just like more than a few firearms retailers could live with outlawing private gun sales, but neither represents anything as insidious as a "loophole."

Proposals to close the "gun show loophole" are designed not to thwart criminals from buying guns at gun shows, but to close down the gun shows themselves. More than 2.5 million Americans attend one or more gun shows every year, but various surveys have found that *few illegally used firearms are purchased at gun shows; many are stolen or bought illegally on the streets.*

Criminals do not buy their guns at gun shows, from collectors, or at Walmart. Regulations designed to "tighten" private gun sale transactions have little impact on criminals and even less on individuals with mental disabilities who should be on who prohibited list within the NICS system and are not.

New Loopholes Whenever It Suits

Democratic Presidential candidate Hillary Clinton, during her campaign stumps, has been heard to speak of a new "loophole." She calls it the "Charleston loophole" and has promised to close it if she makes it to the White House.

The "loophole" Mrs. Clinton wants to close has never existed. She named this supposed "loophole" after a crazed racist who attacked and killed worshippers at an African American Church in Charleston, South Carolina. During an arrest prior to the church shooting, the attacker, Dylan Roof, had admitted to police that he was a meth addict. Mr. Roof passed the mandatory NICS check at the firearms retailer for the simple reason that the FBI had negligently failed to include his drug use information, forwarded to them by the South Carolina police in its database. Thus, the Charleston shooter was able to buy his gun not because of a "loophole, but because federal regulators simply were not doing their job.

Mistakes of this sort happen, especially in an agency with a limited budget and that is, today, responsible for running more than 20 million background checks a year. The results in the case of Mr. Roof were tragic, but it is difficult to imagine how Mrs. Clinton would close this "loophole" unless she nonsensically assumes the FBI let Roof progress through the NICS system on purpose. Or maybe, as President, she thinks she will have the power to ban bureaucratic mistakes. One can be tougher on bureaucracies and their procedures, but electing a new President does not automatically fix the system. (The NRA and other pro-gun groups have supported the NICS system, as well as legislative proposals to reform it.)

Firearms Industry Responsibility

In addition to talking about the gun show and Charleston "loopholes," Mrs. Clinton has spent an inordinate amount of time denouncing her primary opponent, Vermont Senator Bernie Sanders, for "voting with the NRA" in support of shielding firearms manufacturers and dealers from lawsuits for negligence in producing "dangerous" products. In doing so, she seems to claim that Congress exempted gun makers from lawsuits that manufacturers of other products risk on a daily basis.

This is simply not the case. The 2005 Protection of Lawful Commerce in Arms Act (PLCAA) protects firearms manufacturers and dealers from liability *when third parties use their products illegally.* The law does not, as Mrs. Clinton and others imply, eliminate liability for damages arising from defective products, breach of contract, criminal misconduct, and other actions for which they can be held directly responsible. *Any* U.S.-based manufacturer of *any* legal product is held to this same level of responsibility.

PLCAA was passed because anti-gun advocates launched a series of lawsuits designed to bankrupt our domestic gun manufacturers. Attorneys bringing the suits did not expect to win, but it was widely believed the cost of the defense would severely damage and, hopefully, bankrupt the firearms industry. PLCAA was designed not to give gun makers rights or advantages manufacturers of other products lacked, but to put them on the same footing as manufacturers of other legal products and to prevent the abuse of the legal system in an attempt to drive them out of business.

Senator Sanders voted with his state and for PLCAA. Now, as many as one-third of NRA's members are Democrats, but that party's growing antipathy to gun rights dominates the base that led Mrs. Clinton to mischaracterize and attack his positive vote. In a CNN interview with Jake Tapper, on July 5, 2015, early in his campaign for President, Senator Sanders made the case for the act as persuasively as anyone else does:

> *If somebody has a gun and it falls into the hands of a murderer, and that murderer kills somebody with the gun, do you hold the gun manufacturer responsible? Not any more than you would hold a hammer company responsible if somebody beats somebody over the head with a hammer.*

Mrs. Clinton may or may not know just what the Act allows and does not allow, but, as an attorney and former United States Senator, she should be expected to understand and characterize legislation accurately. Her false allegations in this regard are just one more instance in which she has been willing to disregard reality if she believes doing so will prove helpful to her politically. She said what she said not because it was true, but because it suited her to falsely imply that Congress has exempted gun makers from the same potential liability faced by the manufacturers of other legal products.

The Disconnect

Part of the electorate's frustration with establishment candidates in 2016 is that many of the policy proposals coming from politicians are not based on a true understanding of the problems they are supposedly designed to solve. The more one knows about an issue, the more obvious the disconnect between the real world and Washington.

This is true even of government officials charged with executing the laws, as illustrated by an exchange between FBI Director James Comey and South Carolina Republican Senator Lindsey Graham about what is and is not legal or protocol if one wants to buy a gun in response to an Internet ad. The President wants to ban Internet gun sales, suggesting that criminals are essentially free to buy guns from Internet sellers without submitting to a NICS background check. This is only partially possible. The Internet is not the Pakistani arms bazaar any more than is the local gun show, and that is true no matter how the President characterizes it. Internet, gun show, or private party transfer, it is *illegal* for a prohibited purchaser to buy a gun, *illegal* regardless of how such a buyer hears that a gun is for sale or about who is selling it.

Most guns sold through Internet advertisements are sold by FFL holders. At the same time, most private sales resulting from Internet advertising are no more legal or illegal than those sold as the result of a classified ad in a local newspaper.

How Informed Is the FBI?

The Director of the FBI, whose agency runs the NICS background check system, should know, more than anyone else, that gun sales are highly regulated. In December 2015, in the wake of President Obama's attacks on Internet gun sales, FBI Director James Comey appeared at an oversight hearing before the Senate Judiciary Committee on Capitol Hill and was asked a simple question by Senator Lindsey Graham, the South Carolina Republican:

> *Mr. Graham: If I buy a gun on the Internet, is it delivered to my home?*
> *Mr. Comey: If you buy a gun on the Internet?*
> *Mr. Graham: If I try to buy a gun on the Internet, where do I pick it up?*
> *Mr. Comey: I assume it's shipped to you, but I don't know for sure, actually.*

Actually, an interstate firearms transaction effected over the Internet *requires* the seller to have a FFL dealer ship the firearms to an FFL dealer in the buyer's home state. Once received by the buyer's end FFL, the buyer can pick up the gun *only* after passing the NICS background check has been successfully completed—the gun cannot be mailed!

You can see that this supposed "Internet sales loophole" is not big enough to drive a Mini Cooper through let alone a truck, as Mr. Obama and others contend. And, once again, little indicates that criminals buy firearms via this route.

Since the Sandy Hook massacre, anti-gun crusaders have focused most of their attention on the adoption of "universal background checks," a proposal with the most popular support and, therefore, the most likely to pass via referendum and legislative action. How effective such background checks have been in keeping firearms out of the hands of criminals, the dangerously mentally ill, and potential terrorists has been debated for years, yet universal checks remain the favorite proposal of most gun-controllers.

Gun rights advocates argue that background checks have been largely ineffective, because many who should be included in the National Instant Check System are not in the database—and millions who should *not* be thrown into the system are included based on sloppy state government reporting. Still, NICS is used by licensed gun dealers and by some private sellers, who require those who buy from them to allow a friendly licensee to run a NICS check on them.

Various studies have shown that few criminals obtain their firearms from FFL dealers. As *Preventative Medicine* reported in an online article titled "Sources of Guns to Dangerous People: What We Learn by Asking Them," written by Philip J. Cook, Susan T. Parker, and Harold A. Pollack, criminals being held in the Cook County Jail in Chicago get guns from their "social network," i.e., friends and persons known to them, but generally not from the various legal sources available to them.

Science Daily, reporting on September 16, 2015, said:

> *Information from the Cook County inmates lined up with findings in a second study, which identified straw purchasers and gun traffickers as key sources of crime guns in Chicago. Straw purchasers can pass a background check and buy guns that they transfer to others.*
>
> *This study, "Some Sources of Crime Guns in Chicago: Dirty Dealers, Straw Purchases and Traffickers," is forthcoming in the 2015 Journal of Criminal Law and Criminology. The research was supported by operating grants to the University of Chicago from the MacArthur and McCormick foundations, as well as project grants from the Joyce and McCormick foundations and the Fund for a Safer Future.*

(You can read the full article here: https://www.sciencedaily.com/releases/2015/09/150916162916.htm.)

How Many Really Escape a Background Check?

The initial plan when background checks were instituted was to arrest and prosecute those who attempt to buy a firearm illegally and were subsequently caught through the NICS check. In actuality, this rarely happens. The overwhelming majority of those stopped through a NICS check actually have a right to buy the gun they were denied anyway—and once caught in this snare, ordinary citizens must endure a long, bureaucratic process to prove they are not criminals and have been falsely accused. This wastes the resources of citizens and chews up taxpayer money in government time.

Gun-control advocates argue that the bigger problem is that many firearms buyers are not required to face a NICS check, because they buy not from dealers, but from private parties. President Obama, Hillary Clinton, and others have argued for years that as many as four in 10 gun buyers manage to escape the background checks (which these advocates would like to make mandatory) by making their purchases at gun shows (the so-called "gun show loophole"), via the Internet, or from private parties, rather than licensed dealers. The 40-percent figure was gleaned from a sample of a couple hundred gun purchasers (in a survey taken by telephone) in 1994, before the modern FBI-run NICS was up and running. Few who examined the data believed the 40-percent figure when it was first publicized, and even fewer accept it today. In fact, recent studies indicate that perhaps 20 percent of gun owners bought through a family relative, a one-time estate sale, a gun owner selling one gun, or some other non-NICS way. (You can read more about these studies here: https://www.nraila.org/articles/20151022/hillary-adopts-the-40-myth-to-argue-for-gun-control.)

When President Obama first began using the 40-percent figure in 2013, the *Washington Post*'s "fact checker," Glenn Kessler, determined it was "mostly false," awarding the President "three Pinocchios" for using it. Mr. Obama, and now Mrs. Clinton, continue to cite the number as "proof" that the system needs to be tightened.

Hilary Clinton is quick to say that a more reasonable NRA in the 1990s actually supported background checks and that most NRA members, along with 75 to 90 percent of the public, continue to support making such checks universal today. The NRA did support background checks in the 1990s and even helped lobby to get the NICS system up and running, but when it became clear the government was either incapable or unwilling to make it function fairly and efficiently, the NRA and other gun groups refused to support its extension to the individuals and groups it was never intended to include in the first place; the sort of universal checks proposed today by the gun-control lobby was *never* supported by gun advocates.

While we will look at the entire history of background checks later in this chapter, the following will help underscore that which we have already presented. Almost all first-time gun buyers acquire their firearms through a firearms retailer and undergo a NICS check when making the purchase. Any dealer—whether Walmart, a corner sporting goods store, or an individual engaged in the *business* of buying and selling firearms—is required to have a Federal Firearms License (FFL) and to subject anyone buying from them to a NICS check. Though there are NICS-exempt licenses or permits, particularly for law enforcement—18 U.S.C. 922(t)(3)(A)—the mandatory NICS check must be completed and the FFL must receive a "proceed" response before the sale can be completed. "Prohibited persons" are not allowed to buy firearms and can be prosecuted for attempting to do so, although, as we shall see, that rarely happens.

The Manchin-Toomey Gamble

The apparent (or superficial) popularity of the universal background check concept helped persuade the Obama Administration and the Democratic Senate leadership to essentially stake everything on a proposal by New York Democratic Senator Chuck Schumer. This proposal was later modified and co-sponsored by Pennsylvania Republican Senator Pat Toomey and West Virginia Democratic Senator Joe Manchin. Manchin, a former Governor of West Virginia, bragged that he was a life member of the NRA and a long-time Second Amendment supporter but found the Schumer universal background check proposal "reasonable."

The erroneous assumption in this proposal was that gun shows did not require background checks and that all private sellers avoided checks. As we've seen, neither assumption is correct, but Mr. Schumer's amendment would have required criminal background checks for all sales between private parties. The exceptions were few and the logistics odd, so a host of problems were unresolved.

The current rules were ironed out years ago, after two weeks of Senate hearings chaired by then-Democratic Senator Birch Bayh of Indiana, to avoid the pitfalls inherent in a loosely worded amendment such as that considered by the Senate. The universal background check almost always applies not just to sales, but also to simple transfers, where money may not exchange hands. Thus, questions arise if a wife borrows her husband's gun or if, at the range, a shooter asks a friend if he or she would like to try a firearm that shooter has brought with them. Further, if two neighbors or cousins sold a gun out in the rural area where there was no Internet, did they need to drive into town, find a dealer, and undergo a NICS background check before completing their sale? If Lassie was not around and a rattlesnake was nearby, were you allowed to borrow your buddy's gun to kill the snake before it struck? As with most laws, the devil is both in the details and in the way they are interpreted after they are enacted.

Manchin-Toomey was a watered-down version of an earlier universal background check bill introduced by Senate Democratic Leader Harry Reid of Nevada. The Reid bill illustrates the problems one confronts in trying to apply to the real world what only sounds like a good idea. All such bills require background checks not just for sales, but for any kind of physical transfer between private parties, such as lending another one's gun or gifting it to a friend or even a relative. Second Amendment scholar and author of 17 books David B. Kopel analyzed the Reid bill, hypothesizing its impact on a fictional woman who buys a handgun at the age of 24 and who keeps the gun for the rest of her life. As Kopel writes, "She never sells the gun. But over her lifetime she may engage in dozens of firearms transfers."[1] Consider the following:

- She loans the gun to her sister, who takes it on a weekend camping trip.
- While out of town on a business trip, she leaves the gun with her brother for safekeeping.
- If she lives on a farm, she lets her brother use the gun for pest and predator control purposes.
- If the woman is in the Army Reserve and is called up for an overseas deployment, she gives the gun to her brother-in-law for safekeeping until she returns.
- She lends the gun for a few days to a neighbor who is being threatened by a stalker, until the neighbor can get her own gun.
- She becomes a certified firearms safety instructor and takes the gun to a class she is teaching, where students are given an opportunity to hold and handle the gun.

Under each of these scenarios, with a universal background check in place that affects any transfer of a firearm, the unsuspecting gun owner would have committed illegal transfers that could result in her arrest, indictment, and imprisonment.

As Senate colleagues recoiled at the possible consequences of passing the Reid proposal, Senator Chuck Schumer, along with Senators Manchin and Toomey, came up with a compromise that would mitigate some, though not all, of the inherent problems in such a scheme. The defeat of Manchin-Toomey in the Senate was based on the practical consequences of requiring a universal background check, rather than the superficial attractiveness of the idea, and it marked the end of the Obama Administration's immediate post-Sandy Hook attempts to further restrict Second Amendment rights. Unfortunately, it remains at the top of gun-control advocates' agendas.

Another Obama Executive Order

Frustrated by his failure to get Congress to enact the sort of universal background check he favored, President Obama sought, on January 21, 2016, to take executive action to extend such checks to as many potential sales as possible. To accomplish this, he gave federal officials the power to almost arbitrarily decide to declare anyone who sells a firearm a dealer who must possess an FFL and who must subject a purchaser to a background check.

The History of Background Checks

To understand the debate about universal background checks requires an understanding of the history and effectiveness of background checks as we know them now. The concept sounds good to the public, so why have policy makers rejected going down this road each time?

Advocates claim "universal" checks are a reasonable response to "gun violence" that could prevent crime and future mass shootings. These advocates blame the power and money of extremists with the NRA and other pro-gun organizations for blocking them, but the evidence suggests something much different—that universal background checks have been rejected because they have been proven ineffective and burdensome to the general gun-owning public.

The modern background check system was put into place in the 1990s but is a product of the debate over the private ownership of firearms that began in the 1960s. The Gun Control Act of 1968 required record-keeping for all firearms sales by FFLs and required anyone in the business of dealing in firearms to have a FFL. The law allowed federal authorities to prosecute anyone dealing in firearms without a license but did not define the parameters of "dealing."

Without a clear definition, law enforcement officials defined the meaning of "dealing" as they liked. The result was a legal no-man's-land in which federal agents and prosecutors could go after anyone they desired to target.

Most private sales are between relatives, friends, or neighbors, or made by collectors and hobbyists who want to reduce the size of their collections or upgrade from one firearm to another. The problem with not having a detailed, legal definition of "dealing" was that virtually no one knew what might trigger law enforcement to make someone a potential target. So arbitrary was the targeting of "dealers," some collectors were prosecuted for selling as few as two or three guns in a year. At the same time, federal authorities were refusing to renew FFLs held by people who only sold that same number of firearms in a year, because their low sales volume somehow meant they were not dealers.

The abuses resulting from a vague law, combined with prosecutors and federal law enforcers operating under orders from above to make arrests, resulted in a wide, well-documented swath of injustice. Federal agents operating undercover cajoled reluctant collectors into selling one or two guns from their collections so they could then be arrested, prosecuted, and incarcerated as unlicensed dealers. The penalties were harsh under the 1968 law: felony prosecution with a sentence of as much as five years in prison and a fine of up to $250,000. Families were ruined and firearms owners lived in fear of crossing an invisible line that could lead to jail and ruin.

The firearms community's way of dealing with the vague requirements of the 1968 Gun Control Act was to have thousands of collectors and hobbyists acquire FFLs. These FFL holders could buy and sell firearms, though they were subject to severe record-keeping requirements and their home and business could be visited or searched at any time by ATF agents—without a warrant. Nevertheless, applications for FFLs skyrocketed as a means of protection against ATF abuse.

Whom NICS Is Supposed to Stop

The existing NICS system lists nine categories of prohibited purchasers who cannot legally purchase a handgun:

- Anyone convicted of or under indictment on felony charges, but not yet convicted.
- A fugitive from justice.
- A user of illegal drugs.
- An adjudicated mental defective.
- Anyone illegally in the United States.
- Anyone dishonorably discharged from the U.S. Armed Forces.
- Anyone who has renounced their U.S. citizenship.
- Anyone subject to a court order restraining them from harassing, stalking, or threatening an intimate partner or the child of an intimate partner.
- Anyone convicted of a misdemeanor crime of domestic violence.

It is a felony for anyone in any of these categories to purchase a firearm or for anyone to knowingly or with a reasonable suspicion still sell—even in a private sale—to any prospective purchaser who falls into one of these categories. This prohibition exists regardless of whether a background check is performed on the buyer.

Not My Problem
By David Keene

Like many other firearms enthusiasts in the pre-NICS era, I acquired a FFL in the 1970s and dutifully kept records of a few private sales. Most sales were to friends. I sold one gun to a friend of a friend, a U.S. Foreign Service Officer who was subsequently posted to a country that did not allow him to bring his sidearm with him. He secured it in a locked box in a commercial mini-warehouse where he stored his furniture and personal property. On one of his trips back to the States, he discovered the warehouse had been broken into and his gun was among the items stolen. He called the police and filed a theft report.

In due course, police confiscated the gun from an armed robber. ATF contacted me as the last known seller, and the ATF agent demanded the record of the sale, as the law required. When I produced the paperwork and told the agent about the subsequent theft of the gun, he listened politely but impatiently, then curtly said he was not concerned with what happened to the gun after it was sold or how it got into the hands of a criminal. "My only job," BATF said, "is to make sure you haven't broken any laws. What happened to the gun once you sold it is somebody else's business."

This minor incident demonstrates a larger truth. The ATF was interested in enforcing or seeking to demonstrate its power over FFL holders—and tracking down criminals was "somebody else's business."

At that time, anti-Second Amendment groups were arguing that too many FFLs were being issued and that the government should begin revoking them as a "common sense" means of further restricting access to firearms. Within a few years, the number of FFL holders had been reduced by 80 percent, as license holders either had their licenses revoked for not selling enough guns to be classified as a dealer or simply gave them up as ATF harassment of licensees increased.

This was before background checks were mandated in the 1990s, so the new policy of limiting the number of FFL holders had the effect of eliminating the record-keeping system required for most sales. Thus, these sales once again became private sales.

Finally, in February of 1982, after extensive hearings that began in the Senate Appropriations Committee in 1979 and the Senate Judiciary Committee in 1980, the Judiciary's Subcommittee on the Constitution issued a report, concluding:

> *The BATF has primarily devoted its firearms enforcement efforts to the apprehension, upon technical* malum prohibitum *charges, of individuals who lack all*

criminal intent and knowledge. Agents anxious to generate an impressive arrest and gun confiscation quota have repeatedly enticed gun collectors into making a small number of sales—often as few as four—from their personal collections. Although each of the sales was completely legal under state and federal law, the agents then charged the collector with having "engaged in the business" of dealing in guns without the required license.

Malum prohibitum is Latin and means "prohibited by law but not necessarily evil in itself." This existing prosecutorial and bureaucratic abuse, and the ATF's record, motivated Congress to tighten the definition of "dealing" in firearms as a business. It defined "dealers" as those who "repetitively buy and sell firearms with the principal motive of making a profit," thus freeing hobbyists, collectors, and others who buy and sell to improve their collection or to upgrade the firearms they use from record-keeping and agency oversight. A dealer license is required if one "devotes time, attention, and labor to dealing in firearms as a regular course of trade or business with the principal objective of livelihood and profit through the repetitive purchase and resale of firearms." This license requirement is not restricted to full-time dealers—some part-time dealers may well need a FFL—but the abuses of the early 1970s were much reduced by the 1980 legal clarification.

In 2016, by executive order, Obama reversed this fix. He calls the Order a "clarification" of the definition of "dealer," but it in fact reopens the door to precisely the sort of potential for abuse firearms owners were subjected to under the 1968 law. For the rest of Mr. Obama's term—and longer, if Mrs. Clinton is elected President—government bureaucrats can decide who is a firearms dealer on an ad hoc basis, on the spot. Many of those seeking to impose a requirement for universal background checks on all sales and transfers today have given far less thought to the implications of such a regime than the Congressmen and Senators who spent so much time studying the issue in the 1970s and early '80s; what sounds so attractive conceptually loses much of its appeal when those consequences are considered.

The Gun Control Act of 1968 required FFLs to ask prospective firearms purchasers a series of questions in order to determine whether they were prohibited from buying a gun, but there was no requirement for the information those purchasers supplied to be verified and no system in place to provide such verification. That changed with the passage of the Brady Handgun Violence Prevention Act, in 1993. The Brady Law required dealers to submit a potential purchaser's identifying information and answers to a series of questions to law enforcement officials for verification. Law enforcement had five days to get back to the dealer advising an approval or blocking the purchase. The law applied only to handguns.

The Problems with NICS

In 1993, when the Brady Bill passed, the NRA led a successful effort to require the federal government to set up a computerized system that would allow almost instantaneous background checks. The system, run by the FBI and known as the National Instant Criminal Background Check System (NICS) allowed a FFL to submit information on a prospective purchaser to the system electronically. In most cases, the check is completed in a few minutes by 1998.

The operational weaknesses of the early NICS system were that it sometimes broke down, and it never included all the data on potentially prohibited persons. That information on prohibited persons was to be submitted to the system by the federal government and the states, but many states simply dumped arrest records into the system, did not update what they were submitting, or, particularly in cases involving those with mental illnesses that should have been included in the database, flat-out refused to submit any data.

When originally set up, NICS was to include not only felons, but also those who had been adjudicated as potentially dangerous because of a mental illness. But few states included those so adjudicated in the "prohibited purchasers" lists NICS receives from them. Some states simply did not bother. Others responded to pressure from mental health advocacy groups that argued against complying with the law, feeling that inclusion of the mentally ill in the NICS system would "demonize" them.

The controversy over who should or should not be included in the background checks system as a prohibited firearms purchaser goes to the very nature of what NICS is supposed to do. People who are far more likely to misuse a gun than the average citizen should not be able to get a gun, but, invariably, including groups or categories of people based either on who they are or their past conduct will envelop many who are no more likely to misuse a gun than the average man or woman on the street.

There are other problems. The Obama Administration claims that as many as two million people have been denied permission to purchase firearms from NICS checks, implying that those flagged during the check have all been dangerous criminals. This is false. The sloppy nature of the information submitted by many states has led to sale denials based on erroneous data. While a convicted felon is truly a prohibited purchaser under the law, many of those supposedly within this category are men and women who may have been arrested but never convicted of anything, as well as those who were convicted of misdemeanors that do not disqualify them from buying a firearm rather than a felony that does; misdemeanor charges were never meant to trigger NICS or the loss of a constitutional right. Still other denials turned out to be people who might have been arrested or convicted for nonviolent crimes in their youth as long as 40 or 50 years before the attempted purchase, while others have been denied their right to buy a gun because they share a name similar to that of a legitimately prohibited person. In a very different context, this was the same sort of mistake that landed the late Senator Edward M. Kennedy on the federal anti-terrorist no-fly list.

As a result of these erroneous denials, very few charges are ever brought by prosecutors, even though it is a felony for a prohibited purchaser to *attempt* to buy a gun or to provide false information when doing so. In 2012, state and local background checks were completed for more than six million gun buyers, with the FBI turning down 72,659 of these for various reasons. Yet only about 1,500 of these denied persons attempting to purchase a firearm were arrested by state or local law enforcement agencies, and just 44 of these were prosecuted under federal laws. (There is no readily available data on how many of the 44 were eventually prosecuted or convicted.)

The FBI says that, in a typical year, somewhere between one and two percent of potential gun purchasers subjected to a NICS check are turned down, and it appears that far less than one percent of those are prosecuted. These figures, in aggregate, testify to the fact that very few felons, gangbangers, or other prohibited persons actually acquire the guns they want through dealers. The Justice Department's Inspector General has found, in fact, that very few of those caught committing perjury in answering the questions required as part of the background check ever face any penalty other than denial of the purchase they seek. A criminal who actually tries to buy a gun at their local Walmart and is denied the right to do so after a NICS check can, in most cases, just walk away without fear of arrest or prosecution—and then acquire a gun illegally, as most criminals do.

In theory, anyone wrongly denied the right to buy a gun as the result of a NICS check has a right to appeal the denial, although that process can be time-consuming and expensive. Many simply give up on their purchase, and many may not know at all that they have a right to appeal.

The issue of false denials got worse in 2015, as the government, for "manpower and budgetary reasons," simply stopped processing appeals. By the beginning of 2016, more than 7,000 appeals were awaiting action. These potential firearms purchasers, assuming their appeals have merit, are being denied their constitutional rights.

Gun rights advocates familiar with the NICS system believe it is not working, and that if Congress through legislation or the President by executive order requires background checks of millions of firearms purchasers without providing adequate funding to modernize and clean up the prohibited persons list, American gun owners will find it ever more difficult to exercise their rights.

Solutions that Skim the Surface

Background checks remain popular, but public policy is more complicated than a campaign slogan. In many ways, the move to put more categories of people into the NICS system is an extension of the age-old desire on the part of law enforcement and public policy experts to utilize various group characteristics as a predictor of individual behavior. In the past, it was believed it was best to keep an eye on the poor, minorities, and immigrants, because they were the sorts of people "more likely" to become criminals than affluent whites.

Other "categories" followed. In the 1970s, scientists even came up with what was popularly called the "criminal chromosome," suggesting that males carrying it should be monitored because studies suggested they may be more prone to violence and crime than others. This was a variation on pseudoscience that went back much farther in time: consider the British who painted themselves blue in the belief it would scare off attackers; or phrenology, studying the shape and size of the cranium as a predictor of mental abilities and character. The XYY chromosome was even associated with physical characteristics that might make it easier to identify and monitor potential wrongdoers; carriers tended to have red hair and freckles; it did not take much imagination to imagine red-haired Irishmen being turned away by potential employers and pub bouncers, because hiring them or letting them drink could prove risky.

Eventually, the backlash killed the whole idea, but those arguing for it used the same arguments as those who suggest that the poor or African Americans should be more closely monitored by law enforcement because, on a percentage basis, more of them than other members of the general population are somehow "likely" to commit crimes. Still, critics kept asking if carriers of the XYY chromosome were certain to commit criminal or violent acts. Of course, the researchers had to admit that only a small percentage of them ever had, yet they still argued that, since statistically the percentage of red-haired males who might turn violent was greater than the percentage of violence-prone individuals within the general population, monitoring them made some sense. The problem was that actual science was asking Americans to target millions of people who had never broken any law whatsoever. Sound familiar?

As it turns out, and as it is with African Americans or the mentally ill, the vast majority of XYY carriers were, if anything, more likely to be victims of crime than become criminals, though they would still be looked at suspiciously by the rest of us for their *potential* to be criminals. In a sense, that is exactly why advocates for the mentally ill or leaders of racial minority populations are so troubled by similar guesses. When law enforcement begins looking at groups, rather than individuals, for likely criminals, and particularly when a decision is made to target groups because of characteristics that supposedly "make" individual members of the group a potential danger, the innocent suffer.

That is exactly what those who would deny entire groups of Americans the right to own or purchase a firearm argue every day. Consider the list of "prohibited persons" unfairly denied their Second Amendment rights under federal law. With a so-called "logical" reason for including each group, large numbers of people who have never and will never pose a threat to anyone are denied the rights the rest of us enjoy. To illustrate this, examine the seemingly most logical of all prohibitions: the lifetime ban imposed on convicted felons.

A pretty good case can be made for prohibiting a felon who has, say, been arrested, indicted, and convicted of armed robbery or some other violent crime. Given the evidence that individuals convicted of violent crimes are prone to committing another crime and going right back to jail, these criminals are just the sort of people who should not have access to guns or other dangerous weapons.

But what about the 5'4" bookkeeper who embezzled funds from a flower shop in 1952, was quite properly arrested, indicted, and convicted of a felony for doing so, but finished "paying his debt to society" decades ago. It is preposterous to suggest that although that person is indeed a convicted felon, he is someone we should be afraid will commit any act of violence, with or without a gun. And yet, he, like the armed robber or gangbanger, is included as a prohibited purchaser by the federal government.

There are many other symbolic proposals that would have little impact other than to harass gun owners, but they sound good at first. Among the most egregious has been the Obama Administration's proposal to include those whose names appear on the government's various no-fly and terrorist watch lists in the NICS system as prohibited purchasers. Even CBS's *60 Minutes*, no friend of conservatives, broadcast a segment on October 8, 2006, on the inaccuracy of these lists. (You can see the broadcast here: http://www.cbsnews.com/news/unlikely-terrorists-on-no-fly-list/.) Many real and suspected terrorists who should be on these lists are not, while people who have never done anything wrong are included. Bureaucrats from various agencies are empowered, without any real supervision, to add names to the list, and the people they add, along with anyone else with a similar name, are then scrutinized as a potential threat whenever they try to board a plane. Political staffers have been persistently harassed at airports and find themselves on the no-fly list soon after certain legislation is proposed—and yet politicians who believe in the law will not come forward for fear of even more harassment and partisanship.

Even in the best of cases, there is no due process before putting someone on these lists and, therefore, no process for getting off a list. A few years ago, the late Democratic Senator from Massachusetts Ted Kennedy was stopped at Washington, D.C.'s Reagan Airport, because his name was on a government no-fly list as a suspected terrorist. Democratic Congressman John Lewis of Georgia, a civil rights hero to many, was on the list at one time. And Jim Gilmore—former Governor of Virginia, Chairman of the Republican National Committee, U.S. Army Counterintelligence Agent, and Chair of the Congressional Advisory Panel to Assess Domestic Capabilities for Terrorism Involving Weapons of Mass Destruction (nicknamed the "Gilmore Commission")—was detained for hours flying back to Washington, D.C., for an NRA Board meeting. These problems were resolved, but not without a lot of hassle. Had Kennedy, Lewis, and Gilmore been average citizens, rather than elected members of Congress or well-known government appointees, they would have had a far more difficult time straightening out the problem.

No-Fly Lists

Like the demand for universal background checks, proposing that those on the government no-fly list be listed in the NICS system as prohibited purchasers sounds perfectly reasonable on the surface. But such proposals, under review, can be seen as nothing more than symbolic; adding bad data to good will not solve a real problem.

President Obama has said, "People can't get on planes, but those same people, who we don't allow to fly, could go into a store right now in the United States and buy a firearm, and there's nothing we can do to stop them. That's a law that needs to be changed." When Mr. Obama started talking about this a few years ago, reports were that there were fewer than 50 American citizens on the list, and none of those 50 people have ever reportedly tried to buy a firearm or been accused of being or aiding terrorists in any way. On June 20, 2016, U.S. Senator from California Diane Feinstein was quoted on the floor of the Senate that the Terrorist Watch List contains about 1 million names, while the no-fly list has 81,000 names, with fewer than 1,000 Americans. (You can read more here: https://www.congress.gov/crec/2016/06/20/CREC-2016-06-20.pdf Page S4341).

No one outside the government really knows how many individuals are on these lists or how they got there; the numbers change depending on who is reporting. (You can read more here: http://www.washingtontimes.com/news/2016/jun/20/fbi-no-fly-list-revealed-81k-names-fewer-1k-us/.)

According to the December 2015 Senate Judiciary Committee testimony of Alan Bersin, Assistant Secretary for International Affairs at the Department of Homeland Security, about one-tenth of one percent of those on the U.S. no-fly list are U.S. citizens. (Keep in mind that there are only a few circumstances under which non-citizens can buy a gun legally and that the rules for doing so are much stricter than they are for our citizens.)

Bersin was asked if it made sense to use the no-fly lists to deny people the right to buy a gun. He replied that using the list in this way was "like comparing apples and oranges." It seemed obvious from the questioning that Mr. Bersin, who is in charge of the list, had never been asked his opinion by higher-ups in the Administration and did not know the President wanted to use that list to deny firearms to those on it. When news of the Assistant Secretary's testimony broke, a Department of Homeland Security spokesman clarified what Mr. Bersin said to reassure everyone, no doubt including his superiors, that Bersin does indeed support the Administration's position.

Like many proposals emanating from gun-control advocates, using the no-fly lists for NICS checks would do nothing to put an end to terrorism or gun crime. People are put on these lists, *without due process,* by unaccountable bureaucrats. For many, their existence on the lists glosses over the due process problem: they have been denied a fundamental and constitutional right without having been convicted of a crime. (You can read more here: http://time.com/4146025/guns-no-fly-list-constitution/.) Private citizens caught in this trap can attest that honest, law-abiding citizens have an awful time getting off it and even getting the government to admit that they are on it in the first place, let alone why they were put there.

Now consider that a review of the details behind the Boston Marathon and Orlando nightclub attacks has proven that the FBI is currently wallowing in so much information, it now has significant problems investigating potential criminals and terrorists even when it receives specific and credible warnings.

The issue of the no-fly and terrorist watch lists was revived after the Orlando shootings, because the shooter had been put on the terrorist watch list by the FBI and later removed. As a practical matter, because of that removal, he was never flagged when he underwent a NICS background check for the guns he bought and then used to kill 49 people. But anti-gun activists and the media began raising the issue again, falsely charging that a suspected terrorist can just walk into a gun store and buy firearms to murder people with impunity. Mrs. Clinton put it this way: "If the FBI is watching you for suspected terrorist links, you shouldn't be able to buy a gun with no questions asked. You shouldn't be able to exploit loopholes and evade criminal background checks by buying on-line or at a gun show. Yes, if you are too dangerous to get on a plane, you are too dangerous to buy a gun in America."

Within days of the Orlando massacre, liberals and the media initiated what amounted to a massive effort to change the subject from terrorism to guns, arguing that what had happened in the nightclub illustrated why the nation needs additional restrictions on the purchase of firearms. They began arguing almost immediately that new restrictions are needed, not because of crime or to save innocents, but because of "national security."

Jeh Johnson, head of the Department of Homeland Security, was on television within days of the Orlando tragedy, suggesting that because of what happened in there, gun control must be "part and parcel" of any plan to protect the U.S. homeland from ISIS-directed or -inspired terrorists. The argument, echoed by the media and the gun-control community, seemed to be that since the terrorist responsible for the killing of 49 innocents bought his gun legally, the problem had more to do with the laws that allowed him to do so than his motivation, his visits to Saudi Arabia, his ties to known terrorists, or his stated desire to die a "martyr."

Once again, the cry went up for universal background checks, elimination of the so-called "gun show loophole," and a prohibition on firearms purchases by anyone on the government's no-fly and terrorist watch lists—and these cries ignored the reality of what had transpired in the months prior to Omar Mateen's murderous attack that allowed a man who had bragged that he wanted to do what he did on June 12, 2016, was a close friend of known terrorists, and had been both interrogated by the FBI and put on the federal terrorist watch list *to be cleared as no threat to anyone.*

As we have seen, Congress had so far rejected the idea of making inclusion on these lists a sufficient reason to deny anyone their Second Amendment rights—and for very good reasons. An official of the National Counterterrorism Center recently said that government agencies are "leaning very far forward" in adding more names, so the list is expected to grow substantially in future months. (You can read more here: http://www.mcclatchydc.com/news/politics-government/congress/article84037982.html.) Names have been and are added by various agencies without any proof or, in most cases, any reasonable suspicion, that those being added are actual terrorists or even contemplating any sorts of terrorist acts. Because of this, Congress has rejected adding those on a government watch list to the NICS prohibited persons database; anyone added to such a list by a nameless bureaucrat and for unspecified reasons would amount to setting a precedent that the government could restrict one's Second Amendment rights based on secret evidence and without any judicial review. That, of course, would be one very dangerous precedent.

Mr. Mateen made the watch list when the FBI began an extensive background check on him after complaints they received from several witnesses who had heard him make threats against non-Muslims, and because it was believed he might have ties to a radical imam and a suicide bomber. They eventually cleared Mr. Mateen and took him off the terrorist watch list for reasons unclear to just about everyone who has looked into his background since the attack.

The cynical and absurd attempt to blame the NRA and Republicans for the violence in Orlando was led by the *New York Times*. Others quickly followed, and the refusal of Congress, up to that point, to automatically strip anyone placed on the watch lists of their Second Amendment rights without due process was characterized as the crux of the problem. Democrats went on the attack, demanding the law be changed.

A cursory look at the way the watch lists are compiled and used reveals that anyone on any of these lists who tries to purchase a firearm is already scrutinized by the FBI as they undergo the required NICS background check required of all who purchase guns from licensed gun dealers. While such checks usually produce an immediate decision for the dealer on whether to proceed with the sale, the FBI does have extra time to make a decision as to whether a person whose name appears on one of these lists should be able to buy a gun.

When Mr. Mateen walked into a Florida gun shop to purchase a gun, he underwent a NICS check. The dealer called in his identifying information, and the FBI ran that information, by computer, against various databases, including the government watch lists. If the name of a prospective purchaser appears on the list, the FBI takes extra time to determine whether they should allow the sale to proceed. In most such cases, the sale is approved, with the reviewing agents having found no legitimate reason to stop it. Sometimes the FBI takes action to stop the sale, if reason to do so is found, but the agency can also let a sale go through so that they can follow a suspect without alerting the buyer to the fact that the purchaser is actually on the list. Mr. Mateen was not on the list at the time he underwent his NICS check. But there can be little doubt that the FBI botched its investigation of him after being alerted by several people who had encountered him that he might represent a threat. The agency investigated him three times between 2013 and 2014, while he was employed as an armed security personnel at G4S, a firm that, among other things, provides security for nuclear power plants across the country. The Boston Marathon terrorists had also been reported (that time by the Russians), yet dismissed by the FBI and allowed to roam free.

Many of those who knew Mr. Mateen said after the attack that he had often seemed violent and had more than once bragged that he might commit a massacre. This information had to have come to the attention of the FBI during what seems to have been a lengthy investigation but apparently set off no alarms. The agency's final alert in the Mateen case came, as it has in others, not from law enforcement, but from a gun shop or gun range operator who became suspicious.

Robbie Abell, owner of a Florida gun shop, called the FBI five weeks before the attack on the Orlando nightclub after Mateen had come to his shop and raised questions in the gun shop owner's mind, after having been asked a series of bizarre questions by Mateen about the weapons he sought and his desire to purchase body armor not ordinarily available on the civilian market. Abell not only alerted the FBI, he refused to sell Mateen the items he sought. Mr. Mateen eventually purchased his guns elsewhere, after passing a NICS check.

The call for a ban on sales to those on these government lists, like the President's renewed call for another "assault weapons" ban and universal background checks, represents another attempt to exploit a tragedy, rather than deal with its causes and take realistic measures to prevent future tragedy. In the case of the Orlando shootings, motive was all-important. Mr. Mateen was neither a traditional criminal nor a mentally unbalanced shooter. He was a quasi-military combatant at war with America, a fact the President downplayed from the beginning. That Attorney General Loretta Lynch ordered Mr. Mateen's references to Jihad and ISIS deleted from the transcript of his calls from the nightclub during the shooting before releasing those transcripts says all one needs to know.

Innocent Until Proven Guilty?

Connecticut Democrat Chris Murphy led the 15-hour Senate filibuster in June 2016, following the Orlando nightclub massacre, in an effort to get the Senate leadership to allow a floor vote on measures to allow or require those on the government's "no-fly" and "terrorist watch" lists be denied the right to buy firearms and close the so-called "gun show loophole." It was another stark example of the willingness of anti-gun politicians to use the most recent tragedy to promote their favorite anti-gun measures, regardless whether having such measures in place would have prevented the episode.

Finally, Jonathan Karl of ABC News asked the Senator why he and others were promoting measures that would not have prevented what happened in Orlando. "Why," Karl asked Murphy, "are we focusing on things that have nothing to do with the massacres that we are responding to?"

The Senator's response to this simple, logical question was instructive. "We can't get into that trap," he said, "I think if this proposal had been into effect, it may have stopped this shooting, but we can't get into this trap in which we are forced to defend our proposals simply because it didn't stop the last tragedy. We should be making our gun laws less full of Swiss cheese holes so that future killings don't happen."

Karl caught the fact that what Murphy was saying was nonsensical. He pointed out that denying gun sales to those on one of the government lists would not have done much, since the FBI had taken the shooter off the lists before he bought his guns. Murphy simply insisted that his proposals, had they been in effect, might have stopped the shooter.

Usually, public policy proposals are examined before being adopted, in order to determine whether they will accomplish what their supporters say they will, and also to analyze them to provide costs and a spending accountability by the Congressional Budget Office. Senator Murphy said asking for this justification of restrictive gun proposals is a "trap," that applying such a test to proposals to restrict the availability of firearms would somehow be unfair. In other words, we should support gun regulations not because they will do any good, but because Senator Murphy knows better than we do what is good for us.

Just as interesting is the cavalier way in which supporters of the Senate proposals regarding the watch lists treat the constitutional right of due process most of them would accord to most alleged criminals. The anti-gunners would allow the government, without any showing of probable cause, to put one on such a list and then require that person be denied the right to buy or possess firearms. Their idea of due process is that a person denied such rights could, after the fact, ask a court to review the government's denial of those rights but would have to do so without being allowed to know why the government acted as it did in the first place.

The pro-Second Amendment, pro-constitutional rights Senators who opposed these watch list proposals argued that, if constitutional rights are to be denied, there should be an up-front requirement that the government first go to a judge to show justifications for such a denial. In other words, the two sides were arguing not about whether a terrorist should be denied a gun, but whether an accused person should be considered innocent until proven guilty or guilty before being required to prove their innocence.

California Senator Diane Feinstein, one of the most rabid anti-Second Amendment members of the Senate, put her view succinctly and threateningly, when in a *PBS News Hour* interview the day after the Orlando shootings reporter Judy Woodruff stated, "The argument that many of your Republican colleagues have made about this is that there is still the potential that people who are innocent are on a watch list, and they would be prevented from buying a gun . . . ." "Well," the California Senator answered, "then you can petition and prove that you are innocent and get off the watch list." Senator Feinstein has served for 24 years and is well aware that the U.S. Constitution says one is innocent until proven guilty, just as she is aware that many of the problems with the watch lists are the results of people with the same or similar names. She knows that liberties would be taken away under her proposal while an unknown and undetermined process ensued. So much for due process.

A "compromise" amendment promoted by Maine Republican Susan Collins after the more drastic measures the Democrats wanted were defeated won enough support on Thursday, June 23, 2016, to go forward, but even its supporters were reluctant to suggest that it would move forward once the body reconvened after the July 4 holiday break. Meanwhile, gun-control advocates in the House of Representatives were staging a "sit-in" to demand (unsuccessfully) that the House Speaker schedule a debate and vote on their favorite anti-gun bills.

The sit-in allowed Democrats to "change the subject" by diverting attention away from the holes in the Administration's tactics in dealing with domestic jihadists and gave heart to anti-Second Amendment activists in and out of Congress. Senate Democratic Leader Harry Reid of Nevada characterized Senator Collins's temporary procedural win as "a defeat for the NRA," while Senator Murphy crowed after the vote, "Between the Senate filibuster, the House sit-in, and this vote, we have helped create a massive uprising of support in favor of laws to make our nation safer from gun violence. And while I know we are far from the finish line, this has been a momentous last eight days for this crusade."

Obama Déjà Vu

The inability of the President to come up with policy improvements to the regulatory or legal structure surrounding gun ownership is a testament to his unstated view that he does not care about the safe and effective use of guns; his gun-control proposals are not about crime or terrorism, but about guns and the "gun culture." Mr. Obama issued a spate of executive orders on guns in 2013 and continued to use the same, tired language to persuade the public that further restricting firearms would reduce crime and violence when he announced additional executive orders three years later.

Congress refused to enact the Administration's "common sense" restrictions on gun ownership after the Sandy Hook shootings because of one simple question that Senators kept asking: if these restrictions had been in place at the time, would they have prevented the tragedy that took place when Adam Lanza walked into that school in Newtown? Witness after witness admitted that none of the proposals would have prevented the tragedy, but gun-control advocates kept insisting the restrictions should be adopted, because "we have to do something."

Ironically, it was not President Obama or Congress or Michael Bloomberg's groups that decided realistic steps had to be taken to help prevent future tragedies. The NRA, long before background checks were routinely required of retail purchasers, had been urging that those adjudicated as mentally dangerous be included in the NICS system or otherwise flagged so that they would be denied access to firearms. Indeed, when the government dragged its feet on NICS, the NRA pushed to get background checks up and running, and going back further, NRA's official publication had urged action after University of Texas Tower shootings—that was in 1966.

The Canada Problem

Scarcity has not stopped the Obama scare tactics from gathering support either here or abroad. Anti-gun Justin Trudeau followed the pro-gun Canadian Prime Minister Stephen Harper in 2015. Trudeau, like Mexico, is assisting U.S. anti-gun policy-makers build a case for restrictions, even though Canada has an extremely low homicide rate and, under the previous government regime, it had pointedly refused to sign the U.N.'s Arms Trade Treaty because it might interfere with the right of individual Canadians to own and use firearms.

The *Washington Post* reported, on February 16, 2016:

> *[Canadian] Prime Minister Justin Trudeau has promised new regulations and a string of measures to counter gun smuggling, which is regarded in the United States as a dangerous problem underscoring much looser firearm laws.*
>
> *The move comes as police have discovered an increased number of high-powered handguns, semiautomatic, and automatic weapons in Canadian cities.*

What actually happened in Canada is easy to understand. A flood of automatic weapons from the U.S. simply is not possible, since the U.S. essentially outlawed them decades ago; the Canadian "national homicide epidemic" is not about statistics, because the homicide rates in Canada have remained low. The change is a shift in government and ideology.

Interestingly, Canada's new Prime Minister Trudeau decided to delay signing the U.N. Arms Trade Treaty until his country could complete a multi-billion-dollar arms sale to Saudi Arabia, a deal that might have proved problematic under the terms of the ATT due to Saudi Arabia's human rights record and treatment of women. Like most anti-gun politicians, Trudeau positioned himself as a principled believer in international gun control—as long as it meant controlling the activities of governments and citizenries other than his own.

New York

When it comes to gun control, New York's Governor Andrew Cuomo of New York can be seen as more successful than President Obama: he forced a package of truly strict restrictions through the New York legislature, literally in the dark of night, shortly after President Obama called for increased firearms restrictions after Sandy Hook. The next day, pro-Second Amendment men and women in New York announced that they wanted to protest at the state capital. The leaders of the protest called then-NRA President Keene to speak.

It was about 30 degrees and raining in Albany, but between 10,000 and 12,000 protestors had shown up. A veteran Albany reporter claimed he had never seen such a large crowd so quickly assembled in his 30 years of covering New York politics. Mr. Keene told NRA Executive Vice President LaPierre the next morning that he hoped the NRA was prepared for a monster turnout for the NRA Annual Meetings that spring in Houston, Texas.

And it was. The rallies continued, and more than 70,000 Americans attended the Annual Meetings that spring, breaking all attendance records. Gun owners were sending a signal to everyone they could reach that they were never going away, they were not going to roll over and play dead, and their numbers were growing as they brought children and neighbors to join their ranks.

America's gun owners knew they were the real target, just as they do now, and today they are banding together as never before to protect their rights. In the wake of the Sandy Hook shootings, membership in the NRA jumped within months from four million to five million. Gun sales have broken all records, and ammunition cannot be manufactured fast enough. Hundreds of thousands of gun owners attended rallies in support of their Second Amendment rights from one end of the country to the other.

None of this means the campaign to harass and shame gun owners will end anytime soon, but Mr. Holder and his friends are discovering, to their chagrin, that guns are not cigarettes.

[1] *Law, History, and Policy. 53 Harvard Journal on Legislation 303 (2015). http://harvardjol.com/wp-content/uploads/2016/02/HLL105 _crop.pdf.*

CHAPTER 4

A Lesson From Colorado

T he 2013 post-Sandy Hook effort to enact what President Obama liked to call "common sense" gun-control measures was three-pronged. First, everyone knew that to succeed politically, the gun-control movement would have to marginalize the NRA. Second, the anti-gun advocates wanted to divide gun owners in general from those the Administration viewed as "hard-liners," those who seemed to object to *every* gun restriction. Finally, the effort in Congress was to be paired with similar efforts at the state level, with gun-control advocates in the various state legislatures introducing state versions of the restrictions favored at the federal level.

In what are, essentially, one-party states like New York, California, and Maryland, where those who would further restrict firearms rights hold majorities in both houses of their state legislature and typically the governorship, this last effort was generally successful. In addition to these "usual suspects," the Administration needed a victory or two in states that were not historically seen as favoring such measures.

It turned to Colorado, a western state with a liberal Democratic governor and Democratic majorities in both houses of its legislature, as its next target. Vice President Biden got on the phone early with Democratic Governor John Hickenlooper, to persuade him to lead the effort to make his state the Western political poster child for the "common sense" firearms restrictions the Obama Administration was promoting.

A concerted effort by liberals willing to invest millions of dollars to seize control of the Colorado legislature had paid real dividends in 2012. By the time the Vice President began calling the Governor, both Houses were in Democratic hands and could be expected to rubber-stamp anything President Obama and Governor Hickenlooper requested—and this was in a state that, historically, had been friendly to firearms rights. The legislature delivered, steamrolling opposition from the state's gun owners and many state law enforcement officials who opposed the initiatives.

Colorado legislators passed and Governor Hickenlooper signed three bills on March 20, 2013. One banned "high-capacity magazines," defined as magazines that would hold in excess of 15 rounds. Others established a state-run universal background check system and authorized the state to impose the costs of running it on firearms buyers.

Working to Give the People What They Want
By Tom Mason

"Right to carry" or "shall issue" bills were passing in various states, in 1983, while I served as chairman of Oregon's House Judiciary Committee, which has jurisdiction over firearms bills. A majority on the committee agreed that a concealed carry law that required county sheriffs to issue concealed carry permits to law-abiding citizens was a good idea.

The Speaker of the Oregon House at the time, Vera Katz, was vehemently anti-gun. An attractive Jewish refugee from Nazi Germany (via New York), she had clawed up the greasy pole of Oregon politics by representing the urban Portland district next to the one I represented and working with rural legislators when she could find common ground.

As Democratic legislators, Speaker Katz and I got along, so when she wanted criminal background checks for permit applicants, we held hearings. Even supporters had no idea how successful it would be. At one hearing, I asked the Superintendent of the State Police how many permits he thought would be issued, and his answer was about 3,000. The bill received the NRA blessing, passed the House and Senate, and was signed by the Republican Governor Vic Atiyeh, an NRA member. If it is a bill the people want, people work together.

The media focused on the success of the anti-gun battle in Colorado, and the state was seen as a harbinger of similar victories in other states and proof of the Obama Administration's position that the public supported the new restrictions NRA and other gun rights groups wanted to block. But what seemed at first to be a major victory for the restrictionists soon turned into a major defeat that doomed gun-control measures in other states. The passage of the Hickenlooper-backed measures sparked a grass roots backlash that resulted in the recall of several leading Colorado legislators who had backed the proposals. The message to other states was clear: the cost of falling in line with the Obama and Bloomberg proposals could prove politically disastrous.

As the *New York Times* reported on September 11, 2013, the recall of two Colorado State Senators who had backed the newly enacted state firearms restrictions was "seen as a test of whether swing-state voters would accept gun restrictions after mass shootings at a Colorado movie theater and a Connecticut elementary school."[1] Clearly, the voters would not.

The grassroots recall effort attracted both national support and money. Gun-control advocates like former New York Mayor Bloomberg, other wealthy anti-firearms activists, and the Democratic Party poured money into the state and, eventually, saw the Senators being recalled outspend their pro-gun opponents by a margin of six to one. And still they lost. This did not stop National Democratic Party Chair Debbie Wasserman Schultz from claiming, once the votes were counted, that the Senators were recalled because the NRA financed the recall effort. She also charged that gun-control forces were defeated because of "voter suppression," an allegation dismissed by the *Denver Post,* which pointed out that the Senators lost simply because more voters wanted them to be recalled than wanted them to retain their offices.[2]

It was the first successful recall vote in Colorado history, and, as NRA President Keene observed when news of the recall spread, "You could almost hear doors being closed on gun-control advocates in state capitols all around the country."

The recalls marked a turning point. Legislative wins for gun control in the states where such measures had always been popular failed to be duplicated. In fact, state after state passed gun-*friendly* legislation in a largely successful effort to demonstrate that the gun-controllers were not going to get their way.

As the Senate vote of the Obama Administration's "reforms" approached, gun shops and gun shows were experiencing record-breaking business, ammunition was in short supply, and the collapse of the Harrisburg, Pennsylvania, Outdoor Show proved that it was going to be impossible to separate gun owners from the outdoor community. NRA membership was skyrocketing, and President Obama was being described as "the best gun salesman ever."

The Colorado reaction to the Hickenlooper attempt to get his state to buy into the Administration's effort and the rush of gun owners to join the NRA rode along with the U.S. Senate defeat of the Manchin-Toomey universal background check amendment to be seen as the final nails in the coffin of the President's 2013 efforts to restrict gun rights. This reality can be seen reflected in state after state as the debate continues.

In December of 2013, a year after the Sandy Hook shootings, the *New York Times* reported that, during the year, almost every state legislature had considered legislation affecting gun rights. Surprisingly, at least to the paper's reporter, however, most states that year removed, rather than imposed, restrictions on the Second Amendment rights of their citizens. As the paper reported, "Nearly two-thirds of the new laws ease restrictions and expand the rights of gun owners."[3]

Take My Advice

By David Keene

I visited Democratic Governor John Hickenlooper and Colorado's Republican and Democratic legislative leaders before the legislature passed its gun-control package of bills in March 2013. The visits were widely covered by state and national reporters, and when I sat down with Governor Hickenlooper, I told him that I had been cornered on my way in by reporters asking why I was meeting with him. Mr. Hickenlooper asked, "What did you tell them?" "I told them I was meeting with you because you're not Andrew Cuomo [Governor of New York] and I'm here to urge you not to act like him."

The Governor did not take my advice. The next time I saw Mr. Hickenlooper was before the recall vote, at a National Governors' Conference meeting in Milwaukee, where we shared a beer. He raised his glass and said, "We've both had a tough spring, but it looks like we've both survived it." I raised mine in response and said, "So far, Governor, so far." Mr. Hickenlooper did survive and was reelected, but one wonders if he still believes volunteering to impose the national gun-controller's agenda on the people of Colorado was such a great idea.

[1] http://www.nytimes.com/2013/09/11/us/colorado-lawmaker-concedes-defeat-in-recall-over-gun-law.html?_r=0

[2] http://www.denverpost.com/2013/09/13/voter-suppression-in-angela-giron-recall-hardly/

[3] http://www.nytimes.com/interactive/2013/12/10/us/state-gun-laws-enacted-in-the-year-since-newtown.html

PART II

The Arms Trade Treaty: Interference From Abroad

CHAPTER 5

Gun Control Comes to the U.N.—The End of the Cold War, Tragedies, and a Murder

G un control came to the United Nations like the plot of a spy thriller. A bizarre mix of Cold War history, interest group politics going global, and murder, the characters include a con man posing as a count, academics, ambitious politicians, gun-control and gun-rights activists, and world leaders. History's tragic events lit the fuse.

Since the days of Woodrow Wilson and the failed League of Nations, international idealists have hoped that disarmament and world peace might one day be achieved through an international organization that would supersede, or at least ameliorate, the competition among nation states. The U.N., established by the victors following the Second World War, is the vessel into which these hopes have been placed.

U.N. involvement in the campaign to control or abolish the private ownership of firearms has come about as a result of what might best be termed "mission creep," combined with the increasing power of what are known as "non-governmental organizations" (NGOs) within the U.N. The U.N. has, from its inception, been active in working to eliminate or reduce the threat of nuclear war. For decades it focused on the international tensions generated by the Cold War.

The founders of the U.N. placed great hope in what might be accomplished by bringing nations together to iron out their differences. Post-World War II marked the beginning of the Cold War between the United States and her allies, and the Soviet Union and an empire composed of nations she had overrun or captured before, during, and following WWII. Crisis after crisis threatened peace, and with the development and spread of nuclear weapons, the stakes became higher and higher, seemingly with the world on the very knife-edge of destruction. During these years, the U.N. suffered both successes and failures, but was seen my many as the most effective vehicle through which to avoid a global confrontation.

This was particularly true in the United States, where, during the decades of the 1950s and '60s, high school classes were held to "teach" children that their very survival might well depend on their faith in the U.N. These classes made quite an impression at a time when those same children were asked to hide under their desks during air raid drills and warned continually of the consequences of a nuclear confrontation with the Communist world.

The effort to maintain peace, in combination with humanitarian operations, led, over time, to the growth of a huge U.N. bureaucracy that began looking to expand its mission in the days following the collapse of the Soviet Empire. The wars and tensions that now dominate the post-Cold War world may not threaten nuclear holocaust, but they have wreaked havoc within and among the nations involved. These wars have been and continue to be fought not with nuclear and heavy weapons, but with light weapons.

Some years ago, the U.N. began to focus on what might be done to limit the spread of such weapons. In its development, that effort was, as we shall see, refocused to include not just traditionally defined light weapons such as tanks, artillery pieces, and the like, but now also what is defined as small arms, which include pistols, handguns, and rifles, *as well as the right to individual self-defense and the availability of such arms to non-state actors or individuals.*

The role of liberal, anti-gun NGOs in persuading the U.N. to go after private arms cannot be underestimated. Something like 50 to 80 percent of privately owned firearms are owned by the citizens of the United States; the U.S. is also one of the few nations remaining in today's world that recognizes the right to individual self-defense.

There have always been those who believed that disarmament is the key to international peace, and they have tended to blame the existence of the weapons of war, rather than differences between nations or the aggressiveness of tyrants and their penchant for war. Thus, even as Stalin's forces after World War II were threatening a new war and adding nation after nation to the Soviet Empire, many in the West talked about disarmament, even unilateral disarmament, as the only rational policy for those who wanted peace.

This inclination to believe that the elimination of the weapons of war would lead to world peace made those people holding that belief easy converts for those who argued that, if firearms in private hands could next be banned, violent crime would, perforce, vanish.

Gun Crimes and International Reverberations

Looking back, there are two particular points in history that began the international movement toward gun-control.

The first non-Italian pope in 450 years, John Paul II, who had been a cardinal in Poland, united the Polish people in a nine-day trip that culminated, years later, in a huge success in liberation from the Soviet Union. That liberation occurred in June 1989. The Berlin Wall fell in November that year. Then, on December 6, 1989, Marc Lépine massacred 14 women at the École Polytechnique in Montreal, Canada. Lépine hated women and killed as an act of pure misogyny.

The effects of that atrocity are still felt today at the U.N. and in Canada. The leftist government in Canada became an early proponent of gun control. Allan Rock, Canada's ambassador to the U.N. from 2004-2006, called for Canadian and international gun control. Canadian feminists such as Wendy Cuiker have been, and still are, international anti-gun movement leaders.

On October 17, 1992, a New Orleans homeowner killed Yoshihiro Hattori, a Japanese exchange student whom the homeowner mistook for a burglar. Hattori had gotten an address wrong while looking for a Halloween party and tried to get into the defendant's garage. When the homeowner was not convicted in the shooting death of Hattori, the Japanese public reacted with outrage, sending 1.65 million signatures on a petition urging stricter gun-control measures to U.S. Ambassador to Japan Walter Mondale. Hattori's parents joined the cry for passage in the U.S. of the Brady gun-control bill named for President Reagan's press secretary, James Brady, who had been shot in the head during a 1981 assassination attempt on Mr. Reagan.

Spurred on in part by these incidents, the idea of a U.N. effort on gun control called "micro-disarmament" emerged, initially proposed by then-U.N. Secretary General Boutros-Ghali. He was followed by a high official at the U.N. Office for Disarmament Affairs, Swadesh Rana, who adopted international gun control as her pet cause. She lobbied other U.N. and government officials and wrote articles pushing U.N. involvement in international gun control and became a key advocate. A high-caste Indian, Rana was a typical imperious U.N. official who loathes America. She particularly despises the National Rifle Association and voiced her position on occasions small and large, formal and informal. She also allied with Japanese officials, as Japan began financing early gun-control efforts through studies and meetings.

There is no better way to establish a U.N. policy than to pay for it as agencies and offices compete for campaigns and funding. Although disarmament advocates in New York were the first to bring up gun control and micro-disarmament, it did not take long for their counterparts charged with reducing crime to hop on board.

The U.N. Office on Drugs and Crime, since 1955, has held a Congress on Crime Prevention and Criminal Justice once every five years at various locations around the world. During the 1995 Congress in Cairo, Japan introduced the radically anti-gun Resolution 9. (You can read about the resolution here: http://www.un.org/documents/ga/res/50/a50r145.htm.) In attendance during this Congress was one of this book's authors, Thomas Mason, on hand to deliver a report on international environmental crime and, to everyone's chagrin, make a statement in favor of gun rights.

Mr. Mason is the American Executive Secretary for the World Forum on Shooting Activities, an official United Nations non-governmental organization comprised of organizations such as the British Shooting Sports Council, the National Rifle Association, Sporting Shooters Associations of Australia, and the South African Gun Owners Association.

Although the NRA had been monitoring international gun-control advocacy for some years before the 1995 Congress, the organization had never presented at a U.N. meeting. Nor had there been until then within the NRA a sense there was any need to be overly concerned about an international threat to the Second Amendment rights of the American citizenry; the NRA and its members had enough to worry about with the U.S. Congress.

Turning Points
By Tom Mason

Speaking out in favor of gun rights in Cairo was a major turning point in my life. I had been a legislator working on crime issues and teaching at Portland State University. A fellow professor was vehemently anti-gun and persuaded the department's dean to fire me when I returned. My ensuing lawsuit uncovered a secret memo from the faculty member to the dean saying the school could not be associated with the NRA. We settled out of court with compensation.

Led by Jim Hayes, an anti-gun Canadian diplomat, and financed by Japan, the anti-gun forces from the 1995 Cairo Congress set about the work of attaching a firearms "protocol," or companion treaty, to the Convention Against Transnational Organized Crime that the U.N. in Vienna was developing. Not to be outdone, the U.N. Office for Disarmament Affairs in New York started its own series of studies financed by Japan and chaired by Japan's Ambassador Mitsoro Donawaki. The long-term goal: control all small arms.

Underestimating

By Tom Mason

During one of the innumerable meetings in Vienna, Japan's Mission to the U.N. asked me to come discuss the firearms protocol. They were anxious to evaluate the strange phenomenon of a NRA representative at the U.N. A Japanese official named Inomata lectured me on why U.N. gun control would be successful.

"We will outlast you on this issue; you Americans have no patience. We'll take 10 or 20 years. We think there is strong domestic support for gun control in your country." Inomata, like too many American politicians, seriously underestimated grassroots support for the NRA and the Second Amendment in this country.

There are other tragic events that many have used in recent years to aid the anti-gun efforts. In March 1996, Thomas Howard killed 16 children at a grade school in Dunblane, England. The United Kingdom promptly took the opportunity to ban all handguns.

The ease with which Great Britain passed its gun ban is partially attributable to the structure of the parliamentary systems that exists in Great Britain, in many other European countries, and in Australia. It is far easier in these countries for the party in power to support and effect changes in the law than it is in the United States, where its unique constitutional system requires agreement and compromise between the executive and legislative branches of the government.

A bigger difference, however, and one that is perhaps more largely responsible for the easy success of the U.K. ban, lies in the history of the two nations over the last several centuries. Great Britain, as do most European nations, restricts participation in the shooting sports, and hunting in particular, to the landed gentry and to the crown. Wild game in Great Britain is the property of the crown, and commoners who hunted it were subjected to severe criminal penalties. Add to that the fact that most British citizens were never able to hunt or own firearms, and, as a result, there was no significant voter block to demand the retention of "rights" that were, in practice, available only to the few.

This is in stark contrast to the situation in the United States, which developed and was settled by men and women familiar with and dependent on firearms. Firearms ownership and the shooting sports were, essentially, democratized as the U.S. developed; the right to keep and bear arms was not just included in the Bill of Rights, it was equally almost a part of the DNA of the new nation.

Australia soon followed the U.K.'s example. In April 1996, Martin Bryant killed 21 people in Port Arthur, Tasmania, an island state to the south of the mainland. Prime Minister John Howard and the Australian government quickly instituted a compulsory buyback of semiautomatic and other firearms, including pump-action shotguns. Ads appeared in Australian papers saying, "Duck Hunters Turn in Your Pump-Action Shotguns." (No one is sure why these shotguns were singled out. There was an apocryphal story that one of Howard's staff saw *Terminator 2* and mistook Arnold's shotgun, used in the motorcycle chase scene, for a pump gun. Thinking they were particularly deadly, he included them in the new law. Schwarzenegger's gun was actually an old lever action Winchester. In 2016, when an Australian importer brought in lever action shotguns, there was tremendous controversy over whether they should be banned.) But the Australian buyback campaign was not a voluntary operation, such as those that have taken place in several U.S. cities in recent decades, wherein gun owners are offered money by the city or state to turn in their guns. Australia's buyback program was mandatory and accompanied by the threat of prison for those who would not participate.

Through movies like *Quigley Down Under,* the 1990 *Australian* western starring Tom Selleck, and the *Crocodile Dundee* movies, Americans know that the Wild West has a lot in common with the Australian Outback, so this mandatory buyback struck fear in gun owners worldwide. Pictures of thousands of treasured family heirlooms and hunting guns being crushed and shredded sent a horrible message to gun owners—and thrilled anti-gun forces like the Joyce Foundation. Candidate Hillary Clinton has endorsed an Australian–style buyback, and President Obama cites England and Australia as places with "common sense" gun regulations.

The Land Mine Treaty as a Model for Gun Control

In 1997, the Land Mine Treaty banned the use of land mines in warfare. The first disarmament treaty outside of U.N. structure, it was the product of a conference in Ottawa, Canada, held by interested nations and NGOs. U.N. officialdom and the major nations were aghast that an actual treaty could be initiated and put into place without their consent and outside the formal U.N. structure, challenging the body's international status quo. The insult was made worse when Jody Williams and the International Campaign to Ban Land Mines were awarded a Nobel Peace Prize for the accomplishment.

After the Land Mine Treaty Montreal Conference, there was a nearly unwritten agreement among major nations and the U.N. that they would not let such a process get out of hand again. Yet the Land Mine Treaty soon became the model for international anti-gun NGOs and activists who dreamed of winning their own Nobel Prizes for a gun-control treaty. The difference is that unlike private firearms ownership, no one had ever argued in favor of civilian-owned land mines—and such a worldwide consensus on gun control would mean some *four or five hundred million* civilian gun owners would be adversely affected by a small arms treaty that includes civilian ownership.

The Land Mine Treaty was also the product of globalization. The Internet and other cheap communication means have converted domestic issues into worldwide issues, sometimes within the time it takes to Tweet. Anti-gun advocates not only know when an incident that can work in their favor happens, they instantaneously use the information. International telephone and conference calls are relatively inexpensive or free via Skype and similar services, so activism is no longer just for the well financed, having now become globally democratized among those groups making up the NGO activist world. This sea change in political intercourse has profoundly changed the world on many fronts: 30 years ago, gun control for U.S. citizens was recognized as domestic threat; today, that threat is on an international scale.

The tragedy at Columbine High School, on April 20, 1999, when Dylan Klebold and Eric Harris killed 12 students and a teacher, offered up school shootings a vehicle for the sickest minds in any society to go out in a blaze of publicity. For the international disarmament community that had set its sights on "small arms and light weapons," Columbine became a well-timed agent for gun-control advocacy at the U.N., and the various studies in Vienna and New York began to bear fruit in 2001.[1]

It was at that time that three protocols were attached to the Convention Against Transnational Organized Crime as it made its way through the U.N. process. Two focused on the smuggling of migrants and trafficking in women and children, but one was the Firearms Protocol adopted in Vienna, in January 2001. (The Washington, D.C.-based international organization of 35 countries in the Americas is called the Organization of American States—oas. org—and it has its own Firearms Protocol that served as the model for the U.N. Protocol.)

The U.N. Firearms Protocol was more a crime-oriented measure than a strictly gun-control measure, although this did not make it any more palatable to gun rights supporters. Too, many of the proposals to the Protocol made by gun-control groups and anti-gun states were so radical that they were resisted even by Bill Clinton's State Department (although, in this instance, the Clinton Administration followed up with an attempt to impose an age cap on hunting on federal lands in the United States). At one meeting in New Delhi, an Indian delegate suggested there needed to be an 18-to-70-year-old age limit on owning guns and then said that he was making a major concession in that, because he disapproved of killing animals. Another delegate argued that civilian firearms should be limited to single-barrel shotguns kept locked up at a gun club. Fortunately, these types of recommendations were not made part of the Protocol, although they keep bubbling up in other U.N. venues.

As radical and even nonsensical as some of the proposals were, the firearms community's most notable success was that "antique" firearms, defined as those manufactured before 1899, and replicas of antiques modified with safety devices would be exempt from any restrictions in the Protocol.

A major travesty occurred in the creation of the Firearms Protocol that we live with today. Article 8, Section 1(a) of the Protocol initially required that every firearm manufactured be identifiable by a unique serial number. This was a requirement that the firearms community and Western firearms manufacturers endorsed as an act of goodwill (and something China resisted until it was modified, as it might have interfered with her ability to sell guns anywhere in the world[2]).

The Chinese Exception
By Tom Mason

At approximately 11:00 p.m. on March 2, 2001, the last night of the conference to draft the Firearms Protocol in Vienna, the Chinese insisted on meeting with the head of the U.S. delegation, Elizabeth Verville, a human rights specialist from the U.S. Embassy in Vienna, about the serial marking requirement. Ms. Verville knew little about guns and decided not to bring the U.S. delegation's attorney, William Kullman from the Justice Department's Bureau of Tobacco Bureau of Alcohol, Firearms Tobacco and Explosives (ATF).

The Chinese proposed a rewrite of the requirement, which Ms. Verville accepted:

> *At the time of manufacture of each firearm, either require unique marking providing the name of the manufacturer, the country or place of manufacture and the serial number, or maintain any alternative unique user-friendly marking with simple geometric symbols in combination with a numeric and/or alphanumeric code, permitting ready identification by all States of the country of manufacture . . . .[3]*

Only one country had geometric symbols, and the language let it "maintain" its system in fine print, loophole language worthy of the best American corporate attorney.

Kullman and I immediately recognized the problem. As the Conference was closing, Verville pushed to include a requirement for all countries to apply a unique serial number, but China refused. This "Chinese exception" remains and has multiplied into other international instruments like the International Tracing Instrument adopted in 2003.

Good intentions are counterproductive, when inexperienced government officials attempt to write laws in any field they do not understand. American and European manufacturers were betrayed. They had cooperated with the U.N. on the sound idea that every firearm should have a serial number, but an exception for

China meant that its small arms would be difficult if not impossible to trace. Even more objectionable was the fact that a major power could impose its particular will on the U.N. process.

The U.N. "Programme of Action"

In the year 2000, U.N. disarmament "studies" on small arms began to pay dividends for gun-control forces. A major conference was recommended, and in 2001, the Programme of Action to Prevent, Combat and Eradicate the Illicit Trade in Small Arms and Light Weapons in All Its Aspects was adopted.

The U.S. and the firearms community participated in preparatory committee meetings, knowing that regulating civilian firearms was the ultimate goal of the process. The Bush Administration vigorously objected to everything about the conference, starting with its title, and, along with the firearms community at large, demanded that the focus be on "illicit." Even so, the conference title's four crucial words—"in All Its Aspects"— expanded the mandate[4] to include civilian firearms, arguing as only international diplomats can that civilian firearms facilitate "illicit trade." The domestic corollary would be that criminals have guns because citizens have guns, and, if we took all the guns away, criminals would not have guns.

Formalities

By Tom Mason

Political bodies have their own culture. English common law has an elected Parliament, public meetings, and open government. The U.N. is more effete European diplomacy mixed with third-world efficiency, a strange and sometimes even charming combination.

When someone speaks at a U.N. gathering, they are identified by their country or organization. No one uses names and everybody is "distinguished." When that person speaks the first time they must congratulate the chair for being selected before then assuring the chair of his country's cooperation.

> *Chair: The meeting will now hear from the distinguished delegate from Malta.*
> *Malta: Thank you, Mr. Chair. Malta first wants to congratulate you on your assumption of the chairmanship of this important meeting and wants to assure you of the full cooperation of our delegation . . . .*
> *Chair: The Chair wishes to thank the distinguished delegate of Malta, and next we will hear from the distinguished delegate of France . . . .*

All this formality takes up immense time but keeps those per diems, expense accounts, in play.

Here are a few more terms to understand when talking about the U.N. and its processes:

- When participants speak, they "make interventions," an odd, but understandable, term.
- In the U.S., when something is "tabled," it is put off indefinitely, but, at the U.N., "table" means you are proposing something be discussed.
- A "convention" is a broad treaty with many nations, while a "bilateral treaty" is between two nations.
- A "non-paper" at the U.N. is what Americans would call a "position paper"—and the author cannot be held to what was said because it is not considered a paper!
- When your side wants to make a concession or trade, you may say, "It's time to show a little leg on paragraph 20 of the treaty draft" to tempt the other side— something I have never heard in politically correct U.S. politics.
- WEOG—Western European and Other Governments—is one of five regional groups that also include Australia, Canada, Israel, and New Zealand. WEOG boils down to the developed, non-Asian world. The U.S. is an "Observer Member," because it does not want to be formally identified with any region.
- The P-5 countries are those credited with winning WWII, those five permanent members of the Security Council: China, France, Great Britain, Russia, and the United States. Security Council Resolutions have the force of law and are, supposedly, obeyed by all members of the U.N., but P-5 members have veto power over any resolution. This arrangement goes back to the founding of the U.N., in 1945, although Germany and Japan do not like being outranked by the likes of France, and countries are always trying to change the makeup of the P-5, because they have a stronger economy or for whatever other reasons they can argue.
- Very much like the American Southern insult, "She's nice," if two delegates are talking and one says that a third is "hardworking," this is damning. It means that the present company is brilliant, whereas the third person has to "work hard" to achieve the same results. This insult appeals to the snobbery of the diplomatic world.
- A trap for those new to the U.N.: If one mentions a person, state, or organization in an "intervention," that person, state, or organization has the "right of reply," which means an automatic right to respond. This is the same sort of rule applied in the 2016 Republican Presidential primary debates, after the field was winnowed down to Bush, Cruz, Kasich, Rubio, and Trump. If you saw the debates, you remember that those personal mentions do not have to be overtly hostile to invoke the right of reply. The right to reply can, in fact, drop the veil of feigned civility— South Korea versus North Korea, India versus Pakistan, or Israel mentioned by an Arab country. During the 2012 Arms Trade Treaty (ATT) negotiations, the U.S. referenced Iran's record on human rights, to which Iran began

with "You've got a damned lot of gall" and a laundry list of U.S. transgressions. While statements at the U.N. are couched in understated diplomatic terms—one does not say "no," one says "it would not be constructive"—clearly not all statements are understated.

Parallels That Set Precedent

The "Programme[5] of Action" became known as the "PoA." This is where Assistant Secretary of State for Disarmament John Bolton drew a red line, stating in a 2001 speech, in unequivocal terms, that the U.S. would not join consensus if, among other things, the PoA was written to impact civilian firearms and the domestic constitutional rights of the American people. The only provisions the U.S. allowed were in a general U.N. effort not focused on civilian firearms and future meetings—but in a place where a phrase turns into 100 meetings over a decade and turns into a treaty, that was enough. Over its 15 years, the PoA has survived and established itself inside multiple U.N. agencies with "meetings of government experts" in the odd years and "Biennial Meetings of States" in even years.

The most recent was the Sixth Biennial Meeting (BMS6), which took place June 6 through 10, 2016, in New York. Many of the 2001 players attended in a continuing effort to include civilian firearms. Of particular interest was Germany, which submitted an extensive paper[6] referencing gender-based violence and Reaching Critical Will, a project of the Women's International League for Peace and Freedom (WILPF), and then advanced a pre-meeting report,[7] asserting that the PoA was the proper vehicle to address these issues.

Germany's proposition was a difficult and touchy one. No reasonable individual or legitimate organization advocates or makes excuses for domestic violence, a reprehensible and unacceptable behavior, but does the discussion belong at the United Nations? Expanding the PoA to address such violence seems ill-advised, especially because, for all its immediacy and gravity, gender-based violence is a question of national law and the U.N. should be limited to international matters.

But the current U.N. does not recognize sovereign boundaries. Of how much concern is that? In reality, aside from the Security Council, theoretically, the U.N. possesses little power, except to propose treaties and establish programs. However, the U.N. does establish *norms*. For instance, most people are peripherally aware of the U.N.'s Universal Declaration of Human Rights, although few have read it. That said, the letters "U.N." carry a moral cachet and goodwill, so a U.N. declaration or standard becomes an idea backed by political prestige.

Advocates for expanding the PoA assert that the lack of education for women, the tradition of early marriage, high levels of sexually transmitted diseases, and the use of firearms are all indicators of gender-based violence. Firearms are defined as male, men owning guns is defined as power, and that power is power over women, ergo, reducing the number of guns will reduce gender-based violence. The relationship is tenuous and the logic bizarre but common to the U.N., where repetition is success and where totally unrelated themes and issues are incorporated into documents and even full-blown treaties.

The German paper also called for "national arms registers" in digital form and accessible as part of a U.N. database.[8] Registration is an anathema to U.S. gun owners, who own the majority of civilian firearms in the world, and so U.N. involvement with this issue confirms every fear that American gun owners ever had about the organization.

Another PoA proposal that sounds alarms includes a call for the engraving of unique identifiers on each ammunition cartridge. Supporters of this proposal (falsely) believe that regulation of ammunition is sustainable, although the firearms industry has repeatedly explained the technical obstacles. Among other obstacles:

- A gun's "cartridge" consists of a case that holds the powder and bullet. The powder burns to create the energy that sends the bullet through the gun barrel. The bullet is the part that is shot down the barrel. Once the cartridge is put in a gun and shot, the now-empty case gets ejected. That empty case, in most instances, can be reused by adding new powder and another bullet. So cartridges (cases) are reusable and can be reloaded by almost anyone, anywhere. Markings on a cartridge (case) would designate only the initial manufacturer.
- No one really knows how many rounds, another word for cartridges, are manufactured and shot in any year, perhaps 12 to 15 billion rounds, mostly for hunting and sport shooting, but also including military acquisitions. Ammunition manufacturers associations tend to agree on the higher number manufactured but cannot say with exactitude how much is used, reloaded, or stockpiled. Gun owners typically own some rounds for each gun they possess and the military stockpiles. Then consider that the very idea of the defense of an area of land requires that governments keep many rounds for each type of gun, cannon, tank, etc., in numerous and separate areas above and below ground. Tracking the sheer number of rounds produced and consumed every year would overwhelm any system.
- Few of the world's militaries would agree to reveal how much ammunition they buy, stockpile, use for training or battles, and where it is shot. Such data would reveal military strategies, movements, and weaknesses after every

practice or real engagement. Knowing how many rounds any country owns at any given time would be an advantage for any aggressor, and an identifiable shell casing left every time a soldier fired their weapon would act as a "calling card" to be used by enemy intelligence to identify and trace not the ammunition, but the military units themselves.

Cartridges can be kept almost indefinitely, through many kinds of weather, and many even work after they get wet. Modern gunpowder is stable and considered one of the Four Great Inventions of China from the 9th-century Tang Dynasty. Caches of ammunition from World War II are still being found with intact rounds. Land mines still blow up on farmland in Europe. A universal database would be impractical with any inventory that is so widespread and long-lasting. Too, small arms ammunition is basically and fundamentally different from military munitions and explosives, and it does not deteriorate under normal circumstances. Yet the U.N. decided that ammunition stockpiles are subject to "uncontrolled explosions or environmental contaminants." Rigorous tests by the Sporting Arms and Ammunition Manufacturers Institute (SAAMI; www.saami.org) and the International Associations of Fire Chiefs have shown that, even when exposed to fire, small arms and light weapons (SALW) do not pose the same danger as military munitions and explosives, and even military SALW munitions do not have explosive projectiles because they are disallowed by Geneva Conventions. Yet these discussions continue to include the non-explosive civilian ammunition.

Germany, Mexico, and roughly 40 other countries demanded that the discussion of ammunition regulation be included at the BMS6. Both the Bush and Obama Administrations recognized the impracticality of such regulation, and both wanted to protect munitions supplies to groups such as the Syrian rebels, part and parcel of a history going back further than the Lend-Lease policy of World War II, in which the United States assisted the Allies while claiming neutrality.

At the final session of the BMS6 on Friday afternoon, June 10, 2016, in a battle over Paragraph 9 of the meeting's report, advocates for the inclusion of ammunition regulations in the PoA wrote, in cunning language:

9. States noted that some States apply relevant provisions of the PoA to material additional to that mentioned in the ITI (International Tracing Instrument) definition of small arms and light weapons, while recognizing that other States were of the view that such material was outside the scope of the PoA.[9]

The crucial word is "additional," which can mean anything. "Related" or "contemplated by" or any other term would limit what could be added. Like the words of the PoA title ("—In All Its Aspects") and the Chinese exemption to the Firearms Protocol, these small words were devastating and will cost many millions of hours and dollars to fight.

Politics does make strange bedfellows. The two countries most opposed to Paragraph 9 were the U.S. and Iran. The U.S. had done its utmost to keep the word "ammunition" out of the report but did not want to push the issue further publicly or be associated with Iran. When the final report was presented, Iran asked that Paragraph 9 be moved to Section IV, which encompassed a short list of issues that were discussed but not agreed to. The distinction is subtle, but crucial.[10]

For almost 45 minutes, the Iranian delegate requested that the paragraph be moved to Section IV. The Chair, Courtaney Rattray of Jamaica, politely ignored all requests. Throughout the dialogue, Iran never rejected consensus (as it has the right to do at any U.N. meeting). Finally, the Chair said he was going to declare the report adopted. There was a pause, Iran said nothing, and the gavel came down. It was good theater.

In the end, the message from the BMS6 was that ammunition regulation had become the Holy Grail of certain states and NGOs, regardless of any practical realities. The PoA will be revisited, in 2018, in a "Review Conference." At a "conference," unlike a "meeting," as one U.S. official pointed out, everything, literally *everything*, will be "on the table" in 2018. Conferences are for negotiation and will not be restricted by what has happened thus far (which only emphasizes that the 2016 and 2018 U.S. election outcomes are critical to the "start over" mentality)..

Two International Gun-Control Forces

These early efforts at international arms and ammunition control created an international anti-gun NGO community centered around two major groups, Control Arms and the International Action Network on Small Arms (IANSA).

Dr. Edward Laurance of the Monterey Institute for International Studies was an oddity in the disarmament world, a West Point graduate turned academic. He managed numerous projects for the U.N. Office for Disarmament Affairs and, early on, identified small arms control as ripe for an organizational effort. In 1997, about 160 associations from the disarmament and the gun-control worlds held a meeting where a "Preparatory Committee" was established and funding was pursued. Both were very successful, as Dr. Laurence raised $160,000 from various foundations and governments.

The result of Dr. Laurance's effort was the establishment of IANSA, in May 1999 (which gave it ample time to prepare for the 2001 PoA Conference). In 2002, IANSA hired Rebecca Peters as its executive director. Ms. Peters is an Australian attorney and activist who spent much of her time on women's issues and led the Australian National Coalition for Gun Control that pushed the 1997 Australian gun buyback. Her appointment to the IANSA connected that organization's efforts directly to the U.S. domestic gun-control issues, especially as the Australian buyback continues to be a model for anti-gunners, including Hillary Clinton.[11] Ms. Peters next worked for the Open Society Institute funded by billionaire George Soros, who had also helped fund IANSA. Ms. Peters's profile remained extremely high until 2010, when she resigned from IANSA, but she made her presence known again in 2016.

Eight hundred member associations from 120 countries contributed to IANSA in 2016. Even so, IANSA suffered from a lack of funding in comparison to Control Arms and Anna MacDonald, but both have effective permanent offices of "liaisons" (lobbyists) at the U.N. in Manhattan, a tremendous advantage. The first liaison for IANSA was Mark Marge. He was replaced by Michele Poliacof, a grandmotherly, retired U.N. employee who was particularly effective because of her U.N. contacts and a restrained public image in contrast to Ms. Peters. Ms. Poliacof left IANSA in 2013 and was eventually replaced by Rose Welsch.

In 2011, there was a "memorandum of understanding" signed between the U.N. Office for Disarmament Affairs and IANSA in which IANSA would be recognized as the contact point and coordinator of *all* NGO activities on firearms. Americans expect at least an illusion of evenhandedness in government—but the U.N. echoes the French system of criminal justice, where one is presumed guilty and has to prove their innocence. A legislative committee in the U.S. would not openly have an advocacy group schedule and coordinate testimony.

Fortunately, IANSA has not abused its authority often (at least once one gets used to U.N. slights). Firearms community groups do appear at U.N. meetings. Usually, NGOs are allotted a block of time for presentations, and who gets what time is negotiated between IANSA and the firearms community. During the BMS6 PoA meeting, all the NGOs were allocated 45 minutes, and the IANSA's Ms. Welsch allotted almost half the time to pro-gun groups. IANSA brought 52 people, many from Africa, with Rebecca Peters seemingly in charge of the delegation and active in fundraising again.

The Small Arms Survey (SAS) was established, in 1999, by Switzerland, to be a permanent research institute focusing on SALW original research. Switzerland is an enigma. All males serve in the Army reserve, and military rifles are kept in civilian houses. Shooting matches are huge public events, and the Swiss are comfortable with guns. At the same time, SAS is vociferously anti-gun. Now, take into account that, in Switzerland, *everything* is numbered, registered, and regulated. Even its cows have serial numbers. But while guns are registered, the Swiss have no fear of confiscation. Gun are an integral part of the national identity and ethos; many Swiss feel that guns, even with the registration, keep Switzerland free. Thus the culture clash at the U.N.

The ultimate non-polluting, high-profit industry, the Swiss love hosting the headquarters of international organizations. International conference attendees spend in hotels and conference centers—tourism without the hassle of entertaining tourists. The Swiss knew that SALW gun control advocates would need a headquarters institution and that they wanted it based in Switzerland. That foresight has paid off, with the Arms Trade Treaty Secretariat located at the Geneva Graduate Center, so that it has academic support and credibility.

Funded by governments, the SAS and its 36 employees operate under a façade of objectivity. They publish a lavish yearbook on SALW and numerous reports frequently cited at U.N. conferences. They also supply staffing for various U.N. meetings and reports. The BMS6 report, for instance, was written by Glenn MacDonald, senior researcher for the SAS. Sarah Parker played a key role in writing the ATT, and Anna Alvazzi del Frate is considered an international expert in a myriad of crime-related issues. Together, these three exemplify the close relationship between the U.N. and the various think tanks and NGOs in which some consultants swap roles throughout their careers. Numerous other groups support international gun control, among them: Amnesty International (AI), Mine Action Group, and Oxfam. Clare da Silva, a Canadian attorney whose prior vocation was defending accused war criminals in the International Criminal Court, is effective for AI.

The U.S. firearms community, while able to fight intellectual and legal battles in its support of the Second Amendment domestically, has no body or group in place to combat their international enemies. There are no Dave Kopels (Research Director of the Independence Institute in Golden, Colorado) or Don Kates (Independent Institute in Oakland, California) to do the intellectual spade work, although Ted Bromund working part-time at the Heritage Foundation does his best. Moreover, pro-gun groups in the U.S. have to raise money from American citizens, while international anti-gun forces are well funded, often from government monies.

The National Rifle Association Arrives

Prior to 1995, the NRA had informal contacts with the Sporting Shooters Association of Australia. Tanya Metaksa of NRA's Institute for Legislative Action (ILA) had noticed an increased number of foreign manufacturers at the NRA Annual Meetings and the annual National Shooting Sports Foundation's (NSSF's) Shooting, Hunting and Outdoor Trade Show (SHOT Show; www.shotshow.org). Ms. Metaksa called for pro-gun representation at the U.N. meeting in Cairo, and for pro-firearms groups and manufacturers to meet at the annual European equivalent of the SHOT Show, *Internationale Waffen Ausstellung* (International Weapons Exhibition), better known as the IWA and OutdoorClassics Show that takes place in Nuremberg, Germany, each year. The World Forum on Shooting Activities (WFSA) was formed at IWA.[12]

Where There's a Will . . .

By Tom Mason

After the U.N. Crime Congress, in May of 1995, the NRA decided to participate in all U.N. meetings relating to firearms. Preliminary work on the Firearms Protocol was held at the Crime Prevention Branch headquarters in Vienna, Austria. Also in 1995, NRA began the arduous task of applying to the U.N. for NGO status, which was granted in 1996 despite the strong reservations of Japan.[13]

The U.N. is a club of governments, not a democracy or open to anyone for participation—and prior to its being admitted to the U.N. as a NGO, the NRA would *never* have been invited to participate. However, NGOs that are permitted to attend meetings traditionally let members of other allied groups also attend.

Roy Innis, President of the Congress of Racial Equality (CORE), a NGO with the U.N., had walked with Martin Luther King, and both were gun owners. A NRA Board Member, Innis arranged a CORE credential for me. The U.N. knew I was a NRA representative but could not object to this common and accepted practice.

In early 1996, I faxed the U.N., asking if NGOs would be allowed at the first U.N. meeting on the Firearms Protocol, and after several telephone phone calls the answer was a reluctant "Yes."

As I was packed and ready to leave Oregon for a 6:00 a.m. flight to Vienna, the U.N. called at 3:00 a.m., saying the meeting was now closed to NGOs—in other words, do not come!

A Clinton Administration official at the U.S. Mission was put off by the snub of a U.S. NGO and "guaranteed" that the next meeting would be open, and later that year I flew to Vienna and presented my credentials, the letter from CORE designating me. Normally, this is a pro forma process of a few minutes, like getting your passport stamped by an utterly bored official. I waited *three hours* while staff dialed a great number of telephone calls. Finally, a person who seemed in charge smiled and said, "Here's your pass. They are quite amused upstairs that you had to wait."

U.N. meetings typically start at 10:00 a.m., break for lunch at 1:00 p.m., and resume from 3:00 to 6:00 p.m. The morning session was breaking for lunch as I was admitted, so all I could do was introduce myself to the chair of the meeting, who seemed uncomfortable with his new guest.

The afternoon meeting did not start on time; U.N. meetings never do. Told the meeting was open, I sat in the back of the room in what seemed to be a public area. A clerk or assistant appeared immediately, saying the chair had closed the session. Not wanting to make a fuss my first day, I retreated to the lobby and began reading background documents on a table at the entrance. There were no high-level VIPs in the room, nor was the meeting sensitive, but an armed U.N. guard stationed himself at the door.

Turns out the guard was for me! The U.N. was that intimidated by the idea of an NRA representative.

This type of treatment became routine—inquiries were made months in advance, and meeting notices were received at the last minute; I was often told meetings were closed to NGOs only to discover that anti-gun NGOs attended.

I had been lobbied during my 16 years in the Oregon legislature, so I started to campaign. A meeting may be closed, but participants are fair game when going to the toilet! Introduce yourself, say you just want a few words with them, and make your pitch. They will not like it at first but learn you are human. Make friends with anybody possible, especially the opposition. Humans love to gossip and share information often to show just how important they are—and that holds at the local church, any state capital, or in Vienna.

Even in that hostile U.N. environment, people leave documents in the meeting room. After the "closed" meetings, a few smart scavengers pick up tidbits.

Many professionals will work only with people who rank equally or above them. Staff can be amazingly helpful, though, and I introduce myself to everyone and take them to lunch or, better yet, to dinner. An example of how helpful this can be: I believed staff assurances that there were no records of U.N. meetings until I invited a mid-level Crime Prevention staffer out to the best restaurant in Vienna. He (or she—I'm not saying) spontaneously presented me with a meeting transcript that I had been told simply did not exist!

The World Forum on Shooting Activities (WFA) became a U.N. NGO in 1997, followed by the Sporting Shooters Association of Australia. Five other pro-firearms groups have since been admitted:

- Associazione Nazionale Produttori Armi e Munizioni – ANPAM (Italian manufacturers)
- Council of Licensed Firearms Owners of New Zealand
- National Firearms Association of Canada
- Safari Club International
- Sporting Arms and Ammunition Manufacturers Institute (American manufacturers)

There are also other active Second Amendment supporters who can participate in U.N. functions. The National Shooting Sports Foundation (NSSF), the trade association for the American firearms industry, was awarded special consultative status by the U.N. in 2015, following its application for that status with the Committee on Non-Governmental Organizations. Focusing on military commerce, The Defense Small Arms Advisory Council (DSAAC), a military firearms manufacturers association, is a NGO and a reliable partner in revealing some absurd U.N. proposals such as those seeking to regulate ammunition. Major General (Ret.) Allen Youngman is especially effective in representing that organization. A combat veteran, hunter, shooter, and a member of Kentucky law enforcement, he is always a reliable ally.

The WFSA is based in Rome, hosted by the Associazione Nazionale Produttori Armi e Munizioni Sportive e Civili (ANPAM, representing "almost all of the companies belonging to the industrial sector of the weapons and ammunition, and many of those explosives," according to its website, www.anpam.it). It has two executive secretaries, Mauro Silvis of Italy for Europe and the European Union, and one of this book's authors, Thomas Mason for the Americas. It publishes reports and holds workshops to support the continued use of lead ammunition and demonstrates the economic and environmental benefits of hunting and shooting. In 1999, the WFSA established a manufacturers advisory group (MAG), so that firearms makers from around the world could formulate policies and present positions to the U.N. Until 2016, the chair of the group was Ted Rowe, who managed international matters for Strum, Ruger & Co.

The NRA maintains a strong U.N. presence with a few victories, especially for the 2001 PoA Conference, where Ambassador John Bolton cautioned against interference with American gun rights. Aaron Karp, an anti-gun activist involved in the proceedings, wrote:

Even if America's final position at the Conference had been assembled under the leadership of a President Al Gore, the immense clout of one of the country's most effective single-issue lobbies would have been felt. As it was, under the George W. Bush administration, it was just plain huge. At the Conference itself, the NRA emerged as a greater force than all the other 180 NGOs combined, dominating the American delegation to a degree few had imagined to be possible.[14]

The NRA is tolerated, not liked. As one writer put it:

The NRA may not be actively funding gun lobbies around the world—the organization claims its charter prohibits it— but its influence is felt in much more than dollars. It lends support to the anti-gun control effort at the United Nations. It promotes lines of argument, strategy, and political tactics that others adopt for local use. And, if you contact the association, its representatives will come to explain how to get it done. Although many of the NRA's members may not own a passport, their leaders are savvy operators in international politics. For all their red-blooded American pretensions, they have a deep understanding of how globalization works. "We live in a very globalized society," says Thomas Mason, the American gun lobby's top representative at the United Nations. "[Y]ou can't say what happens in Scotland doesn't affect the United States, because it does."

When Thomas Mason arrived at the United Nations, diplomats weren't greeted by the swaggering cowboy they had expected. The former Oregon state representative is the American gun lobby's emissary to the United Nations and other international forums. Over the past decade, he has developed a reputation as a canny strategist and cordial operator, despite the fact that he works in territory that could only be described as hostile.[15]

Headed to Hollywood

By Tom Mason

"Will you hold for Count Albi?"

I had never talked to a count, so I agreed.

Count Albi said U.N. Secretary General Kofi Annan had named him Executive Director of the Eminent Persons Group (EPG) to address small arms and light weapons. Membership included Robert McNamara, former U.S. Secretary of Defense; Michel Rocard, former Prime Minister of France; and Alpha Konare, former president of Mali. He name-dropped, with casual references to Vice President Cheney and Justice Antonin Scalia going to his house for dinner. George Soros was funding the project. Though those claims were true, Mr. Albi's claim to have the most famous Russian General, Michal Kalashnikov, as a member was probably a fabrication.

Mr. Albi said he wanted a "grand bargain" on small arms between the U.N. and the NRA and Charlton Heston. I knew the chances were zero, but the U.N. is all about talk.

"There will be all action and no movement. Don't worry, Russia, China, and the U.S. will never allow their vital interest to be affected. The U.N. needs something to do." This was true. I introduced Mr. Albi to Ted Rowe, chair of WFSA's MAG. Soon, proposals and memorandums spewed out of the EPG.

Mr. Albi was active at the 2001 PoA Conference and once hosted a lunch for Robert McNamara, wearing a vest, a wing collar, striped pants, and a cutaway tail coat, the traditional German diplomatic garb called a "Stresemann," named after the foreign minister of the Weimar Republic but not seen in this century.

A tall, severe-looking man, in 2002 and 2003 Mr. Albi arranged meetings in Paris and London to establish what he called "the Paris Process" with U.S. State Department Officials in attendance. At a spectacular dinner at the Naval and Military Club on St. James Square in London, Mr. Albi introduced his wife, Viola Drath, a wealthy Washington, D.C., doyen 44 years his senior.

After each meeting, Mr. Albi would unilaterally issue a press release claiming that the firearms industry was cooperating with the U.N. Mr. Rowe had to explain to Ruger and other companies what MAG was really doing. The guest of honor at one New York dinner I attended and arranged by Mr. Albi after the 2001 Conference was Michele Rocard, former Prime Minister of France. Robert Glock, the son of Gaston Glock, the founder of the Austrian pistol company that bears his surname, and Mr. Albi spoke in German at dinner and later in the bar. Mr. Glock was an active member of MAG, and after the dinner he called me to say Mr. Albi was a con man. When I asked how he knew, he said by just his manner and that he had "made inquiries." Mr. Glock was right.

Mr. Albi's activities in this realm calmed for a few years, but early in 2004, Mr. Rowe and I received anonymous faxes telling of an Albrecht Muth's criminal record, with run-ins for abusing his elderly wife. We learned that Ms. Drath sent the faxes. Mr. Albi, now Mr. Muth, kept up on email and in one message after the anonymous faxes began included a telephone number in a message. I called it and asked the Washington hotel operator for Count Albi, and after a pause she transferred the call. Mr. Albi/Muth's voice answered, "Concierge." Soon there were reports of him hosting an event for Benazir Bhutto, and even claims that he was helping the new Iraqi government after the U.S. invasion. After he reunited with Drath, they hosted dinners for Washington luminaries in their Georgetown townhouse, where he wore the uniform of an Iraqi general.

On April 11, 2011, Ms. Drath was found strangled in her townhouse. Mr. Muth claimed it was a botched Iraqi assassination, although Ms. Drath had just reduced his allowance from $2,000 to $1,800. The police also found a letter, allegedly signed by her and gifting Mr. Muth $150,000 in case of her death.

Arrested, after a hunger strike and substantial publicity, Mr. Muth was found guilty and, on April 30, 2014, sentenced to 50 years in federal prison. At last report, a movie script was circulating in Hollywood, as good stories often do.

The Fight Goes On

After the 2001 PoA Conference, Aaron Karp candidly admitted what he and others wanted to do:

> *Going beyond the limits of diplomacy, it [the U.N. effort] has to include those small arms already in public hands. It must stress the imperative to minimize the role of small arms in all sectors of society . . . . This approach logically leads to unification of the international small arms and domestic gun-control process. Gun advocates have long spoken as if there were an international conspiracy to get rid of their guns. Perhaps it is time for the advocates of restraint [gun control] to become more as they are described . . . policies should stress the shared goal of reducing the number and visibility of small arms in states and societies.*[16]

We have been warned. The U.N. gun-control effort is a threat to our Second Amendment freedoms, as well as a threat to every gun owner in the world. The advocates of U.N. gun control may not be as violent as the Count, but they are just as much of a threat.

[1] *Ambassador John Bolton has observed that all a U.N. initiative needs is a footnote in a resolution. The footnote becomes a paragraph, the paragraph a resolution, which generates a study then a report then another study or a series of meetings. Finally, a conference where a treaty is drafted. This gradual policy development is called "policy by accretion."*

[2] *AK-47s are ubiquitous in Africa.*

[3] *United Nations, Protocol Against the Illicit Manufacturing and Trafficking in Firearms. . .A/55/383. Add.2.*

[4] *"Mandate" is U.N. for authorization to act.*

[5] *The reason for the British spelling is lost to history.*

[6] *Germany, "Position Paper by Germany," February 2016.*

[7] *Reaching Critical Will, "Preventing Gender-Based Violence Through Arms Control."*

[8] *Ibid.*

[9] *United Nations, Outcome Document of the Sixth Biennial Meeting of states to Consider the Implementation of the Programme of Action A/CONF.192/BMS/2016/WP.1/Rev.3.*

[10] *Included in Section IV is reference to controlling arms transfers to non-state actors. The U.S. has always been opposed to any limitation on such transfers and managed to keep the mentions in Section IV.*

[11] *As of June 2016, Clinton was calling for the ban of "assault weapons" in reaction to the June 12, 2016, shootings in Orlando.*

[12] *Originally the World Forum on the Future of Sport Shooting Activities, later shortened.*

[13] *The U.S. Clinton Administration insisted the NRA be given NGO status. Officials realized that denial could affect UN funding because Republican Senator Jesse Helms of North Carolina, a key player in the question of UN funding and staunch ally of the NRA, and others would be more vocal against the UN.*

[14] *Aaron Karp, "The Small Arms Challenge: Back to the Future," Brown Journal of Foreign Affairs, IX, no. 1 (2002): 186.*

[15] *Morton, David (2006-07-05). "Gunning for the World," Foreign Policy. Retrieved 2008-07-23.*

[16] *Ibid at 190.*

CHAPTER 6

Betrayal and a Constitutional Confrontation

I don't care if you have 90 Senators to oppose the treaty, we're still going ahead.

—U.N. Arms Trade Treaty Consultant Rachel Stohl

...It would become me better than to close./In terms of friendship with thine enemies.

—Anthony, *Julius Caesar*

Hillary Clinton and Barack Obama have created the perfect storm for a constitutional confrontation of international law and the U.N. versus American gun owner's rights. Not only will the current Arms Trade Treaty (ATT) impact every civilian firearm in the world, it will uniquely threaten Americans gun owners. To understand this, we have to review some basic international law, look at what our Constitution says about treaties, and then revisit, in detail, the betrayal of American rights at the U.N. by the Clinton-Obama team in 2012 and 2013.

The Process for Treaties and Agreements

There are two stages to how a country adopts a treaty. First, the country negotiates, agrees to, and signs the treaty. Second, the country ratifies or adopts the treaty. In the United States, the negotiation would be made by the Executive Branch and headed up by the President, while the Legislative Branch, Congress, would accept or reject the treaty. However, according to accepted international law, once a country signs a treaty, that country implicitly agrees to abide by all the sections and language within that treaty. The United Nations adopted the ATT on April 2, 2013, and by September 24, 2014, 50 nations had ratified it. This was the magic number for the ATT to go into effect 90 days later, on December 24, 2014, when all the signatories are supposed to abide by its language, regardless of whether the country ratifies the treaty or not. U.S. Secretary of State John Kerry signed the ATT for the U.S. on September 25, 2013; thus, the U.S. must, theoretically, abide by the ATT, even though it is not a ratified by the U.S. Senate according to our Constitution.

Article 2 Section 2 of the U.S. Constitution states that treaties are to be considered ratified with the "advise and consent" of two-thirds of the members of the Senate present. But during negotiations, 50 U.S. Senators voiced strong objections to the ATT for not protecting the Second Amendment. There is little chance the present Senate (that in place before the 2016 November elections) will ratify the ATT, yet that in no way diminishes its threat.

Just as it was with the Law of the Sea Treaty negotiated by President Bill Clinton, the sitting President of the United States can hold a treaty until a future president has a favorable Congress that would ratify it. The treaty stays in force until rejected, so a treaty is sent to the Senate when the President believes it will be ratified or desires to put the onus on the Senate for not acting. There have been some gargantuan political battles over the ratification of treaties, the most notable being the rejection of the Treaty of Versailles in 1919 that ended World War I.

A U.S. president's power regarding international agreements would seem to be limited by the Senate's role in ratifying treaties, but most international agreements are not treaties. Between 1946 and 1999, the U.S. entered into 16,000 international agreements, of which just 912 were treaties. Then there are also "political agreements" between the executives of states. These agreements can affect those things solely within a president's executive power, such as the power he or she holds as commander and chief of the armed forces. A congressional-executive agreement that affects domestic laws, for example, would be the North American Free Trade Agreement of the Bill Clinton Administration, which Congress voted on when Representative Newt Gingrich was Whip, not yet Speaker.

There is always a tension between the President and the Legislative Branch involving these international agreements. Much of this tension comes from the fact the it is the Executive Branch that negotiates these agreements, while the final power of approval of treaties and congressional-executive agreements rests with the legislature. This is especially true of treaties. Treaties by their nature are the more important agreements. It might also be added that many countries that negotiate with the U.S. on international agreements do not appreciate the role played by the U.S. Legislative Branch, especially the Senate. Typically, the Department of State fails to mention to its negotiating partners that it does not have the final say on whether a treaty will be adopted by the U.S.

Treaties are unique in three other respects. First, once a treaty is ratified, it becomes part of domestic U.S. law. Second, even though a treaty becomes domestic law, it never has to be approved by the U.S. House of Representatives. Finally, the Supreme Court has ruled that the treaty power of the President is a separate power and does not need to be authorized under any other section of the Constitution. In other words, the President can do things under a treaty he or she would not be authorized to do under the rest of the Constitution.

Note that this treaty process may actually be unconstitutional, whereby the Executive Branch, without the Legislative Branch, can determine laws within the U.S. (The writers of our Constitution simply could not and did not predict the scope of international organizations and laws that would affect our citizens without ever clearing Congress.) Thus, even treaties unlikely to ever be ratified can be ticking time bombs; many are followed, but never sent to the Senate. Today's Republican Senate is not likely to ratify the ATT, but, like the 1982 Law of the Sea Treaty that Reagan rejected because it transfers technology and wealth to undeveloped nations, or the 1992 Kyoto Treaty that accepts global warming and man-made climate change and vastly regulates commerce, treaties lie around. Any President with a comfortable majority in the Senate can accomplish, via treaty, what could never pass as legislation. Congress would have to defeat the ratification in a vote to keep such treaties from being considered law.

Already the ATT is the gun-control movement's international vehicle for myriad favorite ploys: control of ammunition, firearms destruction programs, gun bans, gun registration, licensing of owners, and limits on the size of ammunition magazines, to name a few. These are found in standards referred to in the ATT and being drafted by the U.N. as the International Small Arms Control Standards. (ISACS : www.smallarmsstandards.org) Through the ATT, the U.N. and its anti-gun allies are on the verge of achieving massive domestic firearm restrictions.

Few Americans, Israelis, or Russians have ever heard of the ATT. But, like the December 2015 climate change negotiations in Paris, the ATT will change lives without any say by more than a few hundred people.

A final note about treaties and the ATT: anti-gun forces like to claim that an exemption for individually owned firearms is in the ATT, because "lawful ownership" is mentioned in the preamble. Preambles to a treaty are not binding, they merely introduce the actual agreement. Thus, the exemptions in the ATT preamble do not influence the restrictions that appear in the body of the treaty.

Arms Trade Treaty Beginnings

The U.S. finally agreed to participate in the ATT development process only if the process abided by the U.N.'s traditional consensus rule. This rule essentially says that that all countries have to agree on the results of a conference or a meeting, i.e., the consensus rule requires a consensus of the parties, rather than a simple vote, for a proposal to go forward within the U.N. (The resolution authorizing the Conference incorporated the consensus rule in 2012; A/RES/64?48.) When Hillary Clinton herself announced the Obama Administration would join the ATT process, she said it would be on the basis of consensus. On October 14, 2009, Mrs. Clinton said:

> *Consensus is needed to ensure the widest possible support for the Treaty and to avoid loopholes in the Treaty that can be exploited by those wishing to export arms irresponsibly.*

ATT negotiations were held during the Bush and Obama Administrations, from 2006 to 2013. Bush's Chief ATT negotiator, Ambassador Donald M. Mahley, consistently and successfully defended U.S. gun rights and the Second Amendment during these negotiations by refusing to join consensus. Because of Amb. Mahley's hard bargaining, civilian firearms owned under the U.S. Second Amendment were specifically excluded from the ATT. The exception to the ATT for arms held under "national Constitutional protection," i.e., the American Second Amendment, was in the U.N. reports that were the basis for the final negotiations at the ATT Conferences in 2012 and 2013.

The Bush Administration's defense of the Second Amendment at the U.N. was unyielding. At a 2001 U.N. Conference on the Illicit Trade in Small Arms and Light Weapons in All Its Aspects, the issue of regulating civilian firearms possession was the central controversy. The original 2001 Programme of Action (PoA), which we talked about extensively in the last chapter and is the proposed U.N. project to come out of that 2001 Conference, brought strong objections from John Bolton, Bush's Undersecretary of State for Disarmament (later to become U.S. Ambassador to the U.N.). The President dispatched Bolton to New York, to make clear to all involved that the U.S. position would be that there would be no interference with the Second Amendment.

Bolton's speech to the opening of the 2001 Conference was stunningly unequivocal: take possession of civilian firearms out, or the U.S. would not join consensus. Civilian possession of firearms was a U.S. "red line."

Negotiators soon dropped those sections from the PoA,[1] with one anti-gun activist, Aaron Karp, noting that the Conference was essentially over after Bolton had made his speech and that the NGO that had the most impact on the Conference was the NRA. At the end of the Conference, Rachel Stohl, an active member of The *International Action Network on Small Arms* (*IANSA*), a well-funded anti-gun organization, screamed at Enrique Perez, one of the U.S. delegates, as he walked out of the meeting, yelling that he should be ashamed of what the U.S. had done in making sure that possession of civilian firearms was left out of the PoA. Her behavior was a bit stunning: Ms. Stohl had been hired by the U.N. as the chief consultant for the ATT negotiations, and in an American political setting, staff are supposed to at least appear neutral.

"We Know We're Right"

By Tom Mason

U.S. NGOs pay for their advocacy out of private donations. The U.N., which the U.S. taxpayer funds at about a third of the total world budget, hired a U.N. consultant to oppose the U.S. Administration position and American law. When I complained to Daniel Prins, head of the Conventional Arms Branch of the U.N.'s Office for Disarmament Affairs, that his office and the various conference and committee chairs were not even maintaining the appearance of neutrality, Prins replied, "Why should we? We know we're right."

The U.N. Firearms Protocol

Until the adoption of the ATT, most agreements on firearms policies and restrictions have been classified as "political arrangements," non-binding agreements between governments. The ATT, however, is different. It constitutes an unprecedented threat to gun rights worldwide as part of a concerted U.N. effort to advance the agenda of the international gun-control community through a legally binding treaty. The ATT is not the proverbial smoking gun—it is a *loaded* gun pointed directly at the Second Amendment and civilian gun owners in the United States.

The ATT is the first disarmament treaty in history to include civilian firearms, as well as the usual military weapons.[2] It is an all-inclusive instrument affecting everything from strategic bombers to pistols owned for sporting purposes or self-defense. In years of debate and discussion leading up to the ATT, it had become clear that the target of the negotiations was really what they call "small arms and light weapons" (SALW), a U.N. term that includes rifles, sidearms, and even shotguns. The great majority of the world's SALW are legally owned civilian firearms, and a third to a half are owned by Americans.

The American voter pays scant attention to treaties and is unaware of how friendly a venue the U.N. is to international anti-gun forces. For instance, while U.S. gun-control groups have generally failed to outright ban assault rifles and large capacity ammunition magazines, their sister organizations have been writing those very same restrictions into law all over the world. And, as American anti-gun groups lost battles where American voters upheld their right to arm in the state legislatures, where courts supported the right to bear arms in decisions like *Heller*, anti-gun forces became intrigued by the prospect of avoiding the legislative process with a treaty. The resulting treaty the U.N. General Assembly passed in 2013 was the product of diverse political forces coming together in a maelstrom of human rights activism, gun-control politics, large economic interests, and misplaced idealism—and its full results will not be known for decades.

It Is All About Them

By Tom Mason

In 1996, the first person I got to know at the U.N., in Vienna, was a Swedish diplomat attached to the Crime Prevention Branch. I was lonely in those early years, and taking pity on this American, he took me aside one evening as a meeting ended. (The Swedes are big hunters, and I suspect he was sympathetic to the concept of gun rights, at least for hunters.)

"You've got to learn how this process works," he said to me. "It's a world all its own. You need some perspective.

"First of all, everybody is important and every meeting is the most important meeting in the world as far as the attendees are concerned. These people are mid- to lower-level bureaucrats who have flown thousands of miles to deliver what they think is a monumental statement, but they have little power and really cannot do anything on their own. The process is extremely slow, but, in its own way, very effective.

"Flatter them. Call them 'Ambassador,' even if they aren't. Forget how important *you* are. You know the formal term of address for an ambassador is 'Your Excellency'—use it."

He was right. There is an old cliché that, when lobbying in America, it cannot hurt to call everybody "Mr. Chairman." The same applies at the U.N. Addressing everyone as "Ambassador" makes each person feel good and sometimes even gets them to listen. Always start by saying that their time is valuable and you do not want to bother them, but if you could only have a few words . . . .

Later, during the same Vienna meeting, a Canadian took me aside and said, "I

want to congratulate you."
   "On what?" I replied.
   "This issue. You'll retire on this. I'll do pretty well myself. This isn't going away."
That was in 1996.

Costa Rica and Britain Make Big Moves

In 1987, Oscar Arias, the President of Costa Rica, won the Nobel Peace Prize for assistance in settling a number of Central American civil wars. In 1997, Mr. Arias organized a cadre of Nobel laureates to advocate for an international arms trade treaty designed to avoid human rights abuses.[4] Mr. Arias addressed the U.N. General Assembly in 2006, and the first U.N. ATT Resolution 61/89 passed that year.[5]

The U.S. was the only state to vote against what the Bush Administration immediately recognized as a potential threat to civilian firearms ownership in this country, with the U.S. delegation emphasizing that the U.S. already maintained stringent export controls to avoid the very human rights abuses that concerned Mr. Arias. Regardless, through the U.N. Department for Disarmament Affairs, the Resolution asked the Secretary General to seek the views of "member states" and authorized a "group of government experts" to examine the "feasibility, scope, and draft parameters" of a treaty.

In 1997, Britain's Labour Party broke its 18-year losing streak, with the election of Tony Blair as Prime Minister. Under Blair, Britain became a major ATT supporter, largely because the British defense industry was at a disadvantage competing with countries having looser export controls. Like the U.S., the British government reviewed export applications to avoid selling arms to human rights abusers. China, Russia, and Brazil did not have such export restrictions.

Large businesses worldwide tend to look upon regulation as a means to limit competition, and British industry thought the ATT would "level the playing field." Two huge defense companies, Rolls Royce (airplane engines, not cars) and British Aerospace Systems, became early supporters of the ATT, not because British industry was concerned about a half-million-dollar sale of Italian shotguns to the U.S., but of a multi-billion-dollar-equivalent sale of airplanes to Saudi Arabia. (https://quarterly.blog.gov.uk/2013/07/12/the-uks-role-in-the-un-arms-trade-treaty-2/ and https://www.chathamhouse.org/sites/files/chathamhouse/field/field_document/20141215DefenceIndustryArmsTradeTreatyKytomaki.pdf)

Major U.S. defense industry members, meanwhile, adopted a wait-and-see attitude (or followed Britain's lead), while civilian small arms manufacturers saw the ATT as a market threat that would impede international shipping and sales. Military small arms manufacturers, too, were concerned that the regulatory structure would impose an undue burden on their relatively limited operations, when compared with "big defense." The $10 million a company like Boeing might have to spend annually to comply with ATT regulations (if they actually had to) in procuring a multi-billion-dollar airplane contract with Saudi Arabia is a line item, but for the military small arms manufacturer, the same annual $10 million spent for a $100 million contract is a deal breaker.

Once Mr. Arias called for action on small arms, the international anti-gun community mobilized. British anti-gun organizations and NGOs like The International Action Network on Small Arms (IANSA) took an early lead in lobbying for the treaty. Then came Rebecca Peters. In 2004, Ms. Peters debated NRA Executive Vice President Wayne LaPierre at King's College in London (you can read a summary of that debate here: http://www.freerepublic.com/focus/news/1243368/posts), on the topic "Should the United States support the proposed United Nations Treaty that bans private ownership of guns?" Ms. Peters, claiming target shooting with shotguns or semi-automatic rifles are not legitimate sports because they are not in the Olympics, made it clear her goal was to ban firearms, saying:

> *If you miss your sport, take up another sport. Take up a sport that does not require a weapon invented for the specific purpose of killing another human being.*[6]

She is, of course, wrong. And certainly tens of millions of shooters in America, Switzerland, and other countries disagree, including the many thousands who, since 1903, have participated in the annual National Matches at Camp Perry (www.thecmp.org), the leading rifle competition in the U.S.

Oxfam International, another major British-based NGO, took on gun control under a subsidiary organization, Control Arms. Eventually, Control Arms came to dominate the NGO pro-ATT movement. The group's chief spokesperson was Anna MacDonald, who shares Ms. Peters's views and is seen by many of her allies as a publicity hound.

Amnesty International, a number of other NGOs, anti-gun regimes from around the world, and anti-gun groups from the U.S. itself coalesced around the IANSA and Control Arms to fight for the treaty. British Labour Party politicians like Foreign Secretary Robin Cook endorsed the ATT for domestic political reasons. Academics, think tanks, and British gun-control groups helped recruit disarmament departments in foreign ministries. Germany, Australia, and New Zealand endorsed it and became vocal supporters. Canada had been a strong initial supporter but jumped ship with the election of the Harper government in a reversal of what happened in the United States when Barack Obama succeeded George W. Bush as President.[7] African countries blamed many of their problems on small arms and were particularly enthusiastic about the ATT, because they saw it as a vehicle to reducing violence in their countries; established African governments wanted limits on the transfers of arms to rebel groups or "non-state actors," as they are called at the U.N.[8]

Many U.N. member states decided to get into the gun ban business because they saw what had happened during an elite and very public campaign for a treaty banning land mines. In 1997, a conference in Ottawa produced the Land Mine Treaty (notorious for its creation outside the purview of the U.N.), in an effort driven solely by NGOs that, in effect, seized control from actual U.N. members.

While NGOs have tremendous influence at ATT conferences, they are not supposed to participate directly in the "club of states." In fact, member states were warned that if they did not participate in the ATT negotiations, a treaty might well be written by NGOs in a process similar to that which happened with the Land Mine Treaty, and with similarly devastating results. (NGOs did override many state—i.e. country—objections, resulting in the loss of sovereignty for many nations, and that is chilling news around the world, not only among pro-gun Americans. If the U.N. becomes an unelected super government, no nation is safe.)

There are, as you might imagine, many others who've played significant roles in the ATT. Ambassador Roberto García Moritán of Argentina chaired a step in the U.N. treaty development process called the Experts Group, which had been created in the 2006 U.N. Resolution. A perpetually tanned, polo-playing aristocrat known for his expensive suits, haughty attitude, and sexist jokes, he was seen as lazy by many. Amb. Moritán would not take notes at the meetings, simply relying on his staff to draft treaty language.

Despite the smoking ban in U.N. buildings, Amb. Moritán, a compulsive smoker, needed a cigarette every hour. Invariably, Control Arms' Anna MacDonald would join him for a smoke outside and bend his ear. Ms. MacDonald was effective, but very disliked by other anti-gun representatives from smaller organizations, for she was no Birkenstock-wearing British nanny, but rather a spiked-heel, low-neckline carnivore who would be mistaken for a high-paid corporate lobbyist in Congress were it were not for her accent.

Another major player was Ambassador John Duncan, who represented Britain at the early meetings. He was charming, sophisticated, worldly, and willing to say anything to get a treaty favorable to British industry. Amb. Duncan assured all who would listen that the ATT would not impact civilian gun owners but vehemently opposed including such assurances in the actual text of the treaty. His chief assistant through the first few years of the process was

Andrew Wood from the British Ministry of Defense. Wood had left government to become Rolls Royce's chief lobbyist for the ATT.

Amb. Duncan would have dominated the Experts Group had it not been for the chief U.S. representative, Ambassador Donald A. Mahley. Amb. Mahley, a retired Army officer who had managed ammunition dumps in Vietnam, was one of the few negotiators who had actually worked with weapons. His second career was as one of the chief U.S. negotiators for disarmament matters.

Amb. Mahley had played a key role negotiating the Biological and Chemical Weapons Treaties. He had retired but came back on special contract, so he had no vested interest in an arms treaty. He did not need to bolster his résumé and, in more candid moments, would admit the treaty was, in its essence, impractical.

A competitive pistol shooter who adored the theater and was passionate about animals, Amb. Mahley was a Renaissance man and the quintessential American to represent the U.S. He could talk about musicals, tactical nuclear weapons, tell you why the Colt's 1911 was his favorite sidearm, and brag about his NRA Life Membership all in one sitting. He was the only U.S. official willing to communicate with the NRA and the U.S. domestic firearms community who believed protecting civilian arms was essential and whose representatives were present during all the early ATT negotiations.

With the Bush Administration's support, Amb. Mahley was actually able to insert the following into the Expert Group's 2008 report, with no dissents:

> *It was also mentioned that, were an arms trade treaty to be considered feasible, it would need to reflect respect for the sovereignty of every State, without interfering in the internal affairs of States or their constitutional provisions, and respect for their territorial integrity. Exclusively internal transfers or national ownership provisions, including national constitutional protections on private ownership within the State's territory, should not fall under the arms trade treaty.*[9]

The term "national constitutional protections" was pure Second Amendment language—as close to the U.S. Constitution's Second Amendment as the U.N. could get. Amb. Mahley had delivered a message on behalf of the United States that the U.N. could have ATT, but not if it restricted civilian gun ownership. This was a major victory for the firearms community.

Amb. Mahley's language had been included in the 2008 Expert Group's report, because he spoke clearly on behalf of U.S. interests and because he maintained good relations with Chairman Moritán and the other 26 members of the Expert Group. He had also countered Amb. Duncan, revealing that he considered

him a perfect example of "perfidious Albion," a polite term for diplomatic duplic-
ity and treachery on the behalf of the British Empire, Albion being Greek for
Great Britain.

Barack Obama's election in 2008 had a major impact on the U.S. negotiating position, as the Clinton Department of State gave away what had been the
Bush Administration's red line. Making the situation even worse, Amb. Mahley
was diagnosed with pancreatic cancer in 2012. He attended some ATT sessions
while undergoing chemotherapy but died on March 1, 2014, an unsung hero
of the American Constitution.

The U.N. General Assembly, in 2008, created an Open-Ended Working
Group that the U.S. voted against at the end of the Bush Administration.[10] Amb.
Moritán chaired the Group and again named Rachel Stohl as a consultant. With
a Report in 2009, the U.N. General Assembly passed a third resolution creating a
Preparatory Committee for the eventual conference on the arms treaty,[11] though
still retaining a version of Amb. Mahley's "national constitutional protections"
language:

> *Acknowledging also the right of States to regulate internal transfers of arms and*
> *national ownership, including through national constitutional protections on*
> *private ownership, exclusively within their territory* . . . . [12]

While the Obama Administration expressed a willingness to work toward
a treaty the U.S. could support, Hillary Clinton assured Senators in her confirmation interviews that this country's support for such a treaty was still contingent on consensus. Even as she signaled a softening of the red line position
Bolton had clearly established during the Bush Administration, Mrs. Clinton
stuck with the consensus requirement.

At first, this amounted to a fallback red line in the eyes of Amb. Mahley and
others concerned about how such a treaty would impact the Second Amendment. But, by October 14, 2009, Secretary of State Hillary Clinton signaled
that the U.S. would no longer insist on consensus—and without U.S. support,
smaller nations that insisted on consensus were simply ignored. (All nations are
equal at the U.N., but some nations are more equal.) Suddenly, with the U.S.
voters in 2012 giving the Obama Administration a second term, the Experts
Group's 2008 Report and the civilian firearms protection language and consensus positions in the 2009 U.N. resolution were doomed.

National Rifle Association Preparations

NRA Executive Vice President Wayne LaPierre believed that once critics of
private firearms ownership realized they were not going to win in Congress,

whether with regulations alone, in the courts, or in the states, they would redouble their efforts to get a friendly president to use a treaty to impose restrictions on U.S. firearms owners. Mr. LaPierre also believed it inevitable that the NRA would end up fighting gun control in the international arena, as well as domestically, because "Ideologues don't give up. If they fail in one forum, they will seek another, and they will fail here both politically and in the courts."

More than a decade ago, Mr. LaPierre directed the NRA's Institute for Legislative Action (ILA) to begin monitoring anti-gun sentiment and activity within the United Nations and to begin warning NRA members and other American gun owners to add the U.N. to their political watch lists.

Persuading Americans of an international anti-gun enemy had been a difficult sell, when President Bill Clinton and the late Senator Edward M. Kennedy were taking aim at gun owners. It was difficult to fathom that the U.N. could ever pose a risk as great as those posed in the daily assaults by Clinton-Kennedy. But Mr. LaPierre's foresight proved correct. Armed with non-profit, tax-free status and government grants, by the late 1990s, U.S. anti-Second Amendment activists were looking to the United Nations as their best, last hope of implementing the agenda they had pushed in Congress. Anti-gun activists were convinced that the new President Obama would support them, as he had promised before his election, and that, if he could do so politically, would certainly be willing to do so behind the scenes at the United Nations. They were delighted when he chose Hillary Clinton as his Secretary of State, because she, like the new President, was a committed, long-term believer in restricting gun ownership for the average citizen, but not for the State.

Preparatory Meetings

Numerous regional seminars and workshops precede each major meeting at the U.N., in New York. The ATT Open-Ended Working Group morphed into a Preparatory Committee for the final U.N. Conference on the Arms Trade Treaty, with four crucial meetings in July 2010, February and July 2011, and February 2012. The European Union spent close to 2 million Euros (the U.S. Dollar fluctuated during this time, but more than $1.5 million) on regional seminars with foreign ministry officials, NGO activists, and U.N. bureaucrats.

All of this led to the four-week ATT conference, in July 2012, attended by more than 150 countries and 140 NGOs. Preparatory Committee meetings are not small; they typically involve more than 500 people, with 15 in the U.S. delegation alone and including representatives from the Departments of Defense, Justice, and State, and sometimes the White House National Security Council.

(U.S. delegations are headed by Department of State officials, even when the State Department has no particular expertise in the subject of a conference. The State Department has been notorious for ignoring U.S. delegation experts from the Defense Department and the Bureau of Alcohol, Tobacco and Firearms of the Justice Department when the topic is gun-related.)

Diplomats from U.N. member states love meetings in New York, where they spend fat per diems, daily living expense allowances, and housing allowances on shopping, theater, dining, and carousing in the Big Apple. U.N. meetings in New York never finish early. One can see why former U.S. Ambassador John Bolton and the late U.S. Senator Jesse Helms criticized the U.N. bureaucracy for bloat and wastefulness, as each meeting simply follows another.

The Bush Administration sent former Congressman Bob Barr and then-President of the NRA David Keene to the 2012 Conference, to add opinion and negotiation expertise to the dialogue. NRA Executive Vice President Wayne LaPierre, ILA head Chris Cox, and attorney Tom Mason were a part of the NRA NGO contingent.

Conveying the needed information and facts about gun rights and self-defense at the U.N. is tough duty, compared with lobbying Congress or a state legislature. A word about that hated profession, "lobbyist." Salesmen in any field are the least-liked profession of that field, be they car salesmen, pharmaceutical reps, whoever. Lobbyists are hired by associations or corporations on both sides of an issue; for example, you have the health food groups who want pure, organic food and genetically modified food labeling versus food manufacturers and farmers who want to grow and export food without restrictions. Almost every American hires lobbyists every day, as protected in the First Amendment as the right to petition. To lose this important communication channel to Congressmen and, in the case of the ATT, to the U.S. delegation on the Second Amendment is to subjugate our freedoms to the idea that an elected official knows information about every issue by virtue of being elected.

In the case of the ATT and the U.N., the basics of guns, their manufacture, use, laws, and the current regulatory minefield—almost every issue is misunderstood. Think "assault weapon" when a gun has added a hollow plastic handle that could look "military"—and multiply it by every sentence uttered and recorded in four-week meetings.

Guns That Self-Destruct

By Tom Mason

The Libyan Revolution was underway in 2011 when a U.N. official stopped me in the hall.

"I have a question about guns."

"OK. I'll try."

"Can one of you gun manufacturers make a gun that will only be good for, let's say, six months?"

"You're kidding me."

"No, I don't know anything about guns, but there are governments that want to supply arms to the rebels in Libya, but they don't want to add to the proliferation of small arms. We're wondering if you can make a gun that would only be good for six months, then would self-destruct."

"I'll get back to you on that."

U.N. Style

One does not have access to the working areas of the U.N. unless one is invited or has a grounds pass from a recognized U.N. NGO. Fortunately, the NRA had the foresight to become an NGO in 1996. The other major group working hand in hand with the NRA was the World Forum on Shooting Activities (WFSA), which the NRA helped create in 1996. The WFSA was also an official U.N. NGO.

At the U.N., there is no open meetings law or public records law. Delegates to conferences are usually officious mid-level diplomats and not elected representatives who have an implied duty to talk with constituents. The real power at the U.N. is held by the Security Council, whose resolutions are binding on member states. The General Assembly can pass resolutions, establish programs, and authorize conferences to draft treaties.

The style of U.N. meetings is unique. Everybody is "distinguished." Most speeches begin with flowery introductions about how important the meeting is. Speeches are always too long by American standards, except presentations by the U.S. diplomats, who, thankfully, tend to be short and to the point—American efficiency. Unlike country representatives, NGOs are allowed to speak at conferences and sometimes at meetings of the General Assembly committee, but NGOs are time-limited.

Twisted Symbolism
By David Keene

My first visit to the U.N. was an eye-opener. The U.N.'s entrance in New York includes a sculpture of a twisted pistol, meant to symbolize the U.N.'s desire for peace by destroying or banning weapons. The fact that the sculpture emphasizes the destruction not of a tank or artillery piece, but of sidearms, tells you where these folks really want to go. Oddly enough, the sculpture is used by both sides in their printed materials. For the anti-gun people, the sculpture represents what they want to see happen. For the firearms community, it represents what can happen if the U.N. were to ever have its way.

Once you get inside, you understand why the representatives of so many truly repressive regimes want to disarm civilians, because most of them are there representing dictators with a truly healthy fear of an armed populace.

U.N. representatives are appointed, not beholden to voters, so the U.N. is not a rule-bound organization with any pretense of saving the common man. It is an organization harder to follow and less transparent than congressional or state legislatures. Many meetings are closed, and suggested changes are delivered orally or are included in handouts or papers without dates or names. There may be a general discussion about a section of the treaty and proposed changes, then closed side negotiations and meetings on specific topics. Eventually, the chairman releases a draft he believes, or at least hopes, reflects the consensus of the group.

The actual language of the ATT was probably crafted by the consultant, Rachel Stohl, aided by Glenn McDonald and Sarah Parker of the Small Arms Survey, an anti-gun think tank based in Geneva, Switzerland. A draft may bear no relationship to the meeting itself, and the minority rights assured in our Constitution, like an amendment process for adding or deleting language or for and against votes on proposed changes, do not exist.

At the July 2010 Preparatory Committee on the ATT, a subgroup that was to "facilitate" a discussion of the treaty's category scopes or what arms would be covered recommended:

> *With regard to matters which should not be included in the ATT, some States were of the view that there should be a section on scope covering categories not within the ambit of the treaty, i.e., a section on "Exceptions." In this context, the following terms of types of weapons and types of activities/transactions were mentioned:*
>
> * *Internal transfers*
> * *National ownership and regulation of weapons*
> * *Sporting and hunting rifles for recreational purposes*
> * *Antique weapons* [13]

"National ownership and regulation" and "Sporting and hunting rifles for recreational purposes" seemed fair language, but a "Chairman's Draft" on July 22, 2010, ignored the language and moved the "national constitutional protection" language to the "principles"[14] section, where it would be non-enforceable:

Recognizing the sovereign right of States to determine any regulation of internal transfers of arms and national ownership exclusively within their territory, including through national constitutional ownership protections on private ownership.[15]

A civilian firearms exemption had to remain in an "operative" section of a U.N. treaty to require the parties to abide by the words. So, when both the language and the section were moved to the preamble, they became quotable, but meaningless. The final draft language read:

Mindful of the legitimate trade and lawful ownership, and use of certain conventional arms for recreational, cultural, historical, and sporting activities, where such trade, ownership and use are permitted or protected by law . . . .[16]

This put the language and intent of the ATT into direct conflict with the U.S. Constitution's Second Amendment's protection of the right to keep and bear arms, but neither Secretary of State Clinton nor President Obama objected. Pro-firearms lobbyists at the Conference raised this issue innumerable times to the U.S. delegation and were ignored.

The Preparatory Committee met again from February 28 to March 3 the next year. An initial paper[17] was distributed including an "exceptions" section:

IV. Exceptions
The following categories of transfers and weapons are not within the scope of the Treaty:

a) Internal transfers
b) Domestic ownership of weapons
c) Sporting and hunting rifles for recreational purpose
d) Antique weapons

This was potentially positive language, especially since it would be hard to separate "Domestic ownership of weapons" from civilian firearms, and it was in the exceptions section of the treaty draft. But it turned out to be just another delaying tactic to soothe the pro-firearms NGOs: it, too, was dropped from subsequent versions.

The controversy over the inclusion of civilian firearms peaked during the third meeting of the Preparatory Committee, July 11 to 15, 2011, the last substantive meeting and the one in which the draft submitted to the ATT Conference was finalized. The effort to exclude civilian firearms came from Canada, whose representative made the following statement on July 14:

Canada would like to see language in the "Principles" section that explicitly recognizes that there is a legal trade in small arms for legitimate civilian uses, including for sporting, hunting, and collecting purposes. To that end, therefore, Canada would propose the addition of a 20th clause to the "Principles" section that would read as follows: Reaffirming that small arms have certain legitimate civilian uses, including hunting and collecting purposes . . . . We welcome clear and simple categories set out in the Scope section. However, with regard to the inclusion of small arms and light weapons, Canada supports the proposal made by Japan and Italy[18] on March 16 to exclude sporting and hunting firearms for recreational use from the treaty.[19]

Canada knew that the principles section would have no binding impact; to mean anything, the language would have to be moved to the operative sections. Still, it was better than nothing. The Canadians then proposed to put an exclusion in the scope section of the Treaty for real impact, and Brazil, Costa Rica, and Mexico quickly attacked. Mexico led the fight:

- *Mexico considers that the ATT should establish flexible lists that can cover all types of conventional weapons, including small arms and light weapons, hence permitting the development of the concept "conventional arms" together with the future technological developments of the armaments industry. A static treaty would considerably limit its relevance.*
- *It should regulate the trade of arms based on the probable use of it and not on the user. That is, we should not limit ourselves to the analysis of the weapon's guardian, but to the possible use given to it. That is why it is important to maintain control throughout the whole life cycle of the weapon, from its production to its destruction.*
- *All conventional arms must be included in this regulation, regardless of their purpose: there is no distinction between arms created for sports and arms created for military use when in the hands of criminals.[20]*

This was a crucial time, and the U.S. flinched, refusing to support Canada in a clear break from the Bush Administration policy. In early July, Amb. Mahley warned on the Floor of the Conference that the U.S. would not join consensus on a treaty that included civilian arms. But by mid-month, other State Department officials were contradicting him in diplomatic language, saying the U.S. would not agree to any treaty that "impacted" Second Amendment rights. Throughout early July, Amb. Mahley did what he could to protect the Second Amendment, but things were changing.

Language is crucial. With the treaty lacking a specific exemption, the Obama Administration simply asserted that the treaty has "no impact on the Second Amendment," a fiction that remains its official stance. Amb. Mahley continued to support gun owners' rights when he could, but, in private, he began alluding to State Department pressure.

As it became increasingly obvious that the U.S. opposition had shifted to support ATT, the Senate weighed in with two strong letters of opposition. Senator Jerry Moran, a Republican from Kansas, organized a letter with 44 Senate co-signers:

July 22, 2011

President Barack Obama
1600 Pennsylvania Avenue, NW
Washington, D.C. 20500

Secretary of State Hillary Clinton 2201 C St., NW
Washington, D.C. 20520

Dear President Obama and Secretary Clinton:

As defenders of the right of Americans to keep and bear arms, we write to express our grave concern about the dangers posed by the United Nations' Arms Trade Treaty. Our country's sovereignty and the constitutional protection of these individual freedoms must not be infringed.

In October of 2009 at the U.N. General Assembly, your administration voted for the U.S. to participate in negotiating this treaty. Preparatory committee meetings are now underway in anticipation of a conference in 2012 to finalize the treaty. Based on the process to date, we are concerned that the Arms Trade Treaty poses dangers to rights protected under the Second Amendment for the following reasons.

First, while the 2009 resolution on the treaty acknowledged the existence of "national constitutional protections on private ownership," it placed the existence of these protections in the context of "the right of States to regulate internal transfers of arms and national ownership," implying that constitutional protections must be interpreted in the context of the broader power of the state to regulate. We are concerned both by the implications of the 2009 resolution and by the hostility to private firearms ownership manifested by similar resolutions in previous years such as the 2008 resolution, which called for the "highest possible standards" of control.

Second, your Administration agreed to participate in the negotiation only if it "operates under the rule of consensus decision-making." Given that the 2008 resolution on the treaty was adopted almost unanimously—with only the U.S. and Zimbabwe in opposition—it seems clear that there is a near-consensus on the requirement for the "highest possible standards," which will inevitably put severe pressure on the United States to compromise on important issues.

Third, U.N. member states regularly argue that no treaty controlling the transfer of arms internationally can be effective without controls on transfers inside member states. Any treaty resulting from the Arms Trade Treaty process that seeks in any way to regulate the domestic manufacturing, assembly, possession, transfer, or purchase of firearms, ammunition, and related items would be completely unacceptable to us.

Fourth, reports from the 2010 Preparatory Meeting make it clear that many U.N. member states aim to craft an extremely broad treaty. A declaration by Mexico and other Central and South American countries, for example, called for the treaty to cover "All types of conventional weapons (regardless of their purpose), including small arms and light weapons, ammunition, components, parts, technology and related materials." Such a broad treaty would be completely unenforceable, and would pose dangers to all U.S. businesses and individuals involved in any aspect of the firearms industry. At the 2010 Meeting, the U.S. representative twice expressed frustration with the wide-ranging and unrealistic scope of the projected treaty. We are concerned that these cautions will not be heeded, and that the Senate will eventually be called upon to consider a treaty that is so broad it cannot effectively be subject to our advice and consent.

Fifth, and finally, the underlying philosophy of the Arms Trade Treaty is that transfers to and from governments are presumptively legal, while transfers to non-state actors (such as terrorists and criminals) are, at best, problematic. We agree that sales and transfers to criminals and terrorists are unacceptable, but we will oppose any treaty that places the burden of controlling crime and terrorism on law-abiding Americans, instead of where it belongs: on the culpable member states of the United Nations who have failed to take the necessary steps to block trafficking that is already illegal under existing laws and agreements.

As the treaty process continues, we strongly encourage your Administration to uphold our country's constitutional protections of civilian firearms ownership. These freedoms are not negotiable, and we will oppose ratification of an Arms Trade Treaty presented to the Senate that in any way restricts the rights of law-abiding U.S. citizens to manufacture, assemble, possess, transfer or purchase firearms, ammunition, and related items.

Sincerely,
Jerry Moran et al.

Montana Democratic Senator Jon Tester's separate letter had 13 co-sponsors and read:

July 26, 2011

The Honorable Barack Obama
President
The White House
1600 Pennsylvania Avenue NW
Washington, D.C. 20500

The Honorable Hillary Clinton
Secretary of State
2201 C Street NW
Washington, D.C. 20520

Dear President Obama and Secretary Clinton:
As staunch defenders of the rights of law-abiding Americans to keep and bear arms, we write regarding ongoing negotiations of the United Nations' Arms Trade Treaty, and to express concerns about any provisions that could potentially infringe upon those rights.

We support efforts to better regulate the international trade of conventional weapons, but such efforts must be done in a responsible manner. We should do everything we can to ensure these weapons do not end up in the hands of human rights abusers, terrorist groups, insurgents or organized criminal enterprises. Further, we should not allow the unregulated trade of these weapons to continue fueling conflict and instability in nations around the world. The profound human and economic toll from these conflicts is staggering and the subsequent impact on our nation's economic and security interests are increasing. The United States has adopted a rigorous system of arms export controls and it is time for other nations to abide by some of those same standards.

For the past few years, negotiations for the Arms Trade Treaty have progressed. As your Administration continues to engage in these negotiations, we strongly urge you to address a number of our concerns.

First and foremost, the Arms Trade Treaty must not in any way regulate the domestic manufacture, possession or sales of firearms or ammunition. Firearms possession is an individual right guaranteed by the Second Amendment and this cannot be subordinated, directly or indirectly, by any international treaty. We are encouraged that your administration is working to ensure that signatory countries will maintain the exclusive authority to regulate arms within their own borders. That must continue to be non-negotiable. We also oppose any inclusion of small arms, light weapons, ammunition or related materials that would make the Treaty overly broad and virtually unenforceable. Finally, the establishment of any sort of international gun registry that could impede upon the privacy rights of law-abiding gun owners is a non-starter.

As members of the United States Senate, it is our constitutional responsibility to advise and consent on the ratification of the United Nations' Arms Trade Treaty. Before we could support ratification, we must have assurances that our concerns are adequately addressed and that the Treaty will not in any way impede upon the Constitutional rights of American gun owners.

Anything short of this commitment would be unacceptable.

We appreciate your consideration on this issue and look forward to your response.

Sincerely,
Jon Tester et al.

State Department officials hastened to assure Senators that the ATT would not affect Second Amendment rights but refused to clarify the protections in the treaty. Simultaneously, Mrs. Clinton and the Obama Administration reassured the U.N. that the Senate objections could be safely ignored; many foreign delegates do not understand that U.S. treaties must be ratified by the Senate.

Canada and the U.S. Senate had little effect on Amb. Moritán, who released another paper on July 14 that was never endorsed and only sent as an appendix to the Preparatory Committee's Report. The Moritán paper became the working document for the forthcoming ATT Conference. Only the preamble contained a civilian arms section that somehow again contained the "constitutional language":

Recognizing the sovereign right of States to determine any regulation of internal transfers of arms and national ownership exclusively within their territory, including through national constitutional ownership protections on private ownership.[21]

Preambles may sound comforting, but they have no bearing unless there is a disagreement as to the meaning of a later section. We can never know for certain, but it is likely that the "constitutional" language came back into the preamble as a sop to Amb. Mahley by Amb. Moritán. The two had a good relationship, lunching together frequently, and a quiet word between U.S. Ambassador and Chairman in the interest of consensus is typical of the way the U.N. functions.

Representatives of the U.S. firearms community met with other delegations and the U.S. government in New York and Washington, trying to build on the "national constitutional protection" language and the language proposed by Canada. During the July meeting and leading up to the actual Conference a year later, they proposed this language be added as paragraph "3" in Section IV, page 5, of the Chairman's July 14, 2011, paper:

The scope of the treaty does not include arms held under state parties' national constitutional protections on private ownership or antique arms or other arms legally owned, possessed or transported under state parties' national laws, for sporting, hunting, recreational, cultural or other lawful purposes.

The language was the result of extensive consultations between firearms groups and arms manufacturers.[22] There are seven key phrases in this version. The following is an analysis of the language done by members of the firearms community, thus the use of the term "we":

(1) The scope of the treaty does not include . . .
This is to get around the problem that some of the things we want exempted from an ATT are not small arms per se. We originally wrote language that was an exception to "small arms." But, there are things that are legal in both the U.S. and Canada that would not fit into this narrow small arms category—such as military vehicles owned by collectors. This would also take care of the problem of legal automatic weapons in the U.S. and larger non-firearms weapons in Canada.
(2) arms . . .
We should use the term "arms" instead of "firearms" or even "small arms and light weapons." Arms is used in the 7/14/11 Chairman's paper and it is U.S. Second Amendment language which speaks in terms of the "right to bear arms..." and not firearms.
(3) . . . held under national constitutional protections on private ownership . . .
This is basically US Second Amendment language[23] – "...national constitutional protections on private ownership. . ." This crucial phrase was in the 7/14/11 Chairman's paper and was in earlier papers, resolutions and reports.[24] See chapter 8 for the Clinton Benghazi emails that tell the Administration's actual thinking."
(4) . . . or antiques arms . . .
(5) . . . or arms legally owned, possessed or transported under state party's national laws for . . .
This gets us around the definition problem (the treaty having to define the exception) because it refers to national laws. The definitions will essentially be in the various national laws.
(6) . . . sporting, hunting, recreational or cultural purposes . . .
This is Canadian language from the 7/14/11 statement and the reference to "cultural" is for the benefit of museums and the collectors.
(7) . . . or other lawful purposes.
This is for those jurisdictions allowing for self-defense as a reason for owning arms.

The Bush Administration's work, Canada's objections, a majority of U.S. Senators, and these negotiations had absolutely no impact on the Obama Administration's position. Clinton's State Department and the White House continued to assert that the Treaty would not affect the Second Amendment. But anyone who followed the negotiations leading up to the promulgation of the final draft knew otherwise: Second Amendment protections had been eliminated, with U.S. support. The White House and the Administration were lying and everyone involved knew they were lying, but as has happened so often in domestic politics, the Obama Administration repeated the lie forcefully— assuring skeptics they could ignore the proceedings, the draft language, and those who disagreed with assessment and "trust us"—and got away with it, as

Congress first complained, then rolled over.

In an unusual appearance at the U.N., on July 14, 2011, NRA's Wayne LaPierre made clear that blind trust was not enough for the NRA, the Senate, or the American people:

> *Mr. Chairman, thank you for this brief opportunity to address the committee. The NRA was founded in 1871, and ever since has staunchly defended the rights of its four million members, America's 80 million law-abiding gun owners, and freedom-loving Americans throughout our country. In 1996, the NRA was recognized as an NGO of the United Nations and, ever since then, has defended the constitutional freedom of Americans in this arena. The NRA is the largest and most active firearms rights organization in the world and, although some members of this committee may not like what I have to say, I am proud to defend the tens of millions of lawful people NRA represents.*
>
> *This present effort for an Arms Trade Treaty, or ATT, is now in its fifth year. We have closely monitored this process with increasing concern. We've reviewed the statements of the countries participating in these meetings. We've listened to other NGOs and read their numerous proposals and reports, as well as carefully examined the papers you have produced.*
>
> *We've watched and read, listened and monitored. Now, we must speak out.*
>
> *The Right to Keep and Bear Arms in defense of self, family and country is ultimately self-evident and is part of the Bill of Rights to the United States Constitution. Reduced to its core, it is about fundamental individual freedom, human worth, and self-destiny.*
>
> *We reject the notion that American gun owners must accept any lesser amount of freedom in order to be accepted among the international community. Our Founding Fathers long ago rejected that notion and forged our great nation on the principle of freedom for the individual citizen—not for the government.*
>
> *Mr. Chairman, those working on this treaty have asked us to trust them ... but they've proven to be unworthy of that trust.*
>
> *We are told "Trust us; an ATT will not ban possession of any civilian firearms." Yet, the proposals and statements presented to date have argued exactly the opposite, and—perhaps most importantly—proposals to ban civilian firearms ownership have not been rejected.*
>
> *We are told "Trust us; an ATT will not interfere with state domestic regulation of firearms." Yet, there are constant calls for exactly such measures.*
>
> *We are told "Trust us; an ATT will only affect the illegal trade in firearms." But then we're told that in order to control the illegal trade, all states must control the legal firearms trade.*
>
> *We are told, "Trust us; an ATT will not require registration of civilian firearms." Yet, there are numerous calls for record-keeping, and firearms tracking*

from production to eventual destruction. That's nothing more than gun registration by a different name.

We are told, "Trust us; an ATT will not create a new international bureaucracy." Well, that's exactly what is now being proposed—with a tongue-in-cheek assurance that it will just be a SMALL bureaucracy.

We are told, "Trust us; an ATT will not interfere with the lawful international commerce in civilian firearms." But a manufacturer of civilian shotguns would have to comply with the same regulatory process as a manufacturer of military attack helicopters.

We are told, "Trust us; an ATT will not interfere with a hunter or sport shooter travelling internationally with firearms." However, he would have to get a so-called "transit permit" merely to change airports for a connecting flight.

Mr. Chairman, our list of objections extends far beyond the proposals I just mentioned. Unfortunately, my limited time today prevents me from providing greater detail on each of our objections. I can assure you, however, that each is based on American law, as well as the fundamental rights guaranteed by the United States Constitution.

It is regrettable that proposals affecting civilian firearms ownership are woven throughout the proposed ATT. That being the case, however, there is only one solution to this problem: the complete removal of civilian firearms from the scope of any ATT. I will repeat that point as it is critical and not subject to negotiation—civilian firearms must not be part of any ATT. On this there can be no compromise, as American gun owners will never surrender their Second Amendment freedom.

It is also regrettable to find such intense focus on record-keeping, oversight, inspections, supervision, tracking, tracing, surveillance, marking, documentation, verification, paper trails and data banks, new global agencies and data centers. Nowhere do we find a thought about respecting anyone's right of self-defense, privacy, property, due process, or observing personal freedoms of any kind.

Mr. Chairman, I'd be remiss if I didn't also discuss the politics of an ATT. For the United States to be a party to an ATT, it must be ratified by a two-thirds vote of the U.S. Senate. Some do not realize that under the U.S. Constitution, the ultimate treaty power is not the President's power to negotiate and sign treaties; it is the Senate's power to approve them.

To that end, it's important for the Preparatory Committee to understand that the proposed ATT is already strongly opposed in the Senate—the very body that must approve it by a two-thirds majority. There is a letter addressed to President Obama and Secretary of State Clinton that is currently being circulated for the signatures of Senators who oppose the ATT. Once complete, this letter will demonstrate that the proposed ATT will not pass the U.S. Senate.

So there is extremely strong resistance to the ATT in the United States, even before the treaty is tabled. We are not aware of any precedent for this—rejecting a proposed treaty before it's even submitted for consideration—but it speaks to the level of opposition. The proposed ATT has become more than just controversial, as the Internet is awash with articles and messages calling for its rejection. And those messages are all based on the same objection—infringement on the constitutional freedom of American gun owners.

The cornerstone of our freedom is the Second Amendment. Neither the United Nations, nor any other foreign influence, has the authority to meddle with the freedoms guaranteed by our Bill of Rights, endowed by our Creator, and due to all humankind.

Therefore, the NRA will fight with all of its strength to oppose any ATT that includes civilian firearms within its scope.

Thank you.[25]

The reaction to Mr. LaPierre's speech at the U.N. was indignant outrage by some delegates who were not used to the stern language and straight talk that said the Treaty would be rejected if it affected American's Second Amendment rights. As actor Jack Nicholson said to the courtroom in the 1992 movie *A Few Good Men*, "You can't handle the truth." Had the delegates listened to Mr. LaPierre and heeded his warning, the ATT could have been easily modified to and passed as a non-controversial agreement to restrict not civilian-owned firearms, but weapons of war.

The July 2012 ATT Conference

When the actual ATT Conference convened in July 2012, Under Secretary of State for Disarmament Affairs Thomas Countryman replaced the ailing Amb. Mahley as head of the U.S. delegation. The contrast between the two men could not have been greater. Mr. Countryman had worked for the Department of State since 1982 and was notorious for his shaggy, Beatle-like haircut. A relatively young careerist, his agenda was to burnish his reputation by coming away with a treaty at any cost, even if it risked disarming American gun owners. He had little knowledge of firearms or their use but sought a Kumbaya moment with the ATT. How bad could one more treaty be?

Ambassador Mahley was a hardened veteran of the diplomatic Cold Wars. He had no illusions about the process or treaty and wanted to represent the U.S. and the Constitution fairly. Amb. Mahley remained as deputy, but with cancer and discouragement taking its toll, he was too much of a gentleman and a team player to disagree publicly with Mr. Countryman.

Although the British Labour Party had won re-election overwhelmingly in May, the powerful head of the British delegation, John Duncan, was removed suddenly and temporarily named Governor General of the Falkland Islands, the British equivalent of Siberia. Rumors were that the diplomat and the head of a NGO had become too close, but such accusations were never proven. Jo Adamson, a charming but completely unthreatening woman civil servant, replaced Amb. Duncan.

According to U.N. tradition, the month-long conference was to be led again by Amb. Moritán, who was soon out of his depth. Without the two powerful main opposing delegations of the U.S. and Britain losing strength in their delegations, conferees spent the first week arguing over whether and where Palestine should be seated. The controversy was resolved when Palestine was seated as an observer beside the Vatican.

Australia, a major ATT supporter, paid for 50 delegates from Third World countries to attend in a typical method for buying U.N. votes. In a highly unusual move, Australia's official delegation included Sarah Parker, an anti-gun first-stringer.[26] A brilliant, charming, and strikingly beautiful attorney from Australia, she was the brains behind many of the pro-ATT articles and reports preceding the Conference. Australia's active push for the ATT was no mystery, but Australia and Ms. Parker spent much of the ATT Conference currying favor with anti-gun nations as part of the campaign to enable Australia to be voted onto the powerful U.N. Security Council, an enviable advantage in world affairs.

The Conference began with a series of rambling speeches from various delegates on the evils of weapons, especially small arms—Mexico even asked that the Treaty cover non-explosive weapons,[27] such as slings, spears, and bows and arrows. The European Union (EU) wanted to sign the Treaty as a "regional integration organization." China would withdraw its objections to the treaty if the EU would lift the Tiananmen Square arms embargo. Russia was unenthusiastic, even before it began supplying arms to the Syrian civil war. Finally, the U.S. expressed concern about ammunition's inclusion in the ATT's restrictions.

This illustrates one of the inconsistencies in U.S. policy. Until recently, restricting ammunition has been on the gun-controller's agenda, but on this Amb. Mahley's advice held. The Ambassador had managed ammo dumps in Vietnam during his military career and regaled anybody who would listen with stories of how one could not keep track of pallets of 105mm artillery rounds, much less small arms ammunition. U.S. delegates from the Defense Department agreed. Although there are increasing efforts aimed at ammunition regulation as a means of gun control, such as California Lt. Governor Gavin Newsom's ill-conceived ballot measure, they have failed at the ballot box and in practice.

Amb. Moritán could never manage all these real and tangential disagreements, so he appointed seven working groups. Not one could agree on a recommendation. Some countries wanted limits on arms transfers to non-state actors (i.e., rebel groups), while conservative countries were concerned about references to gender-based violence.

The day before the Conference was supposed to end, July 26, 2012, Amb. Moritán released his draft. Even the already weak pro-Second Amendment language in the preamble was weakened further. "National constitutional protections" was gone, with only a reference to "constitutional systems":

> *Reaffirming the sovereign right and responsibility of any State to regulate and control transfers of conventional arms that take place exclusively within its territory, pursuant to its own legal or constitutional systems . . . .*[28]

This rhetorical nod to the U.S. and the firearms community was meaningless, worse than no reference at all. The "responsibility of any State to regulate and control" could actually be read as a *duty* to implement domestically within its own borders gun-control measures included in the ATT, rather than to protect the rights of citizens. The non-binding preamble now read:

> *Taking note of the legitimate trade and use of certain conventional arms, inter alia, for recreational, cultural, historical and sporting activities and lawful ownership where such ownership and use are permitted and protected by law . . . .*[29]

Mr. Countryman and the Obama Administration predictably claimed they had protected U.S. firearms rights. That the President and his Secretary of State could make this claim with a straight face astounds anyone with knowledge of the proceedings or the diplomatic meaning of the words. However, in a surprise move the afternoon of July 27, Mr. Countryman announced that the U.S. could not support the draft. Given the consensus rule and the prestige of the U.S., his announcement effectively ended the Conference. Mexico and 89 other states immediately released a statement claiming the treaty had just needed a little more time.

Ending the Conference in July 2012, in the midst of Obama's re-election, was a stroke of political genius. Mr. Obama gained domestic deniability about the treaty's intention to impose international regulation of American gun ownership. His reelection committee ran television ads in several pro-gun states, which featured the President asserting his belief in the Second Amendment.

Had an ATT come out of New York with the U.S. seal of approval, Second Amendment supporters would have been outraged and might well have hurt President Obama's re-election chances. As it did turn out, those who wanted to could argue to skeptics that the President had actually rejected the treaty. Alas, within a few hours of his re-election, Obama asked in writing for the U.N. to immediately pass ATT so the U.S. could sign it.

[1] *United Nations General Assembly, "The Arms Trade Treaty," Res. A/67/234 B, 2013.*

[2] *Small Arms Survey, Small Arms Survey 2007: Guns and the City (Cambridge, UK: Cambridge University Press, 2007) 39.*

[3] *Ibid., 46.*

[4] *Óscar Arias Sanchez. "The Global Arms Trade: Strengthening International Regulations," Harvard International Review, Summer 2008.*

[5] *United Nations General Assembly, "Toward an Arms Trade Treaty . . ." Res. A/RES/61/89, 2006. Accessed August 19, 2014, http://www.un.org/ga/search/view_doc.asp?symbol=A/RES/61/89&Lang=E.*

[6] *Ms. Peters led IANSA until 2010. Today, she is considered one of the world's most effective, vocal, and controversial anti-gun activists, though she toned down her rhetoric as she and her allies maneuvered within the U.N. for an ATT.*

[7] *Canada reversed its position on the ATT with the election of Justin Trudeau.*

[8] *United Nations General Assembly, "Toward an Arms Trade Treaty: establishing common international standards for the import, export and transfer of conventional arms," Res. A/RES/63/240, 2009. Accessed August 24, 2014, http://www.un.org/ga/search/view_doc.asp?symbol=A/RES/63/240&Lang=E .*

[9] *United Nations General Assembly, "Report of the Open-ended Working Group Towards an Arms Trade Treaty: establishing common international standards for the import, export and transfer of conventional arms," A/AC.277/2009/1, 2009. Accessed August 24, 2014, http://daccess-dds-ny.un.org/doc/UNDOC/GEN/N09/412/00/PDF/N0941200.pdf?OpenElement.*

[10] *United Nations General Assembly, "The Arms Trade Treaty," Res. A/RES/64/48, 2009. Accessed August 24, 2014, http://www.europarl.europa.eu/meetdocs/2009_2014/documents/sede/dv/sede051211unres_/sede051211unres_en.pdf.*

[11] *United Nations, "Facilitator's Summary for Scope," Preparatory Committee for the United Nations Conference on the Arms Trade Treaty, July 12-23, 2010. (No official number or designation.)*

[12] *United Nations General Assembly, "The Arms Trade Treaty," Res. A/RES/64/48, 2009. Accessed August 24, 2014, http://www.europarl.europa.eu/meetdocs/2009_2014/documents/sede/dv/sede051211unres_/sede051211unres_en.pdf.*

[13] *United Nations, "Chairman's Draft Paper, 22 July 2010," Preparatory Committee for the United Nations Conference on the Arms Trade Treaty, 12-23 July 2010. (No official number or designation.)*

[14] *The actual role of "principles," whether they were controlling language, was unclear at the time.*

15 *United Nations, "Chairman's Draft Paper, 22 July 2010," Preparatory Committee for the United Nations Conference on the Arms Trade Treaty, 12-23 July 2010. (No official number or designation.)*

16 *Ibid.*

17 *United Nations, "Chairman's Draft Paper," Preparatory Committee for the United Nations Conference on the Arms Trade Treaty, 28 February 2011. (No official number or designation.)*

18 *Japan and Italy both commented that sporting arms should be excluded from the ATT, but neither chose to pursue the position.*

19 *Canada, "Statement by Canada," Preparatory Committee for the United Nations Conference on the Arms Trade Treaty, 14 July 2011.*

20 *Mexico, "Statement by Mexico," Preparatory Committee for the United Nations Conference on the Arms Trade Treaty, 14 July 2011.*

21 *United Nations, "Chairman's Draft Paper, 14 July 2011," Preparatory Committee for the United Nations Conference on the Arms Trade Treaty, July 11-15, 2011. (No official number or designation.)*

22 *Most of the groups are members of the World Forum on Shooting Activities, including associations from Australia, Denmark, England, France, Germany, Italy, Sweden, South Africa, etc.*

23 *District of Columbia v. Heller, 554 U.S. 570 (S. Ct., 2008) and McDonald v. Chicago, 561 U.S. 742 (S. Ct., 2010).*

24 *The full text of language is: "Recognizing the sovereign right of States to determine any regulation of internal transfer of arms and national ownership exclusively within their territory, including through national constitutional protections on private ownership." As found in the Chairman's 3 March 2011 paper and almost identical language can be found in General Assembly Resolution A/RES/64/48. Paper was misdated 3 March 2010 but is in fact from 3 March 2011.*

25 *National Rifle Association of America, "Statement of Wayne LaPierre," Preparatory Committee for the United Nations Conference on the Arms Trade Treaty, 14 July 2011. Accessed August 24, 2014. http://www.nraila.org/legislation/federal-legislation/2011/7/nra-delivers-remarks-at-united-nations.aspx.*

26 *Australia included Robert Green of the Sporting Shooters of Australia as a member of their delegation, but Parker was the major player with her hand in the till of U.N. policy.*

27 *Mexico, "Statement of Mexico—July 13," United Nations Conference on the Arms Trade Treaty, 2-27 July 2012.*

28 *United Nations. "Draft of the Arms Trade Treaty." A/CONF.217/CRP.1. August 2012. Accessed August 24, 2014 http://www.un.org/ga/search/view_doc.asp?symbol=A/CONF.217/CRP.1&Lang=E.*

29 *Ibid.*

CHAPTER 7

Obama's Second Term

Adjourning a U.N. Conference without consensus would usually stop a treaty cold, but the forces behind the ATT now counted President Obama and Mrs. Clinton in support. Within hours of re-election, Mr. Obama signed a strong letter asking the U.N. General Assembly to take up the treaty and pass it in all haste, even though the U.S. had been the country to stop the last meeting. A resolution in December 2012 calling for a second ATT Conference expressed disappointment that the July Conference had ended in failure and named the second gathering "The Final United Nations Conference on the Arms Trade Treaty." The meeting was scheduled for March 18-28, 2013, and used Roberto Moritán's July 26 last-minute unapproved text as the basis for negotiations.

Amb. Moritán had fallen out of favor in Argentina and was not selected as President. Ambassador Peter Woolcott of Australia replaced him. Rachel Stohl was still a consultant, but a British diplomat, Guy Pollard, was assigned to help with the negotiations. Misters Woolcott and Pollard traveled the world, holding consultations with all the major state players and pro-ATT NGOs before the March meeting. Amb. Moritán clearly favored the anti-gun NGOs. The Australian Mr. Woolcott was comfortable discussing firearms—but he knew his orders, and his mission was to get an ATT at all costs. He could not go against his government. Still, there was chance he might help the civilian gun groups. Hope springs eternal.

The World Forum on Shooting Activities (WFSA) is an official NGO. Founded by the NRA and 40 other gun groups in 1996, WFSA has attended every major U.N. conference involving firearms since its formation. The NRA and the WFSA, including its President, Germany's Herbert Keusgen, attended the Conference. Tom Mason approached Misters Woolcott and Pollard with concerns about civilian firearms being included within the scope of the treaty and with the exclusion language so many Americans and Europeans like President Keusgen thought important.

Both Misters Woolcott and Pollard seemed to listen sympathetically, but then Mr. Woolcott objected in perfect diplomatic code: an NGO might write language, but a government must propose that draft language for consideration.

Although every effort was made, the Clinton State Department would never agree to an exception for civilian gun ownership, and Canada would not ask for insertion absent U.S. support. The path to insertion of the civilian exemption language was closed.

Oops

By Tom Mason

At the beginning of a conference in 2012, I was arranging pro-gun NGO presentations when the U.N. called.

"Mr. Mason, there is a problem with Mr. XYZ."

"I know him, he represents ABC Association, what's the problem?" (He was the same man who wanted self-destroying guns for Libya.)

"He just tried to get through security with a gun in his briefcase."

"Where is he?"

"We turned him over to the police."

"I'll be right there."

This was one of my longest days at the U.N. The New York Police Department charged the man with illegal possession of a handgun. Since I'm an experienced criminal attorney, I could have asked for special permission to appear before the local court, but I would be ignorant of the local law, procedures, and, even more important, the District Attorney and his ways. The legal world calls this being "home-towned." Think of the late 1980s *Matlock* television legal drama starring Andy Griffith as a Southern prosecutor where a know-nothing Yankee from out-of-state defends. Just guess who wins the trial.

"Counsel, it's nice of you to have come from Or-y-gun to represent Mr. XYZ, but we do things a little different here"—as they lock up my client forever because of my negligence. Fortunately, after a few hours of calls, a firm that had defended gun companies sent an experienced defense lawyer to get the defendant released.

Our hero was licensed to carry in a neighboring state and had a 1911 pistol in his briefcase. Instead of flying or taking the train to New York, he had driven, forgetting he had the gun with him. What good a gun in your briefcase would do you is beyond me.

The case went on for months, cost the guy thousands of dollars, but he was eventually able to plead to a misdemeanor and pay a fine. Given Mayor Bloomberg's attitude toward guns, he was lucky.

Not as lucky as I was. The press never got the story, and the only thing I had to suffer was the good-natured harassment of my U.N. friends, who would ask me for months, with a grin, if I was armed.

The March 2013 Conference was as well attended as the July 2012 Conference. Mr. Woolcott released his first treaty draft on March 20, then a second two days later. He was moving things much faster than Amb. Moritán had, and although the March 22 draft did not include the firearms community's language, it at least included a helpful mention of what sorts of arms were to be included in the category of "small arms":

> *Article 5 (4) General Implementation . . . Each party is encouraged to apply the provisions of this Treaty to the broadest range of conventional arms. No national definition of any of the categories covered in Article 2 (1) shall cover less than the descriptions used in the United Nations Register of Conventional Arms at the time of entry into force of this Treaty.*[1]

Because the Register of Conventional Arms only included military arms, this language seemed to allow countries to exclude civilian arms. No one knows how the language made it into the draft, but as soon as anti-gun forces grasped its implications, it was dropped. In the end, the weakest of language in the preamble implied something regarding civilian ownership:

> *Reaffirming the sovereign right of any State to regulate and control conventional arms exclusively within its territory, pursuant to its own legal or constitutional system . . . .*
> *Mindful of the legitimate trade and lawful ownership, and use of certain conventional arms for recreational, cultural, historical, and sporting activities, where such trade, ownership and use are permitted or protected by law . . . .*

The first paragraph saying that a state has the right to regulate arms is a facile statement of the obvious. The only "right" referred to in the language is the right of the state to regulate.

The reference to "constitutional systems" was a slap to the face of the American firearms community. The drafters would mention the word "constitution" but gave it no content or meaning.

The ATT preamble mentions ownership, but not *civilian* ownership. This cannot be an accident. In a worst-case scenario, it could mean ownership by private security firms, or police officers owning their own guns. There is a reference to "cultural, historical, and sporting activities," but no reference to self-defense. Secretary Hillary Clinton and the U.S. delegation knew that the Supreme Court *Heller*[2] case had ruled that the Second Amendment included a right of self-defense, so some nod to this in language is in order. Of all human rights, self-preservation must rank high.[3] The references to "cultural and historical" might refer to collecting antiques and historical reenactments, and the reference to "sporting" reflects the elitist U.N. attitude that the less sophisticated might hunt ducks if they insist on it. The U.N. did not go quite as far as Rebecca Peters and tell us to get new hobbies.

The U.S. Flip-Flop

The general feeling was that the Conference would adopt Mr. Woolcott's March 26 draft, but, on the evening of March 28, as Mr. Woolcott tried to announce a consensus for moving forward and closing the Conference, the unexpected happened: Iran announced that it could not support the draft for its own reasons.

In a dramatic confrontation, Mr. Woolcott verbally dueled back and forth with the Iranian delegate over what that meant. Mr. Woolcott said that even though Iran disagreed with the draft, there appeared to be consensus. The Iranian delegate[4] played him and would then say that Iran disagreed with the draft, and that meant what it meant: the body could not proceed. The Iranian delegate would not say overtly that they were opposed to consensus, but it was clear to everybody that he was invoking the consensus rule. Syria and the Democratic People's Republic of Korea (North Korea, DPRK) quickly joined Iran, and, finally, Russia ended the discussion by saying there was no consensus.

Following U.N. precedent, these objections would have forced Mr. Woolcott to end the Conference, but precedent no longer applied in the rush to have a treaty.

Mexico pointed out that there was no U.N. official definition of consensus and that Mr. Woolcott could proceed. Mr. Woolcott tried to play down the consensus rule until Russia objected, insisting that consensus meant everyone had to agree, just as it always had. Russia had never really supported an ATT, and this was an opportunity to back three of its "bad boy" allies.

Ignoring Russia is not an option.

Although the U.S. remained silent through most of this, it appeared that the need for consensus meant the treaty could not be sent to the General Assembly for a vote. As the Conference came to its tumultuous end, ATT proponents vowed to ignore the consensus rule and ask the General Assembly to adopt Mr. Woolcott's last draft rejected by the Conference.

On April 1, 2013, the U.S. sponsored U.N. General Assembly resolution A/67/L.58, to adopt the draft of the treaty that had been on the table at the end of the Conference. This clear reversal of U.S. policy was a signal that no diplomat could miss. The resolution passed on April 2, 2013, by a vote of 154 to 3, with only Iran, Syria, and the DPRK voting no. Twenty-three nations abstained, including China, Egypt, India, Indonesia, Russia, and Saudi Arabia—more than half the world's population. Abstaining from a vote at the U.N. is a polite way to vote "No," so these abstentions were significant. In voting for the treaty, the U.S. violated its own red line that mandated the ATT be adopted by consensus.

China and Russia are two of the largest arms manufacturers in the world. India and Saudi Arabia are among the world's biggest buyers of arms. Russia publicly rejected the ATT in 2015:

> We decided not to join. We weighed all the pros and cons, and decided that there's no necessity for this," Mikhail Ulyanov told reporters. He called the ATT a weak treaty that still remains a certain burden for its participants.[5]

China will probably never join the treaty, and there seems nothing in it for them. The Chinese are not notorious for their hard bargaining but ignore treaties that do not serve their interests. India and Saudi Arabia want no restraints on arms they export or buy. The firearms community has said all along that the ATT would have no effect on major arms sales; instead, countries and NGOs will need a target country on which to focus, and the easiest target will be civilian firearms.

Had the U.S. supported a consensus and the legitimate outcome of the Conference, it is highly unlikely the General Assembly would have taken it up, much less passed the ATT resolution. The President and his Secretary of State wanted ATT at any cost but without their fingerprints on it. Clearly, President Obama betrayed his campaign promises and Secretary of State Clinton misled and lied to the U.S. Congress. Both Obama and Clinton betrayed their sworn duty to protect and defend the Constitution.

Kerry and the Constitutional Confrontation

Former Democratic Presidential candidate John Kerry replaced Hillary Clinton as Secretary of State, before the ATT was available for her to sign. Kerry signed the ATT on September 25, 2013, parroting the Clinton-Obama claim:

> This is about keeping weapons out of the hands of terrorists and rogue actors. This is about reducing the risk of international transfers of conventional arms that will be used to carry out the world's worst crimes. This is about keeping

Americans safe and keeping America strong . . . . This treaty will not diminish anyone's freedom. In fact, the treaty recognizes the freedom of both individuals and states to obtain, possess, and use arms for legitimate purposes.

None of this is true. A terrorist or rogue actor is in the eye of the beholder. The United Kingdom considered Americans to be rogue during our Revolutionary War. America does not consider the Kurds or the Syrian rebels to be rogue, but Syria and Turkey disagree. Kerry says that the reducing transfer of conventional arms will prevent the "world's worst crimes . . . ."—as if weapons cause wars and guns cause crimes. Kerry ended with the promise that our freedoms are protected, yet every attempt to protect individual freedom, the right to possess firearms, was rejected by the Conference. Mrs. Clinton and her cronies threw it overboard.

When Secretary Kerry signed the ATT, U.S. citizens assumed all its obligations. A future Administration can try to force public compliance in the same way the Clinton Administration used the Kyoto Treaty on global warming to justify regulations, legislation, and executive action without ever sending that treaty to the Senate for ratification.

The ATT is just beginning to be given content. The "standards" referred to in the Treaty are still being drafted, and the programs for regulation and reporting are just being established. The U.S. will be bound by the ATT regulations that are not even written, echoing Speaker of the House Nancy Pelosi's comment about Obamacare: "We have to pass the bill to see what's in it." (www. youtube.com/watch?v=hV-05TLiiLU)

The world's countries number more dictatorships or other governmental structures that dismiss individual rights than there are democracies, try as we might to help our fellow man. Majority rule in the U.N. does not favor the values that make America exceptional. Even in the U.K., the people are subjects, not sovereign. The Second Amendment vests the people of the United States with the right to bear arms, thus having the means to protect themselves and their sovereignty. It is this fundamentally different worldview that separates us from them.

The Truth Starts to Come Out

At a November 7, 2013, State Department Briefing on the ATT, Assistant Secretary Tom Countryman was asked why the U.S. abandoned the strong position that Bush had achieved and why the U.S. gave in on the protection of civilian firearms.

Questioner: Many senators made it clear that the treaty needed to specifically exempt civilian firearms. That didn't happen. How do you explain that?
Mr. Countryman: There were a lot of things I would love to change in the treaty

. . . . There were a lot of good people in New York, but none of them were named Franklin or Washington.[6] (Laughter from the audience.)

Mr. Countryman was admitting that the Bill of Rights did not matter—since none of the Founders were at the ATT Conference, he and Hillary Clinton were free to ignore the Constitution. When Bill Clinton campaigns for Hillary and says how much work there is left to do, be assured that writing ATT international gun regulations without Congressional oversight will be at the top of the agenda. And should Hillary Clinton ever become President, she will have an excuse to impose gun control in order to abide by the unratified ATT, and an inevitable constitutional confrontation over American gun rights and the ATT will ensue.

[1] *United Nations, "President's Non-Paper, 22 March," Final United Nations Conference on the Arms Trade Treaty, 18-28 March, 2013.*

[2] *District of Columbia v. Heller, 554 U.S. 570 (2008).*

[3] *See, David B. Kopel, Paul Gallant, & Joanne D. Eisen, The Human Right of Self-Defense, 22 BYU J. PUB. L. 43, 101-02, 128 (2007).*

[4] *Iranian diplomats at the U.N. have a reputation for two things: being tough and being competent. They know their stuff and they play hardball. They are also noted for never wearing ties! They do not consider themselves Arabs, but proud Persians.*

[5] *"Russia Refuses to Join Major Arms Trade Treaty Citing Documents Weakness," RT Russian Politics, May 18, 2015, found at http:// rt.com/ politics/259625-russia-arms-treaty-weak/.*

[6] *Countryman, Thomas. "The Arms Trade Treaty-Just the Facts," Arms Control Association 7 Nov 2013. Accessed August 24, 2014, http://www.armscontrol.org/events/The-Arms-Trade-Treaty-Just-the-Facts#transcript.*

CHAPTER 8

The Smoking Gun—Clinton's Benghazi Emails

There is an apocryphal story some trace back to the Franco-Prussian War that told of German officers playing "blind chess" to practice for the fog of war. The contest had two boards, and a player could see only the men on his board, while the other board was kept hidden behind a screen. A player would only know where the enemy pieces were at the point of contact. If your opponent's knight took your pawn on a certain square, you would have some information to act on, but you would never know the real situation. It was like the children's game Battleship, but much harder, or three-dimensional chess.

Negotiating with those intent upon restricting the domestic rights of American citizens through the U.N. Arms Trade Treaty is similar.

The non-governmental organizations against domestic firearms restrictions knew that then-Secretary of State Hillary Clinton was an opponent but because of government secrecy and her own duplicitous style of politics never really knew the extent of her opposition (nor how well the game had been rigged and how many people were helping their opponents)—that is, until the U.S. House of Representatives Benghazi investigation revealed that Mrs. Clinton's private computer server and the U.S. Justice Department and courts forced her, after a two-year delay, to turn over her Department of State (DoS) emails.

Buried within the thousands of emails made public are nearly a dozen exchanges confirming her direct involvement with the U.N. Arms Trade Treaty and the effort to bring legal American firearms within the jurisdiction of the U.N. They revealed that Mrs. Clinton, her cronies, anti-gun lobbyists, and leftist academics were intimately and joyfully working to give away the freedoms guaranteed in the Second Amendment. The emails are damning.

Huge sections of the emails are redacted, and with informal exchanges between individuals privy to the topics at hand, the reader is joining the middle of a conversation. They are as cryptic as coded Mafia telephone calls—"Our friend delivered the package, so the problem has been taken care of"—once one knows the players and understands the context. Even so, the 2011 to 2012 emails exchanged during the negotiations for the U.N. Arms Trade Treaty include those between international gun-control groups, Clinton cronies (including some Clinton Foundation funders), and DoS officials, all of which helped Mrs. Clinton create a new legal structure at the U.N. that threatens American sovereignty and the civilian right to bear arms.

An initial exchange between Mrs. Clinton and Burns Strider, a long-time Clinton associate and Director of Faith and Outreach during Hillary's first presidential campaign, was telling. Mr. Strider worked for Representative Nancy Pelosi and Al Gore. He managed the American Values Network and counted Oxfam America, the U.S. affiliate of U.K. Oxfam, as one of his clients. Remember that U.K. Oxfam is the parent organization of Control Arms, run by Anna MacDonald. Control Arms is so powerful it is allowed to participate not only as a favored NGO, but also with the status of a sovereign nation.

As early as 2011, Mr. Strider, working for Oxfam, used his association with Mrs. Clinton to raise funds for another Control Arms member group supporting the ATT and U.N. gun control. The group, Ploughshares, is on the steering committee of Control Arms. In an email dated March 4, 2011, Mr. Strider wrote:

> *Ploughshares has provided a significant amount of funding to us and others . . . . They're in a decision mode now on how much to resource for supporting ATT . . . . My request, if possible/appropriate, is a Thank You letter to them . . . . Here (below) are names and addresses if possible . . . . As always, thank you for considering . . . .*

Mrs. Clinton agreed to help with the fundraising in an email of the same day addressed to her State Department staff and copied to Mr. Strider:

> *Please follow up with Burns and prepare letter(s). Thx.*

Interpreted: Mrs. Clinton is using federal workers and DoS clout to help raise money for a private organization actively supporting the effort to take away American rights at the U.N. Either she already knew about the issue and supported groups like Ploughshares and Control Arms, or she was so close to Mr. Strider she was willing to act without questioning the legitimacy of his request.

On March 30, 2011, Clinton responded to an email from Anne-Marie Slaughter, who had just completed her stint as the Director of Policy Planning for the DoS. In her email, Ms. Slaughter complains about the danger to women from small arms sent to the rebels in Libya. Mrs. Clinton replied:

> *Thx for sending this to me and I'm copying to Melanne. You know we've tried to support the U.N. small arms treaty but we have run into, as usual, fierce NRA and Congressional opposition. But, I believe we have to keep trying. All the best, H*

Clinton does not call the treaty an "Arms Trade Treaty" or "ATT," she calls it the "U.N. small arms treaty," revealing what everyone knew: that although the United Nations stated that the treaty was about trade, a legitimate U.N. area, the real target was "small arms," U.N. speak for "gun control."

This email was sent in 2011, a year before the re-election of President Obama, who was repeatedly declaring full support for the Second Amendment. Mrs. Clinton had no need to bring up the NRA in her reply, but the NRA has been on the top of Hillary's hit list since 1994, when it helped the Republicans take control of Congress. The Clintons have never forgiven the organization for that upset, in which American gun owners, reacting at the polls to the so-called "assault weapons" ban put in place by then-President Bill Clinton, handed the Clintons one of their few political defeats.

The NRA's alternatives were to fight or to accept the U.N. and Obama-Clinton assurances that the ATT would not affect domestic firearms rights—yet clearly one could infer from the tone of her email that Mrs. Clinton was more concerned with defeating the NRA than defending the rights of American citizens at the U.N.

Something that comes out in the emails between Mr. Strider and Mrs. Clinton is what a sycophant he is. That is the polite term. There is no doubt that Mr. Strider knows on which side his bread is buttered. Thousands of emails had to be reviewed to find the ATT correspondence we are referencing here, but in sifting through them there is another interesting observation to be made that has nothing to do with the ATT. The emails reflect what can only be described as the bizarre culture and style of Mrs. Clinton and her staff. Email after email reveal that the Clinton crowd views everything in terms of a battle, with winners and losers, and those in contact with her characterize her every action as "great." We will not bore you with quote after quote, but, for the Clinton crowd, everything is a victory, she hits nothing but home runs, and the record is one wonderful accomplishment after another. We will see just a bit of this coming up.

On May 29, 2012, two months before the ATT Conference in New York, Mr. Strider sent Mrs. Clinton an email regarding the ATT negotiations. More specifically, it was about an article his group was writing on the ATT for the *Huffington Post* titled "The Most Important Treaty You've Never Heard of and How the NRA Wants It Dead." (You can read the article here: http://www.

huffingtonpost.com/eric-sapp/the-most-important-treaty-youve-never-heard-of_b_1544593.html.) He was seeking her tacit approval of the article. The title of the article is the subject line of the email exchange. Although the email has large portions redacted, he writes:

> *I hope you had a good Memorial day . . . . we had a great time Saturday night at [redacted] . . . . I'd love some face time about our next steps, moving forward.*

Mrs. Clinton replied:

> *I'm copying Lona and asking that she work to find time for you to come and see me (and bring [redacted] if you chose . . . .)*

The Secretary of State is personally approving an in-person meeting between a lobbyist promoting the ATT and U.N. gun control that conflicts with our Constitution at a fundamental level and one other person.

Who was the second person? What name could be so damaging that it had to be kept from the public? If Hillary and the Department of State allowed it to be known that she is meeting with Mr. Strider, why not let it be known who the second person was? This could not be a question of national security because no national security issues could possibly be involved. Mr. Strider does not come from the security sector, and his clients have no relationship with sensitive national security issues.

To better put this into perspective: Mr. Strider was a private citizen asking for a meeting with an American official on a public issue. The issue, the subject of the email, was the ATT and how the NRA was opposing it. The best guess is that the second person was Anna MacDonald from Control Arms, the leading group supporting the ATT and gun control at the U.N. One other possible reason for the redacting of her name, if it was MacDonald, is that she is a Brit. Another is that she is part of the notorious British Left that almost always takes anti-American positions. It is common knowledge among those who have been involved in the ATT negotiations that Ms. MacDonald loathed what she frequently called the "gun lobby," i.e., the NRA and other pro-gun groups.

Given who Ms. MacDonald is and was at the time, it would have been embarrassing for the public to learn that the United States Secretary of State was taking advice on a Second Amendment issue from an anti-gun British Leftist. Now, all of this may be conjecture, but, keep in mind, anyone else from Control Arms or Ploughshare would have held the same views as Ms. MacDonald and would have been willing to use the U.N. to destroy the Second Amendment to our Constitution. Also, Mrs. Clinton cavalierly dismisses the ongoing objections to the treaty from a supposedly "equal" branch of government. When Congressional leaders were not listened to by her staff, more than 50 senators signed letters in the summer of 2011 opposing the treaty. Mrs. Clinton and Mr. Obama completely ignored the concerns of almost a majority of the United States Senate, the body that would eventually have to approve the Treaty.

There is an interesting term at the U.N. for governments that do anything they want simply because they have the power: impunity. Given Mrs. Clinton's attitude toward Congress and the NRA, does one think she would act with impunity in an imperial Clinton presidency? Absolutely. Hillary Clinton, with the power of the presidency, is a frightening concept. Even as First Lady during her husband's administrations, she was widely referred to as Bill's "co-President." If, as Secretary of State, she ignored Congress and a huge portion of the American public represented by the NRA, what is she going to do as President? We have already seen how Barack Obama has abused his authority with executive orders. Given that Hillary has a much more aggressive personality, there is almost no limit to what she could do.

The *Huffington Post* article itself is puff piece for Mr. Strider's company and reads in part:

> *A robust ATT would help prevent weapons sales to states that are human rights violators, and create uniform laws and transparency that would put a serious squeeze on black market arms dealers who supply weapons to terrorists.*
>
> *As a result, a large and ideologically diverse coalition has emerged to support this treaty. Some of the strongest voices come from the faith community: The National Association of Evangelicals and National Council of Churches have joined the Vatican and the World Evangelical Alliance to call for a robust ATT. Last spring the American Values Network organized Christians in 48 states from over 3,500 mostly evangelical congregations to join in a day of prayer and fasting for a successful ATT. And numerous services and prayer rallies are being organized around the upcoming July negotiations . . . .*
>
> *You'd think there would be universal support for a treaty . . . . But if so, you haven't met the NRA . . . .*

This is astounding for several reasons. First, the U.S. Secretary of State, her salary paid by taxpayers and under a duty to protect the Constitution, is, literally, being made part of an international attack on an American group trying to protect a constitutional right. Secretary of State is one of the highest offices in the land, fourth in line to replace the President. One would think that she not allow herself be put in this position. Yes, this was an international treaty, and that would certainly be within the purview of the Secretary of State, but she should not have been using her position to promote the interests of an international gun-control organization, when she was charged with the responsibility of negotiating a treaty consistent with U.S. national interests and its Constitution.

The second astounding thing is her obsession with the NRA. Mr. Strider obviously knows this, and that is probably one of the reasons for both the article's title and its focus on the NRA. In a treaty being negotiated by sovereign nations, on what do Mrs. Clinton, Mr. Strider, and Control Arms focus? Not Iran, Syria, Russia, or North Korea, all of which were opposed to the Treaty, but rather on the NRA. The real issue is, and continues to be, civilian-owned firearms, not terrorism or rogue nations.

The ATT, theoretically, will stop transfers of arms to nations that abuse human rights. Yet the treaty will do little to stop arms transfers by nations if they consider such transfers to be in their national interests. To repeat, *realpolitik* will always trump the ATT.

The ATT went into effect December 24, 2014, and the leading country supporting it was the United Kingdom. Within months, the U.K. was selling arms to Saudi Arabia without going through the procedures supposedly required by the very ATT it had advocated. Why? Because those sales were in the U.K.'s national self-interest, and no treaty was going to stop them. Control Arms howled in protest but was ignored.

In May 2012, gun groups were still under the impression that Mrs. Clinton and her Department of State could be reasoned with and might still protect American gun owners' rights. American gun-rights groups have been accused of a lot, but not naïveté, yet the Clinton emails shocked all but the most cynical. Clinton helped raise money to support foreign pro-ATT, anti-gun NGOs and provided direct access to the highest levels of our government *while she was Secretary of State.*

In June, before the July 2012 New York ATT conference, Mrs. Clinton and State Department officials Jacob Sullivan and Rose Gottemoeller exchanged emails suggesting an ATT meeting in New York in July. They copied Jo Adamson, head of the British delegation and leading advocate for the ATT. As we've seen in a previous chapter, the U.K. defense industry wanted the treaty, because it would make British arms more competitive in world markets. Its initial argument was that if all countries had to meet the treaty's so-called "human rights" criteria, then U.K. industry would have a "level playing field." Meanwhile, the British Left wanted the treaty to control military and civilian arms.

The actual ATT conference did take place in July 2012. On July 3, 2012, the U.S. Under Secretary of State for Political Affairs, Wendy Sherman, the fourth-ranking official in the U.S. Department of State, emailed Mrs. Clinton that the Palestinians had backed off their demand to be treated as a state (country) by the U.N. Ms. Sherman complimented Tom Countryman, head of the U.S. delegation, and praised Mrs. Clinton's efforts in support of the ATT:

> *Love it!—Relief today is also successful negotiations to get the Palestinians to back off of seeking change in status at ATT conference. A long ordeal but working closely with Israelis, just achieved success. Rosemary DiCarlo and Tom Country-man were fantastic duo; David Hale and other played a supporting role. Your trip on Friday key I believe to this outcome.*

The status of the Palestinians took up a week of ATT Conference time, because they wanted to be treated as a state, rather than as an observer. One has to put the pieces of the puzzle together, but does "key . . . to this outcome" refer to the ATT? Is the Secretary of State meeting privately with the key major pro-ATT supporters in direct conflict with our Constitution? The Clinton crowd was not beyond giving one another innumerable high-fives.

Toward the end of the conference, on July 28, the Obama Administration's DoS Legal Advisor Harold Koh sent Mrs. Clinton (referred to as "H") an exchange between him and Mr. Countryman. Mr. Koh is a pro-gun-control internationalist. Mr. Countryman had halted the July conference on the grounds that the ATT needed more work, but it was fairly well understood that President Obama did not want what could be interpreted as a U.N. gun-control treaty adopted with his support during his bid for re-election:

> *From: Koh, Harold Hongju . . .*
> *Sent: Saturday, July 28, 2012 8:32 AM*
> *To: H*
> *Subject: Fw: What a job!*
>
> Mr. Koh: *You must be exhausted. Thanks for all you did . . . (July 27, 2012, 8:38 PM).*
> Mr. Countryman: *Thank you Harold; wished we could have reached a little further... (July 27, 2012, 8:45 PM).*

Harold Koh is the former dean of the Yale Law School, alma mater to both Clintons. He has clout in and outside academic circles and was an early advocate for international gun control. In 2003, Mr. Koh wrote a major article for the prestigious *Fordham Law Review*, saying:

> *For in the end, the only meaningful mechanism to regulate illicit transfers is stronger domestic regulations . . . . The greatest challenge we face in this process is to create a legal framework that combines a treaty framework built around*

clear norms with concrete, conforming domestic obligations to be executed by the participating nations.[1]

So Mr. Koh's comprehensive blueprint for international gun control was planned as early as 2003. He wanted a "treaty framework," and that is exactly what he got. The real irony here is Mr. Countryman's phrase, "wished we could have reached a little further." Evidently, he and Koh are working hand in hand for gun control—and one has to wonder: what would they have gotten if they could have "gone a little further"?

Mr. Koh's article criticizes Ambassador John Bolton for his defense of American gun rights at the 2001 PoA Conference. The article was written pre-*Heller,* and Mr. Koh ridicules Bolton and the idea that the Second Amendment confers an individual right. Today, Mr. Koh sees the ATT as a new type of law-making, where "norms" are "downloaded" from one country to another:

Make no mistake: this is not your grandfather's international law, a . . . top-down process of treaty making where international legal rules are negotiated at formal treaty conferences, to be handed down for domestic implementation in a top-down way. Instead, it is a classic tale of what I have long called the "transnational legal process," the dynamic interaction of private and public actors in a variety of national and international fora to generate norms and global interests . . . . Twenty-first century international law making has become a swirling interactive process whereby norms get "uploaded" from one county into the international system, and then "downloaded" elsewhere into another country's laws or even private actors internal rules.[2]

The ATT is a manifestation of this new type of lawmaking; it is transnationalism, a special threat to the U.S.[3] As mentioned, the Left and the media here and abroad love to portray Second Amendment advocates as out of the mainstream of respectable political dialogue. U.S. Senator John Kyl of Arizona writes:

I wonder if we are the only country that has all of the rights embedded in the first 15 amendments to the U.S. Constitution . . . . Does that also make those rights passé? I think not. We are the only country in the world founded on ideas rather than an accident of geography or blood. So the fact that other countries haven't gotten to our level doesn't mean we have to throw in with them.[4]

It can be argued that America's desirable and commendable values should be applicable to citizens of the world, not the other way around. The advocates of international gun control and transnationalism tried this exact argument before the Supreme Court, when they argued the *McDonald*[5] case. They said that the Constitution should only protect those rights that are acknowledged by other governments (or, as they called them, "civilized governments"[6]). In his majority opinion for the court, Justice Alito did not use the word "transnationalism" or mention the U.N., but this was his analysis:

> *Therefore, the municipal respondents continue, because such countries as England, Canada, Australia, Japan, Denmark, Finland, Luxembourg, and New Zealand either ban or severely limit handgun ownership, it must follow that no right to possess such weapons is protected by the Fourteenth Amendment . . . .*

The DoS ignored the legislative branch's objections, but Mr. Koh is a prominent legal scholar advocating that U.S. courts defer to international norms and foreign court decisions. In that light, *Heller* would not be safe in a Clinton Administration.

Mr. Koh was not present during the ATT negotiations that we know of, but, like Mr. Obama, Mrs. Clinton has effectively collaborated with gun-control forces throughout her career. In retrospect, she had no intention of listening to American gun owners or Congress, because she was listening to Burns Strider, Control Arms, and the likes of Harold Koh.

History is full of instances where the real story does not come out until years have passed. Fortunately for us, important parts of the ATT story, of Mr. Obama and Mrs. Clinton giving away American rights at the U.N., came out before this election. Benghazi had nothing to do with the Arms Trade Treaty, but it was the trigger that revealed the Clinton emails.

[1] Harold Hongju Koh, "A World Drowning in Guns," *Fordham Law Review* Vol. 71 (2003): 2354, accessed at http://ir.lawnet.fordham.edu/flr/vol71/iss6/1/.

[2] Quoted in Theodore Bromund, "The U.N. Arms Trade Treaty and the Gun Grab," *The Heritage Foundation* (blog), March 5, 2013, accessed August 25, 2014 at http://www.heritage.org/research/commentary/2013/3/the-un-arms-trade-treaty-and-the-gun-grab.

[3] For a general discussion of the topic, see John Fonte, *Sovereignty or Submission: Will American Rule Themselves or be Ruled by Others?* (New York: Encounter Books, 2011).

[4] Quoted in Sohrab Ahmari, "American Sovereignty and Its Enemies," *The Wall Street Journal*, July 20, 2013, A13.

[5] McDonald v. Chicago, 561 U.S. 742 (2010), 130 S.Ct. 3020 (2010) accessed at http://www.law.cornell.edu/supct/pdf/08-1521P.ZO.

[6] *Ibid.* at 33.

CHAPTER 9

The Arms Trade Treaty Bandwagon

The language of the Arms Trade Treaty as adopted by the U.N. General Assembly opens the door to far more stringent and dangerous proposals. Contrary to most lawful documents, the ATT has no definitions. It authorizes infrastructure and future deliberative meetings without deadlines, budget, or staffing limitations and is unlimited in scope.

Non-Country Participants

From the moment the August 2015 Conference of States Parties to the Arms Trade Treaty opened in Cancun on the 24th to when it closed on the 27th, non-governmental organizations were in a unique position. The initial speakers list included the traditional foreign minister-level officials outlining their countries' positions on various unresolved treaty issues—and Anna MacDonald, which meant Control Arms had the same standing as a sovereign state. Control Arms was complimented constantly by the President of the Conference, Jorge Lomonaco of Mexico, who acknowledged that there would have been no ATT without its hard work. Recognition of a country is rare. Individual recognition is rarer, and to recognize the efforts of an NGO or the head of an NGO is *unprecedented.*

Control Arms brought 80 representatives to the conference, more than any other government or organization; one member of the U.S. delegation referred to Control Arms as "Controlarmsastan." Other pro-ATT NGOs included Amnesty International (AI), the Institute for Disarmament Diplomacy, GRIP (a Belgium pro-ATT/anti-gun think tank), the Norwegian Parliamentary Forum, the Stimson Center, the Stockholm International Peace Research Institute, the Swiss Small Arms Survey, and Reaching Critical Will.

Clare da Silva and Sarah Parker of AI and the Swiss Small Arms Survey, respectively, announced the release of books analyzing the ATT. Also, Control

Arms and the Stimson Center announced plans to institutionalize ATT efforts, or to shift from advocacy to using the ATT to further their policy goals. This is not unheard of in political and nonprofit sectors; it keeps the advocates employed. The heads of these efforts are Anna MacDonald, head of Control Arms, and Rachel Stohl, an actual drafter of the ATT.

Control Arms' effort in this matter is an annual publication, *ATT Monitor*, on how the ATT is being implemented. *ATT Monitor 2015* was released in Cancun. Rachel Stohl's Stimson Project is called the ATT Baseline Assessment Project, with annual reports on how ATT signatory countries are meeting their responsibilities.

In the U. S., liberal NGOs receive funding from foundations such as MacArthur and George Soros's Open Society Institute. U.S. pro-gun advocates must rely on private, individual donations, while international NGOs rely on government funding, a huge advantage. The largest private donation is a mere rounding error to a government. According to *The New York Times* (Eric Lipton, "Foreign Power Buy Influence at Think Tanks," *The New York Times*, September 6, 2014, found at http://www.nytimes.com/2014/09/07/us/politics/foreign-powers-buy-influence-at-think-tanks.html), Stimson receives money from such diverse foreign governments as Canada, Norway, Sweden, Switzerland, and the United Arab Emirates. Stimson supports a staff of 57 people, considered very large in U.N. circles. Because of Stohl, Stimson retains its strong advocacy access to the ATT Secretariat. Thus, the two largest pro-ATT players have well-funded, new, permanent organizations to continue their advocacy. Although MacDonald and Stohl are intensely disliked within even their own circles, there is no substitute for success.

In contrast, pro-gun groups like the Ammunition Manufacturers' Institute, Defense Small Arms Advisory Council, National Rifle Association, Second Amendment Foundation, and Sporting Arms and Ammunition Manufacturers' Institute (SAAMI) attended the 2015 conference but were largely ignored. Boeing and the European Defense Association represented big industry.

Participants

Russia had announced it would not participate in the August 2015 Conference of States Parties to the Arms Trade Treaty in Cancun, and during the meeting, China announced Beijing would neither sign nor join the ATT, stating that abandoning the consensus rule in adopting the treaty set a bad precedent, before Beijing's representatives left the conference.

With the U.S. as a signatory to but unlikely to ratify the ATT, the biggest arms producers in the world are not party to the treaty. India and the Arab countries have little enthusiasm for the ATT, so it will have little effect on trade in military weapons, especially on major purchases from the big producers. With committed funding and so many well-funded ATT advocates, the Secretariat, the ATT state parties, et al. will have plenty of resources with which to focus on "small arms and light weapons," i.e., civilian firearms. The rhetoric in Cancun presages an ominous fight, this time not from behind closed doors with bored diplomats, but from a well-funded, multi-country assault through media or legislators or any other means the anti-gun forces decide to employ. Former U.S. Attorney General Eric Holder's claims that the American gun culture's days are limited may well be next made from the U.N. headquarters in Vienna and Geneva.

Location of the Secretariat

Intense competition surrounded the vote on where to locate the ATT Secretariat. Geneva, Trinidad and Tobago, and Vienna had all hosted preparatory meetings, and Trinidad and Tobago seemed to have the public commitments of most of the states (countries). Then, contrary to U.N. procedure, Mr. Lomonaco arranged for a secret ballot. It would take a two-thirds majority on the first ballot for one of the three locations to win.

Trinidad and Tobago received a majority on the first ballot, with Geneva next and Vienna third. On the second ballot, most of the Vienna votes switched to Geneva, and it won. Although publically committed to an isolated Caribbean capital, Geneva won because participants would rather spend their expense accounts in a luxurious European city.

The next meeting of the Conference of State Parties will be in Geneva, on August 22, 2016, presided by Emmanuel Imohe from Nigeria.

Head of the Secretariat

England's Guy Pollard had staffed the actual ATT Conference and was the initial favorite for temporary head of the Secretariat. Mr. Pollard knows the ATT and is a competent and experienced Geneva diplomat, but South Africa's Simon Dladla, a relatively unknown Defense Department official, was selected, largely in a reaction to the European location selected for the Secretariat. As Mr. Dladla's one-year term ends, the Conference of State Parties will conduct a more formal selection process.

Three full-time professionals and a support staffer will initially staff the offices with the stated goal to keep the ATT Secretariat as small as possible. This is completely misleading, as accounting, clerical, information technology, and other functions will be contracted out on an unlimited budget.

The work plan for the Secretariat seems simple but casually mentions a provision of the Treaty Article 17 .4 (a-d) that leaves the Secretariat free to do what it wants:

4. *The Conference of States Parties shall:*
(a) Review the implementation of this Treaty, including developments in the field of conventional arms;
(b) Consider and adopt recommendations regarding the implementation and operation of this Treaty, in particular the promotion of its universality;
(c) Consider amendments to this Treaty in accordance with Article 20;
(d) Consider issues arising from the interpretation of this Treaty;

What, Me Worry?

Mad magazine was the Saturday Night Live of the 1950s generation. The fictional but recognizable Alfred E. Neuman on the covers proclaimed, "*What, me worry?*" when worry was sometimes the most reasonable reaction to the world that *Mad* poked fun at so effectively.

Congress passed legislation prohibiting U.S. tax money from being used for ATT. Yet the head of the U.S. delegation, Mr. Countryman, claimed the U.S. will continue to support the Treaty and its implementation.

Yes. Be very, very concerned.

What the Paris bombings by ISIS in November 2015 have shown is that although citizens with guns stop many violent acts worldwide every year, the French reaction was to begin *to take away* more gun rights, not to have more good guys with guns. Europe is reacting like ISIS's dreams.

Turkey's third largest airport was hit on June 30, 2016, killing 42 people. The airport opened the next day. Israel has the same policy—get back to business—so that the terrorists do not change the country's culture. Compare those two to the U.S. government's reaction, wherein it renewed its efforts to allow for more spying on U.S. citizens. That may sound useful to stopping ISIS, but what if you are pro-gun and find yourself in a position contrary to the next Presidential Administration and the U.N.? How does spying on U.S. citizens without a court order and with unlimited budgets sound now?

While Congress banned the funding of the ATT, Obama officials were quick to point out that the U.S. taxpayers will support countries that *are* implementing the ATT. Money is "fungible"—what we fund, other countries do not have to pay for, so there is more money for them to fund the ATT. The U.S.—you—also provide 25 to 35 percent of U.N. funding (and many say more in New York real estate and international aid to funders). The U.N. is not running out of money soon, and it already funds the international anti-firearms lobby in Geneva. When your money is being used to fund your enemies, why worry?

The Obama Administration and any new Clinton Administration will try to implement the ATT regardless of Congress. Remember, Mr. Obama and Mrs. Clinton have named Australia and the U.K. as "common sense" examples of good gun policy, in which no citizen is allowed to own guns. In-between steps will be more gun registration, stopping trade in guns and ammunition, the kinds of enemies lists Mrs. Clinton has already kept in her diary and made partially public in the 1990s, and harassment of gun owners, which we saw in Mr. Obama's "clarification" executive order of January 2016.

Signing the ATT gave domestic gun-control advocates new credibility, research, and pockets of funding for their campaigns. During the November 14, 2015, debate, candidate for President Hillary Clinton argued for "common sense" gun-control legislation. The Associated Press fact-checked her comments and found not one of her "facts" was true. Such misstatements are deliberate and the only way the gun-control conclusion makes sense, but with the U.N. on her side and unlimited money from Europe and countries like Australia, where citizens have never hunted because their ancestors were hungry and shot all their game, we have cause to worry.

Mexico

One of our biggest enemies is actually closer to our own borders. The ATT has been greatly aided by Mexican authorities, who will claim their country's violence is a direct consequence of firearms purchased in the U.S. and smuggled into Mexico, and also that the U.S. signed the ATT promising to do something to solve the problem. Political grandstanding by Mexican leaders has put pressure on the U.S. to adopt stricter gun laws, backed up by reports from the ATT Secretariat that the U.S. is committing human rights violations when citizens have firearms. The U.S. can reasonably expect the Mexican government to demand action whenever we have discussions with Mexico on immigration, trade, and drugs.

Even if the United States never ratifies the ATT, it could require other nations to refuse to export sporting arms to us. If the Secretariat interprets the term "end user" to include retail purchasers of sporting arms, which seems more than possible, it will be virtually impossible for the average American to buy firearms from some of the world's greatest firearms manufacturers. The rich could, perhaps, maneuver their way through the regulatory maze, but the average duck hunter would be out of luck—and once your children never learn how to hunt, they will forget how to vote for the freedom to hunt.

All is not lost, but the future will require vigilance, watchfulness, in the face of treachery.

Throughout this book we have referred the actions of the Obama Administration. Now it is time to turn to the actions we the people need to take to preserve our freedoms.

PART III

We the People

CHAPTER 10

What Can I Do?

Those of us who spend a great deal of time involved in and obsessing about politics are prone to forget that not everyone shares our interest. This is as true of hunters, shooters, and other Second Amendment supporters as it is of most Americans. Second Amendment voters turn out in slightly higher percentages than members of other voter groups, but their turnout numbers sky-rocket when they know their rights are threatened. It is up to those of us who "get it" to let everyone know the consequences of not voting this year. That is, in part, what this book is about.

Let us look more specifically about what each of us can do not just in this very important election year, but in all the months and years after.

Vote Realistically

The National Rifle Association, like other pro-gun groups, works hard to get Second Amendment supporters to the polls every year, but this year, 2016, more than ever. Chris Cox, the Director of all NRA political efforts, is the first to admit that the NRA formally represents only about 10 percent of those who will vote on the gun issue when they realize the Second Amendment is truly being threatened. This political saliency lies in the demonstrable fact that Second Amendment voters will turn out, cross party lines if need be, and do whatever is needed to protect our rights.

The odds are that the 10 percent of Second Amendment voters who do belong to the NRA, and realize the nature of the threat we face, know or come into contact with the other 90 percent of voters who will vote when they know the score. NRA members run into the 90 percent at the gun range, in the field, or at breakfast before they take to the field, at field trials where they run their dogs, at gun shows and in sporting goods stores, and just about everywhere else those involved in the shooting sports are likely to congregate. If you are an NRA member or are already planning to vote this fall because of the threat to your rights, share your concerns with everyone. Do not simply assume that your fellow sportsmen "get it," are registered to vote, or *will* actually vote this fall. Talk to them and urge them to do what needs to be done to preserve their firearms rights. In this country, it is up to those with a stake in the outcome to make sure our elections are fair—and no one has a bigger stake in 2016 than gun owners and Second Amendment voters.

Did you know that more than 100 percent of the eligible voters living in some precincts and congressional districts voted in 2014? In spite of claims to the contrary, voter fraud is a continuing problem in many parts of the country. The old jokes about the dead voting in Chicago are not funny at all, because they are based on fact.

You can do something to make sure that votes are accurate: be a poll watcher this fall. You will not make much money doing it, but your state or jurisdiction will pay you a little for this incredibly important job. You will be assigned a precinct and spend one long, but valuable, day. The vast majority of the people working for the government believe in what it does. It is human nature to want to work without interference, so sometimes poll watching is a "closed" system. It is not well advertised, its training sessions are held months in advance of the vote (time to forget what you learned before election day), and it results in a long day at the polls toiling for less than the minimum wage. With so many two-income families, poll watching is not popular—but it is necessary. The job is amazingly important to our election process, because there are votes stolen every election.

A few votes here or there will not change an election, but elections do get stolen in this country, and the threat that they will be stolen has increased with the push for same-day registration, driver's licenses for illegals, and long mail-in ballot campaigns. Sometimes, busloads of "voters" will arrive at a polling place, jump to the front of the line, cast their votes, and re-board their buses to be carted off to another polling place where the process will be repeated. Yes, *this* happens, and you can help prevent it by calling your newspaper, taking a picture of the license plate number and people on the bus, or volunteering to serve as a poll watcher.

Voter integrity receives little protection here. Ironically, our tax dollars fund programs around the world to prevent voter fraud. It was our government that persuaded Mexico to require a government-issued photo ID to vote and Iraq to require voter identification and to ink the thumbs of voters. The same Members of Congress who attack every attempt to protect the integrity of our elections as being racially motivated are often the same people who vote for funding intended to ensure elections in other countries are conducted fairly.

Take Your Friends to Hunt

Like many Americans who live in Washington, D.C., or who own businesses, the authors receive help from interns. The research for this book and others is often done by young Americans who do not get overt credit or an acknowledgment in the thank-you section. Make sure your interns, employees, and contractors are thanked. How about a day of shooting? Take your children, your grandchildren, your friends' children. Not a word has to be spoken about politics, and your neighbor may never have handled a gun, especially if they grew up in the suburbs. But take that time, let them see what the outdoors and the shooting sports have to offer. It is hard to demonize gun owners or fishermen or hikers if you have seen them at the sport.

Seeing is Believing
By David Keene

One summer, my wife had two interns, a hunter from the Upper Peninsula of Michigan and a Cuban American from south Florida who had never touched a gun. I took my intern and a few others with these young ladies to the 24-hour range at the NRA. The Cuban initially hung back, but, by the end of the session, she did not want to leave. She was amazed at how much fun it was to hit a target. As we were leaving the range, she tugged at my sleeve and asked, "Mr. Keene, how much would one of those 1911s cost?"

Our grandson asked his mother for months if he could learn to fish, and as soon as my wife learned of it, he was out in the cold fishing, with breaks for hot chocolate and homemade mac-and-cheese. Whether five or 85, we like to be outside for the day, and what a terrifically fun way to get to know your friends and family.

You Cannot Ask Someone to Do It For You

President John Kennedy of Massachusetts, Governor Rick Perry of Texas, Senator Jeff Sessions of Alabama, Congresswoman Marsha Blackburn and her husband of Tennessee, and countless others sold door-to-door through college summers. One of the companies that recruits and trains students and helps them learn goal setting and a positive mental attitude is the Southwestern Company, established in 1855. A recruiting technique of the company is the "Everywhere You Go Approach," and in our high-tech world, it is an amazingly effective tool for campaigning.

The post office line, grocery store, literally anywhere and everywhere you can strike up a conversation works with this method, which is about starting and having the conversation. You can start by bringing up the United Nations, this book you've just read, or even by commenting on the photos you see on the front of *People* magazine as you wait to have your milk and bread bagged. Somewhere in that exchange you can weave in "While I was hunting . . ." or "Just got back from the gun show . . ." or whatever. You just have to start it.

It is said that people decide on their views all too often after seven contacts, not just one. That is why political ads repeat over and over. But you, talking to only one person a day, will have more impact than many ads. People also make decisions in four basic ways: family and friends agree, you personally feel it, "the data prove it," and "most people agree." So someone knowing *you* have an opinion can make a difference on guns.

In politics, perhaps more than any other profession, everyone has an idea about how things *should* work. Friends often visit politicians, telling them how to accomplish whatever it is *they* want, regardless of whether it in any way is a good thing for the district the politician represents.

We would counter this by asking, are you perfectly able to do something about the problem yourself? Then do it. Never waste your time asking someone else to do what you can do. Every nonprofit, every business, began with an idea. Yes, recruit others, but lead the charge, at least for a while. A letter to the editor is easy enough to write—but it gets read. And, believe it or not, election officials pay attention to the calls, letters, and emails they get from their constituents.

One of the reasons the Obama Administration's 2013 assault on the Second Amendment failed was that millions of gun owners stepped up to the plate to let elected officials know that they care about their rights. The hundreds of thousands who attended rallies around the country that spring, wrote to their Senators, and confronted them at town hall meetings when the politicians were home all added up. Many constituents actually came to Washington to meet their representatives in their offices, destroying the President's argument that gun owners actually wanted his "common sense" reforms. So let your elected officials know how you feel. They work for you and know that if they ignore you, their jobs can be at risk.

The 2016 elections should be all about freedom, the Constitution, and the makeup of the United States Supreme Court. The Founders wrote the First, Second, and Fourth Amendments knowing that the day would come when free speech and religious rights protected by the First Amendment, the rights protected by the Second Amendment, and many of the guarantees written into the Fourth Amendment (those having to do with unreasonable search and seizure, among other rights) would eventually be threatened. If the Founders had not witnessed what they had in Europe, they would not have included the protection of these rights in the Bill of Rights, because there would have been no need.

The threat to these fundamental rights is a threat to the very nature of our country. The next President will reshape the Constitution, because, as some maintain, the document only means what the court says it means. Whoever occupies the White House for the next four years is probably going to name as many as three or four new Justices but will only need one to alter the way the court views our constitutional rights today.

This means that every believer in the Second Amendment and the rights it protects should be working to make certain the next President of the United States is committed to appointing Justices who will protect the Constitution passed down to us, rather than rewriting it to reflect an ideological political agenda that would have horrified the Founders.

Poll data tell us that more than 50 million American voters will vote to protect their Second Amendment rights if they know those rights are truly threatened. If you have read this book to this chapter, you now truly know what we are facing, but there are many others who share our values and simply do not understand the seriousness of this threat.

Crime Is Not Increasing—Change the Perception It Is

America has spent time and effort on retread proposals to reduce gun crime or firearms violence that, in fact, only threaten the rights of Americans and have been proven ineffective. What we have not done is spend enough time on measures that deserve support and may make an actual difference. Some of these measures have been tried in the past and proven workable, while others are just now being developed to deal with the growing recognition that mass shootings in particular are perpetrated not by traditional criminals, but by people with severe and often identifiable mental problems.

The most progressive "gun control" measures, including the January 2016 executive orders by President Obama, have nothing to do with crime, nor will they save lives, as he claims. They are about a hostility toward firearms, gun owners, and the Second Amendment more than any real effort to deal with either "gun crime" or, as the President likes to call it, "gun violence." The cop on the street, the sheriff on the trail, parents, and any reasonable voter know these laws would have no real impact on the actions of a mentally dangerous shooter who has decided to take innocent lives.

Over the last few decades, the murder rate has dropped precipitously, even as more and more Americans have been purchasing firearms. If the easy availability of firearms has even a causal relationship to murder or violent crime rates, one would expect both rates to have skyrocketed, as more and more firearms have been purchased by people from one end of the country to the other.

President Obama's persistence in blaming firearms in private hands for crime and urban violence has no basis in fact. Second Amendment supporters like to argue that there is a causal connection of the opposite sort, that, as more and more people arm themselves, criminals and violence are deterred and crime rates *drop*. This is far too simple an explanation for the decrease in violent crime that began in the 1990s, but there is some evidence that the possibility that a victim has a gun, combined with heavy and certain punishment of criminals who use firearms illegally, has had an impact on crime rates.

Many crimes are deterred or stopped by good guys with guns each year, yet most are never reported nor found in any Google search. (You can read one article here: http://www.washingtontimes.com/multimedia/collection/good-guy-gun-stopped-bad-guy-gun/.)

Let us look at the crime and homicide rates over the last few decades. According to the Justice Department, Americans owned about 192 million guns in the early 1990s. Today, although it is impossible to say with any degree of certainty just how many firearms are in private hands in America, estimates center somewhere around 300 million. That is 192 million 15 years ago compared to an estimated 300 million now; that is a third more guns in private hands today, and yet firearms homicides have been *cut in half* during that same time. In 1993, the firearms homicide rate was seven per 100,000 people, according to the Centers for Disease Control and Prevention, but, by 2012, the homicide rate had dropped to 3.5 per 100,000 people.

These are statistical facts, but the continual coverage of gun crime and the rhetoric from Mr. Obama and others has had its desired affect: the public *believes* that gun crime has increased. In 2013, Pew Research asked people if they believed gun crime has increased or decreased in the last 20 years. Of those polled, 56 percent said gun crime had increased; only 12 percent thought it had decreased.

In politics, perception often trumps reality. Given enough money and time, politicians create their own reality. Even with the drug- and gang-related increases in the murder rates in a few cities like Baltimore, Chicago, and Los Angeles, Americans overall are much safer than they were 20 years ago. They just do not realize it.

Given the decrease in the U.S. murder rate, gun-control advocates lump everyone killed by a gun together. Yet reality shows that more than, we hear 40 percent, two-thirds, this is conservative, of the nation's "gun deaths," that all-encompassing category, are suicides, rather than murders. To bolster their "data," gun-control advocates also insist not only on including suicides, but also criminals killed in encounters with law enforcement officers or in the commission of a crime.

During its bus tour, Mayors Against Illegal Guns, funded by former New York City Mayor Michael Bloomberg, even included Boston Marathon bomber Tamerlan Tsarnaev, who was killed during a gunfight with Boston Police, in its list of "victims of gun violence." When a rally leader read off the names of "victims of gun violence" on Tuesday, June 18, 2013, the Concord, New Hampshire, crowd fell apart, shouting, "He's a terrorist!" according to the *New Hampshire Union Leader*. (You can read the article here: http://www.unionleader.com/article/20130619/NEWS07/130619169&template=mobileart.) The group finally apologized and removed Tsarnaev's name from its list of gun victims.

New York State Assemblyman Kieran Michael Lalor noted:

> *Bloomberg's apology is disingenuous at best. He has been misleading the American people to score political points. A quick look at the list would have revealed there were many criminals on it. Bloomberg's list includes a man shot by police while threatening to kill a two-year-old girl he had snatched from her mother in a parking lot. This is a group that doesn't distinguish between a gun being used to save a kidnapped child and the victim of a crime. They're just concerned about making a political statement.*[1]

While gun-control advocates, when caught in such lies, might be willing to reduce their "victim count" including terrorists and murderers killed in gun battles with police, they persist in including those who commit suicide. They argue that, but for the availability of a gun, many, and perhaps all, of these suicides might have been prevented. In January 2016, *Reason* magazine's Brian Doherty deconstructed this argument in an article titled "You Know Less than You Think About Guns," finding it less than persuasive. Doherty noted that, while 21,175 Americans killed themselves with a gun in 2013, making guns the choice method by a better than two-to-one margin over the next method preference, the availability of firearms was not the *reason* they committed suicide. (You can read the article here: http://reason.com/archives/2016/01/05/you-know-less-than-you-think-a/1.)

The *Washington Post*'s fact checker awarded Connecticut's Democrat Senator Chris Murphy three Pinocchios for conflating homicide and suicide totals during his effort, after the Orlando nightclub shootings, to get the Senate to revisit gun-control measures it had previously refused to enact. Throwing together murders, suicides, accidental shootings, and even those killed in resisting police and calling the total the result of "gun violence" rather than "gun crime" makes it far more difficult to look realistically at what might be done to deal with suicides, homicides, or accidental shootings. (You can read the article here: https://www.washingtonpost.com/news/fact-checker/wp/2016/06/17/fact-checking-three-democratic-claims-on-assault-rifles-and-guns/.)

Doherty, in his article on reason.com, reports that, while firearms are an "efficient" choice for those seeking suicide and there are more guns here than in other countries, it does not follow that the suicide *rate* is affected by the choice of method. To shed some perspective on this, according to the U.N., Japan, Korea, and India have fewer gun suicides, but far higher suicide rates than the

U.S. In those and other countries, most suicides are by hanging. Hanging is the second most popular choice of suicides in the U.S. Suicides are tragic, but banning rope or autos because of self-inflicted death by them is not the Left's agenda.

Doherty concludes his article with the findings of a 2012 study published in *Sociological Spectrum*, which examined what the authors referred to as the "opportunity model" and concluded that "the accessibility of firearms does not produce more homicide or suicide when other known factors are controlled for." (You can read the article here: https://www.researchgate.net/journal/0273-2173_Sociological_Spectrum.) This finding is echoed by University of Utrecht psychologist Wolfgang Stroebe, also cited by Doherty, who reviewed the literature and, in *Aggression and Violent Behavior*, in 2013, rejected that possession of firearms as "a primary cause of either suicide or homicide."

Searching for a one-size-fits-all solution is not the way anyone seriously interested in solving problems would proceed. So, without data to prove guns lead to more crime, violence, or suicide, one must accept that ideological hostility, rather than empirical evidence, is what motivates those opposed to private ownership of firearms and the Second Amendment. The evidence demonstrates fairly and conclusively that gun-control advocates rely on scary rhetoric, rather than actual facts, to persuade people of the wisdom of their "common sense solution" to regulate guns.

Katy Bar the Door

By David Keene

There are many citizen watch programs where the police will show you and your neighbors the vulnerabilities in your homes and security measures you can easily undertake, what the most likely crime in your neighborhood is, and how to avoid being a victim. As an added bonus, the meeting will help your neighbors all meet one another, which is a huge deterrent to crime.

My wife is a fan of neighborhood watch. When she invited our neighbors over, the policeman showed them that the developer's sliding glass doors could be forced open from the outside. A week later, she was alone and heard a *click-click*. Going downstairs to investigate, she confronted a young man trying to get inside the sliding glass door! Luckily, she has installed the simple wooden bar across the bottom that the would-be intruder could not see in the dark.

Demand Your Government Prosecute Crimes

As a society, we know how to reduce "gun crime," even though some policymakers and elected officials seem blind to the proven solutions. An armed robber who uses a gun to rob a convenience store has committed a state and a federal crime. The robbery itself is a state-level felony, and, once arrested, the criminal faces trial in state court and a state sentence. Using a firearm in the commission of a crime is a federal felony and can be prosecuted in federal court. A convicted felon can also be prosecuted in federal court for the mere posses-sion of a firearm—and a good percentage of armed robberies are committed by recidivists, criminals who have been tried, convicted, and released and who then go on to commit other crimes.

Some, but not many, U.S. Attorneys actually prosecute gun crime under existing federal statutes, and, when they do, criminals within their jurisdictions begin to think twice about using or even carrying a gun. *Crime goes down.* Pro-fessional criminals are pretty rational in their own way; they make their living preying on others and are as capable of making what amounts to a cost/benefit analysis as non-criminals. If they think they can get away with using a gun, they will. If not, they do not.

Plainly, criminals who use firearms in the commission of their crimes do not give up their guns simply because it is illegal for them to have one. In a recent study of gun-related arrests in two large Florida counties, researchers discovered that 62 percent of violent gun crime arrests were to individuals not legally permitted to have a gun at the time. (You can read the study here: http://content.healthaffairs.org/content/35/6/1067.abstract.) People who use guns in the commission of a crime are, by definition, criminals! They have demonstrated a willingness to break the law. Changing that behavior, that will-ingness, requires making it clear that the penalty for using a gun is too severe to risk the crime. Unfortunately, that is not clear to criminals in Baltimore, Chicago, or other major American cities with unacceptable levels of murder and violence.

In 2015, Chicago, the city run by President Obama's former Chief of Staff Rahm Emanuel, now mayor, prosecuted fewer gun crimes under exist-ing federal laws than any other jurisdiction in the United States. The result of this benign neglect of criminals with guns has been predictable. Chicago is a battlefield, where gangbangers and thieves never hesitate to carry and use a gun against innocents.

This does not happen where law enforcement and the courts take gun crime seriously and dedicate themselves to taking armed criminals off the street.

While there may not be a causal relationship between crime and the avail-ability of firearms in the general population, there is an irrefutable direct correla-tion between crime and leaving known armed and potentially violent criminals to roam free. Former prosecutor Rudy Giuliani turned New York City, during his time as Mayor there, from one of the most crime-ridden cities in the world to a place where the streets were safe. It took the prosecution of jaywalkers, kids milling on the streets or breaking windows, and all manner of minor crimes.

As criminals came off the streets, crimes plummeted. Sure, some guns were confiscated, but they were tangential to the people committing crimes.

During the Clinton years, the NRA argued that our country does not need new restrictions on firearms, that it instead needs to enforce those already on the books. To illustrate the impact that enforcing existing laws might have on crime, NRA's Executive Vice President Wayne LaPierre went to Richmond, Virginia, at the time one of the "murder capitals" of the United States. He found a U.S. Attorney there willing to work with local law enforcement and with the NRA.

Together, they announced a program they called "Project Exile." The NRA publicized the program through billboards and other media, and the U.S. Attorney pledged that every criminal caught illegally with a gun or who used one in committing a crime would be prosecuted. There would be no plea bargains, and every one prosecuted would receive at least the five-year minimum sentence demanded by the law.

The program went into effect in 1997, with the support not just of the NRA and local law enforcement, but with support of the anti-gun Brady Campaign; it was one of the few times the two groups found themselves on the same side. The message "An illegal gun gets you five years in Federal Prison" was featured on billboard, radio, television, print ads, and public service announcements and printed on more than a million grocery bags. Prosecutors promptly demonstrated they were going to follow through. Within a year, gun homicide in Richmond had dropped by 33 percent, followed by an additional 21 percent drop the next year. Armed robberies dropped that first year by 30 percent. The program was a success, but its extension into other areas was opposed by then-U.S. Deputy Attorney General Eric Holder in the Obama Administration as "a waste of prosecutorial resources." Mr. Holder, like Mr. Emanuel, was more interested in gun control than in a solution to crime control.

Early rumors in the winter of 2015–'16 were that President Obama could include, in his January 2016 executive actions, new restrictions on firearms ownership and use without going to Congress—this was no surprise. The silver lining, it was hoped, was that he might also include an order to U.S. Attorneys, who work for the Justice Department, to copy the program Richmond had found its success with in the 1990s: prioritize and prosecute gun crime under existing federal laws. This was something the NRA and other pro-gun advocacy had been urging for years, and NRA spokesmen were prepared to applaud the President for doing so, or to at least "welcome him to the table," as one put it.

Unfortunately, the provision did not make the cut, as the White House decided once again to focus its attention on the guns criminals use, rather than on the criminals themselves. The missed opportunity again revealed that those opposed to the private ownership of firearms were not to be diverted in their mission by resorting to measures that have been proved successful in the fight against crime and violence. Results do not further their anti-gun agenda.

Mass Shootings—A Problem for Both Sides

The stickiest problem pro- and anti-gun advocates face involves the mass shootings that have gotten so much publicity in recent years and have triggered presidential, congressional, and media efforts to curb Second Amendment rights. While mass shootings are obviously crimes, those involved in them are rarely if ever "criminals" in the traditional sense. Criminals are rational and do respond to criminal sanctions. But unless the mass shooter is a committed jihadist, he or she is invariably someone with severe mental problems that, in most cases, have gone unreported until too late. Most mass shooters buy their firearms legally, and almost all of them get them from licensed FFLs. They pass the required background checks and acquire the weapons they want, even in states with restrictions in place such as those the President would impose nationwide, states like California, Colorado, and Connecticut.

Preventing such people from obtaining the weapons they need to carry out their attacks is a challenge that has proven conceptually and practically almost impossible.

Predicting future behavior by category is always dangerous and usually unjust, yet law enforcement officials and policy makers have been trying to do just this for centuries. Over the years, crime has been blamed on the poor, immigrants, racial minorities, red hair, and even men carrying a chromosome supposedly linked with criminality. The problem with such categorization is that, while it may be true that, statistically, members of any of these groups commit more crimes than Ivy League or military academy graduates, ministers, or priests, *most in each category never have and never will commit a crime*. The result is that aiming proposals and regulations at groups, rather than individuals, does a disservice to all of us.

At one level, policy makers and the public perceive that losing some freedoms along the margins is a risk worth taking to protect the public from what they see as "preventable violence." Most agree that citizens with a felony conviction should be prevented from acquiring a gun. Even here, though, there are difficulties. In a conceptual sense, we are supposed to treat those who have paid their debt to society as if the payment of that debt somehow allows them to re-enter society on an equal footing with the rest of us. As then-Attorney General Eric Holder told a group of prosecutors at the Brennan Center in New York, "There can be no excuse for denying a fundamental right to one who has 'paid his or her debt to society.'" (You can read more about Mr. Holder's speech here: https://nyelectionsnews.wordpress.com/2016/05/11/brennan-center-holder-pafilla-on-voting-refotom-tonhold-may-18-session/.) At the time, Holder was talking about restoring voting rights, but he could have been talking about other fundamental rights—like the Second Amendment right of a citizen "to keep and bear arms."

When it comes right down to it, however, policy makers know that many felons, once released, go right back to doing what put them behind bars in the first place. So, it makes some sense to make it harder for an armed robber to acquire a gun and use it as he has in the past. But the same category of criminals that would prevent just that also includes *nonviolent* felons, who lose their Second Amendment rights for life. These include the more than 4,500 federal statutory and regulatory felonies enacted by Congress over the years, many of which do not even require *mens rea*, the intention or knowledge of wrongdoing, like planting crops on a "wetlands" when a farmer drains a field.

One might argue that including these felons in the system is unjust; are we, as a society, willing to accept the nonviolent felon who loses their "shall not be infringed" gun rights, when so many violent felons have had their voting rights fully restored? We do this in the name of public safety?

The Left would rather take away everyone's gun and let everyone vote.

Support Mental Health Reform

Mental health advocates and experts claim, quite accurately, that most of those among us with mental health problems are no more likely to shoot up a school or do anything else violent than anyone else. That is *inarguably* true. Indeed, it is far more likely that the mentally ill end up a victim of a crime, rather than a perpetrator. Still, as among felons, there is within that broader group a subset of people who represent a danger to themselves and those around them.

These are the people we find in our jails and prisons and living on the street among the homeless, without adequate diagnosis or treatment. These individuals are responsible for as many as a thousand homicides a year, and thousands more commit suicide. That they escape diagnosis and the treatment they deserve is a tragedy, as is the fact that their numbers include the usually undetected or undetectable potential mass murderer. Members of this subgroup should be in the FBI's NICS system. But simply lumping together anyone who is "different" or has gone through some sort of formal counseling or treatment for a mental disorder into NICS is painting with too broad a brush. The question, then, is how to narrow the criteria in a way that will both protect society and respect those whose rights would be affected by unfairly including them on a list that denies people their constitutional rights.

After the Sandy Hook shootings, while Congressional Democrats and President Obama were demanding the usual litany of gun-control measures, the Republican House leadership asked Pennsylvania Congressman Tim Murphy to examine the flaws in our current mental health system so that we can better identify and treat the most dangerously mentally ill within our society and reduce the chances that they will become either victims or perpetrators of violence.

Mr. Murphy was elected to Congress in 2002, after a stint in the Pennsylvania State Senate, but had been a practicing clinical psychologist for 30 years and authored two books on child psychology. He was the obvious choice for the assignment and took it very seriously, spending a full year researching and interviewing experts on how the current system is failing and developing reforms to improve the way the nation deals with our mentally ill.

The resulting Helping Families in Mental Health Crisis Act would overhaul a failing and incredibly expensive mental health care system that seems to focus on making patients who have had a bad day happy, while ignoring the severely and potentially dangerous mentally ill. Representative Murphy discovered that, while the U.S spends $203 billion annually, including $125 billion in federal money, on what he found can only loosely be described as mental health "care," much of what we are doing is wasteful, misdirected, and even counterproductive. The perhaps 11 million men and women with truly severe mental problems that too often lead to violence, arrest, prison, and suicide are too often ignored in favor of minor mental health issues that improve the statistics for government agencies. One class of drugs prescribed for these more minor mental health issues are opioids, which are experiencing an exponential rise in use and abuse. Therefore, some 300,000 of those diagnosed as severely mentally ill are not, as they should be, in treatment facilities, but in our jails and prisons. In every single state, there are more people diagnosed as severely mentally ill in penal institutions than in all the state's public and private treatment centers. An additional 250,000 live on the streets, and about 38,000 of them a year commit suicide.

These are the paranoid schizophrenics, the seriously bipolar, and others who cannot cope with life in the real world and who too often become a real threat to themselves and to others. Our country provides them little help or treatment until it is too late. Many would have been hospitalized before governmental reforms instituted beginning in the 1960s closed down treatment centers and refocused mental health care spending on problems that seemed more tractable.

Jails and prisons are not set up to treat mental health issues, and many unfortunates come out of such places in worse shape than when they were sentenced. Take sixty-two-year-old William Spengler, who had spent seventeen years in prison for murdering his grandmother. He found life on the outside difficult. He could not stand his sister. On Christmas Eve 2012, Spengler ambushed and fatally shot two firefighters called to a burning house, where police later found the charred remains of his murdered sister. Cornered by police, Spengler killed himself but left a letter in which he wrote, "I still have to get ready to see how much of the neighborhood I can burn down, and do what I like doing best, killing people."

Spengler had spent a good deal of time in prison, but like Adam Lanza in Connecticut, James Holmes, charged in the killing of 12 theatergoers in Aurora, Colorado, and Aaron Alexis, who killed 12 at the Washington Navy Yard, Spengler was very, very sick—and he was wandering around free without treatment.

Mr. Murphy's reforms include much more but would essentially refocus mental health care spending on those who truly need intervention, allow the institutionalization of the severely mentally ill, and encourage assisted outpatient treatment, which would require the severely mentally ill who can nevertheless cope if they take prescribed medications to take them or face institutionalization. Assisted outpatient treatment works. The severely mentally ill receiving treatment in states with such programs in place fare very well, with a 55-percent drop in suicides, a 47-percent decrease in attacks on others, a 74-percent reduction in homelessness, 83-percent fewer arrests, and an 87-percent decline in incarceration.

In spite of the evidence, patients' rights advocates are opposed to such programs. Many actually continue to insist that there is no such thing as a mental illness; after Sandy Hook, a major mental health organization called the NRA to protest its calling Lanza "crazy" in describing his killing 26 people. Mr. Murphy even discovered that the federal government is using taxpayer money to subsidize these groups. His bill would cut off that funding.

Mental health laws can be abused and have been in the past, but that is no reason to deny treatment to those who need it, especially when they might pose a threat to themselves and others. We should never demonize the mentally ill, but as 38,000 suicides a year demonstrate and the fact that tens of thousands end up as victims, rather than perpetrators, of violence, denying them treatment or arguing that they are not really ill does little to either help or to protect society. Mr. Murphy's bill is designed to fix a system that has failed them, as well as society as a whole.

Mr. Murphy wants to fix the problem. Any Congressman who actually examines a problem and tries to solve it is worth our serious consideration. His Helping Families in Mental Health Crisis Act may not be perfect, but it is more than just a step in the right direction. Tell your Congressman you support this bill.

States that have implemented laws requiring those diagnosed as potentially dangerous to themselves or others, but who can function normally when they take their medications, and have required them to do so or risk being sentenced to involuntary inpatient treatment have reduced crime and violence in these populations to a remarkable degree. Measures that target those who commit specific criminal acts—such as felonies involving firearms, violent armed drug dealers, and criminal gangs—reduce crime. Measures championed by Congressman Murphy and others target those who pose a demonstrable danger to society, rather than condemning whole groups of people and demanding they surrender their constitutional rights for mere membership in such a group. The problem is that the ideological commitment on the part of the anti-firearms lobby to blame everything on guns makes it difficult to win consideration for reforms that might actually make our streets and schools safer without restricting the constitutional rights of law-abiding Americans.

School Shield—A Real Solution

That gun owners are informed and vocal about the real solutions to crime is vital to stopping those who use crime and violence as a barrier to gun ownership and to actually keeping us safe. This was nowhere more evident than in the Obama Administration and media reaction to NRA Executive Vice President Wayne LaPierre's expressed belief after Sandy Hook, in 2013, that America should consider ways to protect children attending our schools, even if that meant providing them with armed security.

The first reaction to Mr. LaPierre's suggestion was that it was crazy, but there then came the realization that most urban schools *already* have armed security in the form of School Resource Officers. Such schools have not been the targets of mass shooters, who have focused on suburban schools lacking such protection.

The result of the NRA concern was the establishment of the School Shield Program, which actually works with law enforcement, school administrators, educators, and parents to provide real-world protection for our nation's school-age children.

Reasonable and Immediate
By David Keene

A few years ago, I was invited to meet with the group Prosecutors Against Gun Violence, to examine ways in which they might work with pro-Second Amendment groups to find areas of agreement. Many attendees were in general agreement with the proposition that we should find ways to help individuals who can be shown to be potentially dangerous based on their past activities or mental problems, and to devise ways to limit their access to firearms without impinging on their due process rights or casting too wide a net.

One of Mayor Bloomberg's groups made a presentation and demanded backing for a proposal that would deny Second Amendment rights for 10 years for anyone arrested for or convicted of drunk driving. It was just another way of expanding the universe of "prohibited persons," and I asked what led anyone to believe that a driving while intoxicated (DWI) arrest marked a driver as likely to rob a 7-11 convenience store, murder their wife, or shoot up a theater.

That was a question they could not answer, and most of the prosecutors present seemed to agree that the proposal was off the mark. To further the conversation, I pointed out that there are instances in which it might be appropriate to suspend one's Second Amendment rights for a short time, for instance, during a psychotic break or because, even without an adjudication of dangerousness, there was reason to believe an individual should be denied access to a firearm while a deeper background check is completed. I cited the "naked man" rule the NRA supported in Colorado, as an example of a reasonable approach to this problem, one that focused once again on *individual* dangerousness and due process.

In Colorado, as in most states, the local sheriff decides whether an individual should be granted a concealed carry permit. In some instances, it was decided that a sheriff concerned about someone's mental fitness could deny the permit but would then have to submit the denial to experts within a day or so for a determination as to the applicant's fitness. It is known as the "naked man" rule, because, hypothetically, a sheriff might legitimately question the fitness for a permit of a naked man sitting on the courthouse lawn, wearing an aluminum hat, and claiming to be talking to space aliens.

The NRA found this rule reasonable, because it allowed reasonable *immediate* action, and it required the state, rather than the applicant, to seek approval or disapproval of the action within a set time so that due process rights would not be compromised.

Mr. LaPierre observed that every school could bring parents, teachers, administrators, and local law enforcement officials together to assess their schools' needs. "The best way to stop a bad guy with a gun is a good guy with a gun," Mr. LaPierre told reporters at a press conference the Obama Administration and gun-control advocates panned. Mr. LaPierre announced that former U.S. Attorney, Arkansas Congressman, Drug Enforcement Administrator, and Undersecretary for Border & Transportation Security at the U.S. Department of Homeland Security Asa Hutchinson would lead the effort. The project, named School Shield (www.nationalschoolshield.org), would determine best security practices for public and private schools, develop a manual and course of training by which experts could assess an individual school's needs, and raise funds to help schools without sufficient resources to improve security.

Mr. Hutchinson resigned as head of School Shield when he was elected Governor of his native Arkansas in 2014, but requested that David Keene succeed him. Today, School Shield's highly acclaimed assessors and trainers work with school administrators, School Resource Officers, and local police departments to help develop enhanced security procedures for our nation's students.

The Israeli Example
By David Keene

As it happened, I was in Israel touring a training facility for school security personnel, when the news of the Sandy Hook shootings reached me. In the 1970s, terrorists had targeted Israeli schools, and the nation responded by first tasking the military, and then the police, with providing security but finally decided that each school should take responsibility for its own protection. Today, each Israeli school's budget includes funds to hire private trained and certified security personnel to protect its students.

As I went through the facility, and even before hearing of the shootings in Connecticut, I wondered why we do not provide similar protection to our American schools. The motives of those who might attack an Israeli school might differ from those who would attack ours, but, in either case, armed security can serve as a real deterrent.

Fortunately, the attempt to shame gun owners and demonize gun-advocacy groups has not worked, but the threats continue. In 2016, Mrs. Clinton called for the formation of an anti-gun/pro-gun regulation group that would attract "responsible" gun owners comfortable with the "common sense" gun restrictions the Obama Administration supports. Similar efforts to replace or neutralize the NRA and to draw members away have proven unsuccessful. In every election cycle, anti-gun candidates establish sportsmen's groups to offset the impact of NRA opposition, but these efforts never seem to make much difference on election day.

The prospect of using taxpayer funds in one way or another to establish such a group is a real fear. Michel Bloomberg's efforts to establish a mass anti-gun movement have consistently failed, but he has established a number of what are called "grass top" rather than "grass roots" groups that get media attention because they purport to represent responsible gun-control advocacy. The prospect of such a group with money and a President constantly showcasing its activities would add another dimension to the ongoing struggle to preserve the Second Amendment This becomes even more important in reflecting on Part II of this book, when we saw that U.S. Obama dollars combined with the resources of other governments are attacking civilian gun ownership.

Despite these things, public support for the NRA and the Second Amendment has grown, rather than lessened, in the wake of the current battle over gun control. In the 1960s, most polls reflected strong public support for gun control, but, in recent years, that support has dwindled. A recent Pew poll shows stronger support for private firearms ownership than at any time in recent history, and a 2015 CBS poll reflected, for the first time, a majority opposition to laws that restrict private ownership of the AR-15 and other long guns anti-Second Amendment advocates like to call "assault weapons." (You can read more here: http://hotair.com/archives/2015/12/11/backfire-cbsnyt-poll-shows-majority-opposes-assault-weapons-ban-for-first-time-ever/.)

The campaign against assault weapons begun in the 1990s resulted in a 10-year ban on guns that looked like military firearms. Politicians continue to rail about weapons designed "only to kill other human beings on the field of battle" in an anti-gun public-relations ploy, erroneously including guns that only "look" military.

More Americans are beaten to death each year than are killed by all long arms, including the hated "assault weapons." An AR-15, by proper definition, is a semiautomatic version of the military rifle version, a version that can be utilized as an automatic machine gun through the flipping of a switch on the firearm. But that is the *military* version. The many variations of the AR-15 available to U.S. civilians can *not* be fired automatically. Yet gun-control advocates imply, and sometimes actually claim, that a gun like the AR is "fully automatic." It is not. There is no magic switch on AR variations available to U.S. civilians. More than 4.5 million Americans own this gun, because it is comfortable to hold and use for hunting, sport and competitive shooting, and home defense.

A very few fully automatic weapons are in civilian hands in the United States, because actual automatic weapons require an extensive background check, a special tax, then a special government permit. On top of that, the supply of legally transferrable fully automatic firearms in civilian hands is finite, thanks to the Firearms Owners Protection Act of 1986. Firearms manufactured or converted to full-auto after the implementation of this act can be imported by and transferred only to U.S. government, law enforcement, and FFLs needing such firearms as sales samples for governmental and law enforcement entities. A legal, fully automatic machine gun can cost more than $20,000, certainly more than a typical gangbanger or drug cartel pays for their weapons. So support school shield for your community and help others know their guns.

And Vote!

If you have read this far, you know the time has come to stand up and protect your constitutional rights. It takes work, and much of that work comes down to alleviating misperceptions about crime, speaking up in the most individual way, and spending time with your friends in nature. Oh, and *vote*.

Let us consider the worst-case scenario from the perspective of those of us who, like our nation's founders, are hunters and gun owners, and believe in "the right of the people to keep and bear arms." If Hillary Clinton is elected President, there can be little doubt that she will attempt in every way possible to deliver on her threat to appoint Supreme Justices who will eviscerate the Second Amendment or render it meaningless. Her repeated statements on this issue for years are in direct contrast to her nomination acceptance speech where she said she believes in the Second Amendment.

However, she would have to get the Senate to confirm her nominee or nominees. If she appoints an outrageously outspoken opponent of firearms ownership, it is at least possible that a Republican Senate would refuse to confirm her nominee. This could happen, but is frankly unlikely. Presidents, liberal and conservative alike, are given deference in their appointments by the Senate; the seat that opened up with the death of Justice Scalia has remained open because Republicans insisted that it not be filled until after the 2016 election and a President Clinton will probably nominate someone who will prove difficult to defeat on the Senate floor.

Once this happens, the Court, as we have detailed earlier, could seek out a case that will allow the new anti-gun majority to do as Justice Ruth Bader Ginsburg hopes and reverse *Heller* outright or simply approve or refuse to review state and federal regulations on gun ownership masquerading as "reasonable" under the *Heller* decision.

If the November 2016 election flips the Senate from Republican to Democratic control, the Second Amendment as a guarantee of an American citizen's right to gun ownership will be a thing of the past, and the Second Amendment will no longer serve as the protection of the rights we have always believed it to be.

That would not be the end of the battle over firearms ownership in this country. Even if the courts eviscerate the Second Amendment, as many as three hundred million firearms will remain in private hands, and the newly minted Clinton Administration will have to decide what to do about those guns and the families that own them, as well as the million or so guns that are being sold every year as firearms ownership and the shooting sports become more popular.

Mrs. Clinton admires the mandatory confiscation regimes implemented in Great Britain and Australia, but she cannot unilaterally order and implement such a scheme in this country. Congress would have to go along with her, and, absent a real change in thinking in both Houses of Congress, that seems unlikely. Her plans for confiscation via Australia-like mandatory buy-backs, increased taxes on firearms and ammunition, registration, etc., will require Congressional cooperation, and gun owners can fight and possibly even defeat her scheme there. The individual states may try it, however, without the Supreme Court and the *Heller* decision to limit what states do.

Even without the constitutional and legal protection now in place, gun owners can still fight politically to prevent the new Administration from taking our guns. The NRA, the many other gun groups, and gun owners defeated President Obama's assault on their rights as his second term began, and there is reason to believe that if we remain united and are willing to fight we will defeat Mrs. Clinton's assaults, as well.

Gun owners would just rather not have to have that fight. It will be an incredibly tough battle and waged every day the new Administration holds power. We can expect more extensive executive orders because Mrs. Clinton will never be at all constrained by the Second Amendment, and we can expect a massive public campaign financed by Michael Bloomberg and his friends to cow Congress as a President Clinton demands new laws restricting our rights.

But America's gun owners have been fighting against massive odds for decades and have won more often than lost. We have to dedicate ourselves to fighting every single one of Clinton's anti-firearms initiatives by rallying those who already agree with our right to keep and bear arms and by persuading those with no real interest one way or another that the age-old right of a people to defend themselves, their families, and their homes is argument enough to defeat confiscation and restrictions that target gun owners rather than gun criminals.

The story of the public's change in attitudes toward the role of privately held firearms in a free society has been remarkable. Many who back in the sixties would have rallied to Mrs. Clinton's anti-gun crusade today side with gun owners. More Americans have guns in their homes for legitimate purposes today than at any time in our history, every state has adopted a form of concealed carry law, and groups that have never been particularly strong firearms supporters are buying guns to protect themselves and discovering that the shooting sports are a lot of fun.

This trend can be expected to continue regardless of the 2016 election. Women, gays, and minorities are taking to firearms ownership as never before. Crime is down in most of America, but as a society we face new threats that simply cannot be dealt with unless private citizens have the right and the means to defend themselves. The evolving environment in which we live has changed many minds.

During the first Clinton Administration, from 1993 to 1996, Ronald K. Noble served as Assistant Secretary and then Undersecretary for Enforcement at the U.S. Treasury Department. This made him the direct supervisor of the main federal gun control agency, the Bureau of Alcohol, Tobacco and Firearms (BATF). Noble played a major role in the Clinton Administration's very aggressive gun-control program, including changing ATF licensing practices for Federal Firearms Licensees to deny the majority of applicants license renewal. He then became the first American Secretary-General of Interpol.

What Noble saw in the wake of the 2013 terrorist seizure of a shopping mall in Nairobi changed his mind on the value of guns in private hands. During the attack, the terrorists killed more than 60 shoppers, but Noble believes that but for the assistance of armed private citizens, the death toll would have been in the hundreds.

Noble even made a video on what happened titled *Armed Citizens Can Help Stop Terrorist Massacres Like Nairobi and Paris*. He says, "This is not an American argument, nor a political argument. In these horrific situations, law-abiding armed citizens have helped protect others and literally saved lives, and the world should be made aware of this reality. . . . In the hands of law-abiding citizens, guns can and do save lives." Most Americans agree with his sentiments.

The bottom line is that even if Mrs. Clinton is elected and even if her Supreme Court reverses *Heller*, the battle over gun rights will continue—so there is reason for optimism.

Following the Sandy Hook tragedy and the Obama Administration's unsuccessful, but well financed and heavily lobbied, effort to impose restrictions on the rights of gun owners, a liberal blogger asked why it is that every time he and his anti-gun allies confront the "gun lobby," the confrontation ends with them accomplishing little and polls showing that more Americans support private gun ownership than ever. When a debate such as the one following the Sandy Hook tragedy takes place, the public realizes that critics of Second Amendment rights make little logical sense and have no proposals that would actually solve the problems they claim they would solve. That will not change based on who sits in the White House.

The bottom line is that Second Amendment supporters have no reason to be despondent. The American people are still with us, and we can still gain protection for our rights from Congress as long as the public remains with us and we stand together. We will win, but it will require all of us to engage on the issue of our rights, to make our case with the general public, and to keep letting our elected representatives know just how strongly we feel about our rights and our freedoms.

At the beginning of this book, we quoted former President Ronald Reagan's observation that "Freedom is never more than one generation away from extinction. We didn't pass it to our children in the bloodstream. It must be fought for, protected, and handed on for them to do the same." We need to fight for freedom each day on many, maybe too many, levels, knowing that the future is in our hands.

[1] *As quoted in subscription-based sources.*

ABOUT THE AUTHOR

David A. Keene

While serving as President of the National Rifle Association, Keene, along with NRA's Executive Vice President Wayne LaPierre, led the "All-In" Campaign to elect Second Amendment supporters to federal and state office in 2012, and worked tirelessly to keep the U.S. from adopting further gun-control legislation in 2013. NRA membership grew from four to five-plus million members during his two traditional one-year terms. Keene remains on the NRA Board and chairs the Publications Policy Committee and the National School Shield program.

From 1982 to 2011, Keene volunteered as the elected Chairman of the American Conservative Union (ACU), the nation's oldest and largest grassroots conservative advocacy group. ACU is the major organizer of the annual Conservative Political Action Conference (CPAC) that draws more than 11,000 conservative activists to Washington, D.C., each winter to hear conservative leaders and to network with fellow conservatives from around the country and the world.

Keene remains on the boards of The Center for the National Interest, The Constitution Project, and The Montana Policy Institute, and has served as the National Chairman of Young Americans for Freedom, among other groups. He has been a John F. Kennedy Fellow at Harvard University's Institute of Politics, a First Amendment Fellow at Vanderbilt University's Freedom Forum, and a member of the Board of Visitors at Duke University's Public Policy School.

After earning his law degree from the University of Wisconsin, in 1970, Keene served as a Special Assistant to Vice President Spiro Agnew during the Nixon Administration, Executive Assistant to New York Senator Jim Buckley, and advisor to the presidential campaigns of Ronald Reagan, George H.W. Bush, Bob Dole, and Mitt Romney, as well as many state and local campaigns.

For more than 10 years, Keene wrote a regular column for *The Hill*, which focuses on America's Capitol Hill activities. He has also written extensively on politics, civil liberties, and criminal justice issues for the *Boston Globe, National Review, Human Events,* the *American Spectator,* and others, and has contributed to numerous books and hundreds of radio and television programs. Currently, he serves as the Opinion Editor of the *Washington Times,* the nation's largest conservative newspaper.

Keene is married to Donna Wiesner Keene, and they enjoy the company of five children, seven grandchildren, and a great-grandchild. They work in Washington, D.C., and protect their sanity with extended trips to Montana and West Virginia to hunt, fish, and enjoy the outdoors.

ABOUT THE AUTHOR

Thomas L. Mason

Thomas L. Mason is an attorney representing clients before international bodies. He is the American Executive Secretary for the World Forum on Shooting Activities, an official United Nations non-governmental organization comprised of organizations such as the British Shooting Sports Council, the National Rifle Association, Sporting Shooters Association of Australia, and the South African Gun Owners Association. Mason has represented the NRA and other firearms community groups at every Arms Trade Treaty meeting and conference for two decades and has appeared before the U.N. General Assembly's First Committee and the U.N. Office on Drugs and Crime, among others.

Mason is a member of the Oregon, 9th Circuit, and U.S. Supreme Court bars and has prosecuted and defended cases. A Democrat, Mason served the voters of Portland in the Oregon House of Representatives for 16 years and authored the first vote-by-mail law for a U.S. state. While an associate professor of the Administration of Justice at Portland State University in Oregon, he published *Governing Oregon: An Inside Look at Politics in One American State* (Dubuque, IA: Kendall Hunt, 1994).

Mason hunts, raises roses, reads history, and plays with his one-year-old granddaughter, Tamsin Mason, when not on the road. He and his wife, Patricia Amedeo, met while both were serving in Oregon state government and have one daughter, Jessica Mason, an Oregon lawyer. They live in Oregon and California.